NON-INTERNATIONAL ARMED CONFLICTS IN INTERNATIONAL LAW

YORAM DINSTEIN

D1457239

CAMBRIDGE
UNIVERSITY PRESS

CAMBRIDGE
UNIVERSITY PRESS

University Printing House, Cambridge CB2 8BS, United Kingdom

Cambridge University Press is part of the University of Cambridge.

It furthers the University's mission by disseminating knowledge in the pursuit of education, learning and research at the highest international levels of excellence.

www.cambridge.org
Information on this title: www.cambridge.org/9781107050341

© Yoram Dinstein 2014

This publication is in copyright. Subject to statutory exception and to the provisions of relevant collective licensing agreements, no reproduction of any part may take place without the written permission of Cambridge University Press.

First published 2014

Printed in the United Kingdom by Clays, St Ives plc

A catalogue record for this publication is available from the British Library

Library of Congress Cataloguing in Publication data
Dinstein, Yoram, author.
Non-international armed conflicts in international law / Yoram Dinstein.
pages   cm
Includes bibliographical references and index.
ISBN 978-1-107-05034-1 (hardback)
1. War (International law)   2. Intervention (International law)
3. War victims – Legal status, laws, etc.   4. War crimes.   5. War.   I. Title.
KZ6355.D56   2014
341.6 – dc23   2014020934

ISBN 978-1-107-05034-1 Hardback
ISBN 978-1-107-63375-9 Paperback

NON-INTERNATIONAL ARMED CONFLICTS IN INTERNATIONAL LAW

This dispassionate analysis of the legal implications of non-international armed conflicts explores the rules regulating the conduct of internal hostilities, as well as the consequences of intervention by foreign States, the role of the Security Council, the effects of recognition, State responsibility for wrongdoing by both Governments and insurgents, the interface with the law of human rights and the notion of war crimes. The author addresses both conceptual and specific issues, such as the complexities of 'failing States' or the recruitment and use of child-soldiers. He makes use of the extensive case law of international courts and tribunals, in order to identify and set out customary international law. Much attention is also given to the contents of available treaty texts (primarily, the Geneva Conventions, Additional Protocol II and the Rome Statute of the International Criminal Court): what they contain and what they omit.

YORAM DINSTEIN is a Member of the *Institut de Droit International* and Professor Emeritus at Tel-Aviv University. He is a former President of the University (1991–9), as well as former Rector and former Dean of the Faculty of Law. He served twice as the Stockton Professor of International Law at the US Naval War College in Newport, Rhode Island. He was also a Humboldt Fellow at the Max Planck Institute of International Law in Heidelberg, a Meltzer Visiting Professor of Law at New York University and Visiting Professor of Law at the University of Toronto.

CONTENTS

PREFACE

Due to their preponderance and intensity, non-international armed conflicts are currently very much in the public mind: often, more so than international armed conflicts. The present volume serves as a comprehensive introduction to the international legal regime of non-international armed conflicts, proceeding strictly in light of what the contemporary law is (as distinct from what the present author or anybody else would like it to be).

Non-international armed conflicts raise a raft of issues that need to be addressed, including in particular their preconditions, thresholds, diverse forms and configurations; the discordant perspectives of the international and domestic legal systems; as well as the application of treaty and customary law to non-State actors. In addition, it is necessary to examine the consequences of intervention by foreign States; the role of the Security Council; the effects of recognition; State responsibility for wrongdoing to the installations or nationals of foreign States, etc. The interface between the law of international and non-international armed conflicts is a matter of crucial concern. There are also numerous specific problems, from the complexities of 'failing States' to the recruitment and use of child-soldiers.

The main thrust of the book relates to the law regulating hostilities. Conduct of hostilities in non-international armed conflicts, once virtually overlooked by international law, is currently ingrained in the *lex lata* to an ever-increasing extent. The process is primarily the outcome of a substantial body of case law delivered by international courts and tribunals.

There is an inevitable intersection between the law of non-international armed conflicts, human rights law and international criminal law. To avoid confusion, it is necessary to look carefully for guidelines indicating which legal norms are applicable in any given situation.

Much attention will be devoted in this study to available treaty texts: what they contain and what they do not; what they mean and what can perhaps be read into them. Customary international law coincides with many treaty provisions, but sometimes custom either goes beyond treaty law or falls short of it.

The present book serves as a companion to three other volumes published by Cambridge University Press, dealing respectively with the *jus ad bellum*,* the *jus in bello* in international armed conflicts** and the law of belligerent occupation.*** When taken together, the four volumes – largely speaking – cover the general spectrum of the law of armed conflict in its various aspects. To minimize repetition, matters explored in detail in the companion volumes are not rehashed here.

There is one important omission, namely, the treatment of internees (either in international or in non-international armed conflicts). The reason is that the topic calls for a juxtaposition and analysis of international legal rules affecting diverse categories of civilian detainees – in peacetime and in armed conflict; in inter-State as much as in intra-State strife; and in occupied territories – plus the special status of prisoners of war. Such a comparative survey has to be done methodically, and it will not be undertaken in the present book (just as it was not attempted in the companion volumes).

The numerical cross-references in the text of the book (as distinct from the indices) are to paragraphs and not to pages.

To facilitate syntax, generic pronouns relating to individuals are usually drawn in masculine form. This must not be viewed as gender-specific.

January 2014

* Y. Dinstein, *War, Aggression and Self-Defence* (5th edn, 2011).
** Y. Dinstein, *The Conduct of Hostilities under the Law of International Armed Conflict* (2nd edn, 2010).
*** Y. Dinstein, *The International Law of Belligerent Occupation* (2009).

TABLE OF CASES

(References are to page numbers)

TABLE OF TREATIES

(References are to page numbers)

TABLE OF SECURITY COUNCIL RESOLUTIONS

(References are to page numbers)

TABLE OF GENERAL ASSEMBLY RESOLUTIONS

(References are to page numbers)

ABBREVIATIONS

AC	Appeal Cases
AFLR	Air Force Law Review
AIDI	Annuaire de l'Institut de Droit International
AJIL	American Journal of International Law
AP/I	Additional Protocol I [to the Geneva Conventions]
AP/II	Additional Protocol II [to the Geneva Conventions]
ATT	Arms Trade Treaty
AUILR	American University International Law Review
AUJILP	American University Journal of International Law and Policy
AULR	American University Law Review
Berk.JIL	Berkeley Journal of International Law
BUILJ	Boston University International Law Journal
BWC	Convention on [the Prohibition of the Development, Production and Stockpiling of] Bacteriological (Biological) Weapons
BYBIL	British Year Book of International Law
Can.YIL	Canadian Yearbook of International Law
Car.LR	Cardozo Law Review
CAT	Convention against Torture
CCCW	Convention on [Prohibitions or Restrictions on the Use of] Certain Conventional Weapons
Chi.JIL	Chicago Journal of International Law
CLF	Criminal Law Forum
Coll.	Collegium
Common Article 3	Article 3 Common to the four Geneva Conventions
Cor.ILJ	Cornell International Law Journal
CPCP	Convention for the Protection of Cultural Property
CRC	Convention on the Rights of the Child
CSR	Convention Relating to the Status of Refugees
CWC	Convention on [the Prohibition of the Development, Production, Stockpiling and Use of] Chemical Weapons

CWRJIL	Case Western Reserve Journal of International Law
Den.LJ	Denver Law Journal
DPLR	DePaul Law Review
DukeJCIL	Duke Journal of Comparative and International Law
ECA	European Conventions and Agreements
ECHR	European Court of Human Rights
EJIL	European Journal of International Law
Em.LJ	Emory Law Journal
Fl.FWA	Fletcher Forum of World Affairs
Fo.ILJ	Fordham International Law Journal
Ga.JICL	Georgia Journal of International and Comparative Law
Ger.YIL	German Yearbook of International Law
HILJ	Harvard International Law Journal
HPCR	Harvard Program on Conflict Research
HRQ	Human Rights Quarterly
Human Rights Instruments	*The Raoul Wallenberg Compilation of Human Rights Instruments* (G. Melander and G. Alfredsson eds., 1997)
IAC	international armed conflict
ICC	International Criminal Court
ICJ	International Court of Justice
ICJ Rep.	Reports of the International Court of Justice
ICLQ	International and Comparative Law Quarterly
ICLR	International Community Law Review
ICRC	International Committee of the Red Cross
ICTR	International Criminal Tribunal for Rwanda
ICTY	International Criminal Tribunal for the [Former] Yugoslavia
IJRL	International Journal of Refugee Law
ILC	International Law Commission
ILC Ybk	Yearbook of the International Law Commission
ILM	International Legal Materials
ILQ	International Law Quarterly
ILR	International Law Reports
ILS	International Law Studies
IMT	International Military Tribunal
Ind.JIL	Indian Journal of International Law
Int.Aff.	International Affairs
Int.Leg	*International Legislation: A Collection of the Texts of Multipartite International Instruments of General Interest* (M.O. Hudson ed., 1931–50)
IRA	Irish Republican Army

IRRC	International Review of the Red Cross
Is.LR	Israel Law Review
Is.YHR	Israel Yearbook on Human Rights
It.YIL	Italian Yearbook of International Law
JCSL	Journal of Conflict and Security Law
JICJ	Journal of International Criminal Justice
L&E	Law and Equality
Laws of Armed Conflicts	*The Laws of Armed Conflicts: A Collection of Conventions, Resolutions and Other Documents* (4th edn, D. Schindler and J. Toman eds., 2004)
LCP	Law and Contemporary Problems
LJIL	Leiden Journal of International Law
LNTS	League of Nations Treaty Series
LONIAC	law of non-international armed conflict
LOS Convention	Convention on the Law of the Sea
LPICT	Law and Practice of International Courts and Tribunals
Man.LJ	Manitoba Law Journal
Mel.JIL	Melbourne Journal of International Law
Mil.LLWR	Military Law and Law of War Review
Mil.LR	Military Law Review
MINUSMA	United Nations Multidimensional Integrated Stabilization Mission in Mali
MPEPIL	*The Max Planck Encyclopedia of Public International Law* (2nd edn, R. Wolfrum ed., 2012)
MPYUNL	Max Planck Yearbook of United Nations Law
NATO	North Atlantic Treaty Organization
NDLR	Notre Dame Law Review
NIAC	non-international armed conflict
NILR	Netherlands International Law Review
NSAIL	Non-State Actors and International Law
NTC	National Transitional Council
NYUJILP	New York University Journal of International Law and Politics
PASIL	Proceedings of the American Society of International Law
PCIJ	Permanent Court of International Justice
PGM	precision-guided munitions
POW	prisoners of war
R2P	responsibility to protect
RCADI	Recueil des Cours de l'Académie de Droit International
RDI	Rivista di Diritto Internazionale
RGA	Resolutions of the General Assembly

RHDI	Revue Hellénique de Droit International
RIAA	Reports of International Arbitral Awards
Rut.LJ	Rutgers Law Journal
Sas.LR	Saskatchewan Law Review
SCSL	Special Court for Sierra Leone
Supp.	Supplement
TGS	Transactions Grotius Society
TLR	Texas Law Review
UChi.LR	University of Chicago Law Review
UN	United Nations
UNESCO	United Nations Educational, Scientific and Cultural Organization
UNHCR	United Nations High Commissioner for Refugees
UNJY	United Nations Juridical Yearbook
UNTS	United Nations Treaty Series
UPenn.JIL	University of Pennsylvania Journal of International Law
Van.JTL	Vanderbilt Journal of Transnational Law
VCLT	Vienna Convention on the Law of Treaties
Vill.LR	Villanova Law Review
Vir.JIL	Virginia Journal of International Law
WCR	*World Court Reports: A Collection of the Judgments Orders and Opinions of the Permanent Court of International Justice* (M.O. Hudson ed., 1934–43)
YIHL	Yearbook of International Humanitarian Law
YJIL	Yale Journal of International Law

The framework

I. Introduction

A. NIACs and IACs

1. Every armed conflict is either international or non-international in character (see *infra* 70). Non-international armed conflicts (NIACs) – often called internal armed conflicts or, in the past, civil wars – are an older phenomenon than the modern nation-State. The Roman Republic was subverted and ultimately destroyed by enervating civil strife. The late Roman Empire was shaken to its foundations by near-constant bruising fights between rivals who wished to assume the purple. The Islamic Caliphate went through the turmoil of *fitna*; and in the long history of the Chinese Empire regimes and dynasties often succumbed to aggressive warlords. Throughout medieval and early modern Europe, internal conflicts between barons and kings, interspersed by many a *jacquerie* and *fronde*, were commonplace. In a multitude of countries the animosities and fervour of such ruptures (exemplified by the War of the Roses in England) fed them for long periods of time. In the contemporary era, NIACs like the American Civil War (1861–5) or the Spanish Civil War (1936–9) left scars of self-inflicted wounds not healed for generations.

2. In the past half-century alone, NIACs led to genocide and appalling massacres in Cambodia, Congo, Rwanda and the former Yugoslavia. In the same (post-colonial) period, abundant losses of life and tangible damage to property were caused by incessant ordeals of NIACs (meeting the preconditions set out in Chapter 2) in scores of other countries all over the globe.[1] Some of these NIACs were (or are) exceptionally brutal; others were (or are) less harsh. Some are still in progress; others are definitely

---

[1] The following list can be compiled in alphabetical order: Afghanistan, Algeria, Angola, Azerbaijan, Bahrain, Bolivia, Brunei, Burkina Faso, Burma, Burundi, Central African Republic, Chad, Colombia, Comoros, Congo, Congo-Brazzaville, Cyprus, Djibouti, Dominican Republic, Egypt (Sinai Peninsula), El Salvador, Ethiopia, Fiji, Gambia, Georgia,

over; and still others are in danger of re-eruption. Then, there are places of unrest and confrontation (not listed here) that are teetering on the brink of a NIAC.

3. It frequently happens that an incumbent Government – averse to being tarnished with the stain of a revolt – is prone to shy away from an unwelcome truth, clinging to the fiction that internal violence is sporadic and that no genuine NIAC is underfoot.[2] Governments may go to some lengths to deny the existence of a NIAC even in the face of overwhelming evidence to the contrary. The international community, too, may recoil at the thought of recognizing what is actually happening. Thus, for a considerable time, there was an indisposition to concede that a NIAC had begun in Syria in 2011.[3]

4. Official reluctance by an incumbent Government to acknowledge that a NIAC is ongoing may be a counter-productive stance, inasmuch as the Government may then be held to more stringent international legal standards of behaviour (for an illustration, see *infra* 114). But, in any event, the outbreak of a NIAC has to be determined on the basis of objective criteria rather than subjective predilections.

5. NIACs are certainly much more pervasive today than international armed conflicts (IACs). The carnage and devastation that they leave behind are liable to be calamitous. For sure, not every NIAC necessarily ends up in a catastrophe. But the societal tissue may not mend for a long time following outbursts of implacable hatred and enmity among inhabitants of the same national space. Winning domestic peace subsequent to a sanguinary NIAC may be a slow and arduous process. A NIAC that is ostensibly over can flare up again at a different period, perhaps in a reconfigured manner.

6. Although a NIAC is an intra-State – rather than an inter-State – affair, traditional international law could not be entirely oblivious to its external reverberations. In particular, NIACs had to be woven by the international

Guatemala, Guiana, Guinea, Guinea Bissau, India, Indonesia, Iran, Iraq, Ivory Coast, Kyrgyzstan, Laos, Lebanon, Liberia, Libya, Mali, Moldova, Mozambique, Nepal, Nicaragua, Niger, Nigeria, Oman, Pakistan, Papua New Guinea, Paraguay, Peru, Philippines, Russia (Chechnya), Senegal, Sierra Leone, Solomon Islands, Somalia, South Africa, South Sudan, Spain (Basque region), Sri Lanka, Sudan, Suriname, Syria, Tajikistan, Thailand, Turkey, Uganda, UK (Northern Ireland), Western Sahara and Yemen.

[2] There are a host of instances (see E. La Haye, *War Crimes in Internal Armed Conflicts* 42 (2008)). For a recent one, see B. Zawacki, 'Politically Inconvenient, Legally Correct: A Non-International Armed Conflict in Southern Thailand', 18 *JCSL* 151–79 (2013).

[3] See L.R. Blank and G.S. Corn, 'Losing the Forest for the Trees: Syria, Law, and the Pragmatics of Conflict Recognition', 46 *Van.JTL* 693, 725–30 (2013).

legal system into the fabric of the principle of non-intervention (see Chapter 5), the concept of recognition (see Chapter 6), and the norms of State responsibility (see Chapter 7).[4] Yet, for centuries, international law brushed aside the principal issue of streamlining the conduct of hostilities in the course of a NIAC.

7. All this changed abruptly in 1949 (see *infra* 20). Since that date, the international regulation of the conduct of hostilities in NIACs has undergone tremendous growth, becoming the fulcrum of contemporary interest. In large measure, the normative corpus apposite to NIACs may be seen as an extrapolation of the more robust *jus in bello* applicable in IACs (a body of law whose genesis had already occurred a century earlier). But, as we shall see (*infra* 701 *et seq.*), the relationship between the two legal regimes of IAC and NIAC law of armed conflict is characterized not only by convergence: close attention must be paid to the built-in divergence between them.

B. LONIAC

8. Throughout the present volume, usage will be made of the acronym LONIAC standing for 'law of non-international armed conflict', which must be understood as synonymous with the common expression IHL ('international humanitarian law'). The locution LONIAC is preferable by virtue of its dispassionate connotations. LONIAC avoids a false impression (implicit in the 'humanitarian' limb of IHL) that the rules governing NIAC hostilities are *de rigueur* humanitarian in nature. It is an irrefutable fact that, even though humanitarianism is always a consideration, many of these rules are engendered primarily by military necessity.

9. The operation of LONIAC seems to create a psychological problem for incumbent Governments, which naturally desire to uproot all vestiges of rebellion against their writ. From the inception of LONIAC, the international community has recognized that this set of rules does not question a Government's right to suppress an insurrection by force.[5] The sole purpose of LONIAC is to impose meaningful restraints on both the Government and those rising against it: all parties must refrain from employing means or methods of hostilities that are banned by international law.

---

[4] See J.H.W. Verzijl, IX *International Law in Historical Perspective* 501–2 (1978).
[5] See *Commentary, I Geneva Convention* 61 (J.S. Pictet ed., 1952).

10. Additional Protocol II to the Geneva Conventions (AP/II) of 1977 – which is dedicated in its entirety to LONIAC (see *infra* 21) – sets forth in Paragraph (1) of Article 3:[6]

> Nothing in this Protocol shall be invoked for the purpose of affecting the sovereignty of a State or the responsibility of the government, by all legitimate means, to maintain or re-establish law and order in the State or to defend the national unity and territorial integrity of the State.

Congruent language is used in Article 8(3) of the 1998 Rome Statute of the International Criminal Court (ICC):

> Nothing in paragraph 2(c) and (e) shall affect the responsibility of a Government to maintain or re-establish law and order in the State or to defend the unity and territorial integrity of the State, by all legitimate means.[7]

11. The phrase 'by all legitimate means', appearing in both texts, must be underscored. It connotes that, although the beleaguered Government has a right and a responsibility to restore law and order, it is not allowed to utilize means and methods that do not cohere with LONIAC.[8] There is a delicate balance here. LONIAC ordains restraints in fighting, yet there is no denial of the existence of 'imperative military reasons' (*infra* 471) or 'necessities of the conflict' (*infra* 572). The incumbent Government is vested with a prerogative of acting vigorously in putting law and order back on track, but it can do so only on condition that its conduct is on the same page as LONIAC.[9]

C. No NIAC jus ad bellum

12. LONIAC is the counterpart in intra-State hostilities of IAC *jus in bello*. But there is no NIAC counterpart to the *jus ad bellum*, which determines the legality of an armed conflict between States. A prohibition of relying on force as a mode of settling disputes in international relations

---

[6] Protocol Additional to the Geneva Conventions of 12 August 1949, and Relating to the Protection of Victims of Non-International Armed Conflicts (Protocol II) (AP/II), 1977, *Laws of Armed Conflicts* 459, 461–2.

[7] Rome Statute of the ICC, 1998, *Laws of Armed Conflicts* 1314, 1321.

[8] See A. Zimmermann, 'Article 8(3)', *Commentary on the Rome Statute of the International Criminal Court: Observers' Notes, Article by Article* 502, 503 (2nd edn, O. Triffterer ed., 2008).

[9] See M. Bothe, 'War Crimes', I *The Rome Statute of the International Criminal Court: A Commentary* 379, 424 (A. Cassese *et al.* eds., 2002).

is enshrined in Article 2(4) of the Charter of the United Nations (UN)[10] and is embedded in current customary international law as *jus cogens*.[11] However, '[t]he use of force solely within a State is not covered' by that prohibition, so that it is not unlawful either (i) for the population to unleash an insurrection within a State; or (ii) for the incumbent Government to use its extensive resources in furtherance of the suppression of the revolt.[12]

13. The fact that international law is content with a ban on recourse to inter-State force – without a cognate prohibition of resort to intra-State force – may seem surprising, given the frequency, ferocity and far-flung fallout of NIACs. But this is the indisputable, albeit grim, reality. The domestic law of every State is dedicated to the preservation of internal order: it forbids taking violent action designed to topple the powers that be. But international law does not impose on the population of a country any obligation to desist from an insurrection. The flip side of the coin is that there is no international legal right to rebellion, and international law does not deny the entitlement of the incumbent Government to stamp out an insurgency by force.[13] It has been suggested that international law should at least require the parties to a NIAC to settle their dispute amicably (through negotiation, mediation or arbitration),[14] but even that does not seem to be in the offing.

14. The absence of *jus ad bellum* has far-reaching consequences affecting the whole vista of NIACs. Preeminently, the concept of a right to self-defence as an exception to the prohibition of the use of force – which plays a central role in IACs[15] – has no traction in the context of NIACs.

15. The Security Council's powers under the UN Charter have been exercised in a manner catching NIACs in the Council's net (see *infra* 276). But this speaks more of the towering authority of the Council and less about the ripening of any new general precept in international law concerning the illegality of NIACs. It has been contended that the Council's practice is indicative of 'the possible emergence of *jus ad bellum* norms governing the recourse to violence in internal disputes' (especially

[10] Charter of the United Nations, 1945, 9 *Int.Leg.* 327, 332.
[11] See Y. Dinstein, *War, Aggression and Self-Defence* 95–8, 104–5 (5th edn, 2012).
[12] See A. Randelzhofer and O. Dörr, 'Article 2(4)', I *The Charter of the United Nations: A Commentary* 200, 214 (3rd edn, B. Simma *et al.* eds, 2012).
[13] See A. Bellal and L. Doswald-Beck, 'Evaluating the Use of Force during the Arab Spring', 14 *YIHL* 3, 12 (2011).
[14] See R. Wedgwood, 'The Use of Force in Civil Disputes', 26 *Is.YHR* 239, 248–9 (1996).
[15] See Dinstein, *supra* note 11, at 187–302.

when democratically elected Governments are liquidated by force).[16] But the record of the Council clearly discloses that it does not purport to enlarge the scope of Article 2(4) to NIACs.[17]

16. The only faint echo of a NIAC *jus ad bellum* may be detected when a treaty is concluded by a group of States – applicable in their relations *inter se* – designed to leverage their combined military assets, extending mutual support for extinguishing an insurgency against any one of them (see *infra* 254). But such a treaty would be (i) regional rather than global; (ii) contingent on the consent of the affected States at every stage of its adoption and implementation (see *infra* 252–3); and (iii) confined to military assistance granted to the incumbent Government, in contradistinction to those taking up arms against it (see *infra* 238 *et seq.*, 264 *et seq.*).

II. The legal strata of NIAC law

17. LONIAC and other branches of international law establish a solid corpus of juridical norms related to NIACs. These are embodied either in treaties or in customary international law (or in both). Treaties and custom are the principal strata of international law.

18. Treaties and custom are commonly adduced as 'sources' of that law, but this popular appellation only complicates the discussion. The term 'source' – literally associated with a fountainhead from which a stream of water issues – does not do justice to the role that treaties and custom play within the international legal system. Treaties and custom are not the sources but the very streams of international law, flowing either together or apart from each other. The coinage 'strata of international law' articulates the idea that treaties and custom *are* international law.[18]

A. Treaty law

19. Under Article 2(1)(a) of the 1969 Vienna Convention on the Law of Treaties (VCLT) – a treaty 'means an international agreement concluded

---

[16] K. Samuels, '*Jus ad Bellum* and Civil Conflicts: A Case Study of the International Community's Approach to Violence in the Conflict of Sierra Leone', 8 *JCSL* 315, 338 (2003).

[17] See O. Corten, *The Law against War: The Prohibition on the Use of Force in Contemporary International Law* 132–3 (2010).

[18] For more on this subject, see Y. Dinstein, 'The Interaction between Customary International Law and Treaties', 322 *RCADI* 245, 260–1 (2006).

between States'.[19] In the words of the Permanent Court of International Justice (PCIJ), in its 1926 Judgment, in the *German Interests in Polish Upper Silesia* case:

A treaty only creates law as between the States which are parties to it.[20]

States must express their consent to become Contracting Parties to treaties (see *infra* 214).

20. The framers of the four Geneva Conventions for the Protection of War Victims (concluded in 1949 and currently in force for every existing State) ushered in a new era by crafting for the first time an agreed-upon text relating directly to LONIAC. This is Common Article 3 of the four Conventions (*infra* 409). Admittedly, the language chosen by the drafters consists in the main of broad brush strokes rather than specifics (see *infra* 413–14), but it must never be forgotten that it was Common Article 3 which blazed a new trail in the terrain of NIAC law.

21. After the adoption of Common Article 3 in 1949, it took almost three decades before the need to go beyond mere generalities with respect to LONIAC became firmly implanted in the international legal mindset. In 1977, AP/II was appended to the Geneva Conventions, comprising more concrete stipulations and assigned in its entirety to the subject of NIACs. Yet, as will be shown *infra* 118 *et seq.*, the scope of application of AP/II is narrower than that of Common Article 3.

22. AP/II is twinned with Additional Protocol I (AP/I), which is devoted to IACs.[21] On balance, there is no comparison between the breadth or depth of AP/I and AP/II. AP/II norms (which will be examined in detail in Chapter 8) have been described as 'a debilitated replica'[22] or 'a pale shadow'[23] of the AP/I rules curbing IACs. One can belabour the perception that AP/II is 'a sadly flawed document',[24] compared to what it might have been in a perfect world. But, no less, one can pinpoint the positive

---

[19] Vienna Convention on the Law of Treaties (VCLT), [1969] *UNJY* 140, 141.

[20] *Case Concerning Certain German Interests in Polish Upper Silesia* (Merits) (Germany/Poland), I *WCR* 510, 529.

[21] Protocol Additional to the Geneva Conventions of 12 August 1949, and Relating to the Protection of Victims of International Armed Conflicts (Protocol I) (AP/I), 1977, *Laws of Armed Conflicts* 711.

[22] G.I.A.D. Draper, *Reflections on Law and Armed Conflict: Selected Works* 146 (M.A. Meyer and H. McCoubrey eds., 1998).

[23] L. Condorelli, 'Remarks', 85 *PASIL* 90, 95 (1991).

[24] W.J. Fenrick, 'Remarks', 2 *AUJILP* 473, 475 (1987).

achievements of AP/II against the backdrop of the shortfalls of Common Article 3.

23. AP/II does not supplant Common Article 3. Instead (in the words of Paragraph (1) of Article 1 of AP/II; *infra* 118), it 'develops and supplements' Common Article 3, 'without modifying its existing conditions of application'. The provisions of Common Article 3 thus continue to apply to every NIAC, whether or not it is also covered by AP/II with its narrower scope of application.[25]

24. The great majority of States – albeit not all – are Contracting Parties to AP/II. As far as non-Contracting Parties are concerned, the dominant question is whether relevant stipulations of AP/II are currently viewed as declaratory of customary international law. The answer to the question varies from one section of AP/II to another, and we shall come back to it *infra* 654 *et seq.*

25. Quite a few additional treaties also appertain to LONIAC. Most of them will be cited in context, but it is useful to mention the following instruments at this preliminary juncture:

(i) Article 19 of the 1954 Hague Convention for the Protection of Cultural Property in the Event of Armed Conflict (CPCP)[26] says, in Paragraph (1), that '[i]n the event of an armed conflict not of an international character occurring within the territory of one of the High Contracting Parties, each party to the conflict shall be bound to apply, as a minimum, the provisions of the present Convention which relate to respect for cultural property'. The passage is invigorated by Paragraph (1) of Article 22 of the 1999 Second Protocol to the CPCP.[27] Whereas it may be inferred from Article 19 that some (unspecified) provisions of the CPCP do not apply in a NIAC, Article 22 'makes it clear that the Protocol applies *in its entirety* in the event of an internal conflict'.[28]

(ii) Article 8(2) of the 1998 Rome Statute of the ICC sets out in Paragraphs (c) and (e) (*infra* 559, 572) a detailed roster of war crimes – coming within the jurisdiction of the ICC – committed during NIACs.

---

[25] See D. Schindler, 'The Different Types of Armed Conflicts according to the Geneva Conventions and Protocols', 163 *RCADI* 117, 149 (1979).

[26] Hague Convention for the Protection of Cultural Property in the Event of Armed Conflict (CPCP), 1954, *Laws of Armed Conflicts* 999, 1007. The CPCP was sponsored by UNESCO.

[27] Second Protocol to the CPCP, 1999, *Laws of Armed Conflicts* 1037, 1045.

[28] A. Gioia, 'The Development of International Law Relating to the Protection of Cultural Property in the Event of Armed Conflict: The Second Protocol to the 1954 Hague Convention', 11 *It.YIL* 25, 32 (2001). Emphasis in the original.

B. Customary international law

26. Customary international law, to repeat the well-known formula appearing in Article 38(1)(b) of the Statute of the International Court of Justice (ICJ), is defined as 'evidence of a general practice accepted as law'.[29] Two elements are condensed here: (objective) general practice and (subjective) *opinio juris sive necessitatis* (i.e. 'a belief that this practice is rendered obligatory by the existence of a rule of law requiring it').[30]

27. As the ICJ held in 1985, in the Libya/Malta *Continental Shelf* case: 'It is of course axiomatic that the material of customary international law is to be looked for primarily in the actual practice and *opinio juris* of States'.[31] Earlier, in the 1969 *North Sea Continental Shelf* cases, the ICJ pronounced that State practice – 'including that of States whose interests are specially affected' – has to be extensive.[32] Extensive or 'general' does not coincide with universal or unanimous practice.

28. It has been pointed out by the Appeals Chamber of the International Criminal Tribunal for the former Yugoslavia (ICTY), in the landmark *Tadić* Decision of 1995, that the formation of NIAC customary norms must rest primarily on 'official pronouncements of States, military manuals and judicial decisions', rather than the conduct of troops in the field (which may be in breach of the law).[33]

29. Unlike treaties, general customary international law is binding on all States, irrespective of their consent (unless a State has the status of 'persistent objector' at the time of the consolidation of the custom).[34] NIAC customary international law has grown side by side with treaty law, and to a large degree thanks to it. A treaty may reflect customary international law at the time of its drafting, but it can also generate custom at a later stage.[35] That is to say, the general practice of States (with an emphasis on the practice of non-Contracting Parties) – supported by *opinio juris* – may, in time, adapt itself to the treaty legal regime. If so, the treaty (in whole or in part) becomes declaratory of customary international law.

---

[29] Statute of the International Court of Justice, Annexed to the Charter of the United Nations, 1945, 9 *Int.Leg.* 510, 522.

[30] See Dinstein, *supra* note 11, at 266–7.

[31] *Case Concerning the Continental Shelf* (Libya/Malta), [1985] *ICJ Rep.* 13, 29.

[32] *North Sea Continental Shelf* cases (Germany/Denmark; Germany/Netherlands), [1969] *ICJ Rep.* 3, 43.

[33] *Prosecutor* v. *Tadić* (Decision on Jurisdiction) (ICTY, Appeals Chamber, 1995), 35 *ILM* 35, 63 (1996).

[34] See Dinstein, *supra* note 11, at 282–7.   [35] See *ibid.*, 346–76.

30. Over the years, multiple treaty provisions relating to LONIAC have generated customary international law binding on all States. In the 1986 *Nicaragua* case, the ICJ rendered judgment that Common Article 3 expresses 'minimum rules applicable to international and to non-international conflicts';[36] in other words, it gives vent to customary international law applicable both in IACs and in NIACs. A Trial Chamber of the ICTY, in the *Delalić et al.* case of 1998, clarified the international legal progress in the following way:

> While in 1949 the insertion of a provision concerning internal armed conflicts into the Geneva Conventions may have been innovative, there can be no question that the protections and prohibitions enunciated in that provision have come to form part of customary international law.[37]

Earlier, in the *Tadić* Decision of 1995, the Appeals Chamber of the ICTY went even further:

> some treaty rules [governing internal strife] have gradually become part of customary law. This holds true for common Article 3 of the 1949 Geneva Conventions, as was authoritatively held by the International Court of Justice (Nicaragua Case ...), but also applies to Article 19 of the Hague Convention for the Protection of Cultural Property in the Event of Armed Conflict of 14 May 1954, and ... to the core of Additional Protocol II of 1977.[38]

31. The fact that Common Article 3 is regarded today as declaratory of customary international law, and that it straddles both IACs and NIACs, is sometimes a source of confusion. To be sure, the substance of Common Article 3 is a minimum standard applicable in any armed conflict. But, contrary to what is occasionally asserted,[39] that does not mean that LONIAC *eo nomine* applies irrespective of territorial boundaries (see *infra* 74).

32. The declaratory standing of treaty provisions must be appraised on the basis of their success in presenting a true mirror image of custom. Although a treaty as such is always binding solely on Contracting Parties, non-Contracting Parties are obliged to comply with declaratory

---

[36] *Case Concerning Military and Paramilitary Activities in and against Nicaragua* (Merits) (Nicaragua/USA), [1986] *ICJ Rep.* 14, 114.

[37] *Prosecutor* v. *Delalić et al.* (ICTY, Trial Chamber, 1998), para. 301.

[38] *Prosecutor* v. *Tadić*, *supra* note 33, at 63.

[39] See J. Cerone, 'Jurisdiction and Power: The Intersection of Human Rights Law and the Law of Non-International Armed Conflict in an Extraterritorial Context', 40 *Is.LR* 396, 412 (2007).

norms embedded in the text: not because but, as it were, despite their incorporation in the treaty.[40]

III. The triple classification of violence during a NIAC

33. Violence during a NIAC is rampant, but it has to be subdivided into three separate categories: (i) hostilities; (ii) ordinary crimes; and (iii) war crimes. After pointing out the differences between these categories – from the vantage points of both LONIAC and domestic law – we shall take a look at the practical significance of the classification.

A. Hostilities

34. A NIAC signifies that hostilities are taking place between two or more opposing sides, chiefly insurgents and the incumbent Government (we shall discuss *infra* 87 an additional scenario of fighting between organized armed groups *inter se*). The hallmark of NIAC hostilities is that they are regulated by LONIAC. Hostilities conducted in conformity with the prescripts of LONIAC, even if their consequences are lethal (to persons) or destructive (to property), are not deemed criminal by international law.

35. The gist of hostilities is violence: its preparation, planning and execution at all levels (including command and control). But hostilities also consist of ancillary non-violent operations, such as the gathering of intelligence about the opposing side, logistics (delivering to fighters armaments, equipment, transportation, food, fuel and other essentials), and running a network of electronic or other communications: these measures, albeit non-violent, are indispensable to the successful mounting of a military campaign.[41]

36. Violence involves human casualties or (more than nominal) destruction of property. The injury or damage can be caused kinetically, with explosives, bullets, etc. Consequential violence may also be produced by cyber attacks (gaining control of enemy computers and inducing crashes, explosions, and so forth). Nevertheless, cyber operations – in and of themselves – will not suffice for triggering a NIAC.[42] This

---

[40] See Dinstein, *supra* note 11, at 351.

[41] See R. Otto, *Targeted Killings and International Law with Special Regard to Human Rights and International Humanitarian Law* 273–5 (2012).

[42] See *Talinn Manual on the International Law Applicable to Cyber Warfare* 85 (M.N. Schmitt ed., 2013).

is due to their inability to meet the preconditions required. In particular, they will usually not be sufficiently protracted (see *infra* 96). But there may also be an issue with their intensity (see *infra* 107).

B. Ordinary crimes

37. Ordinary crimes are common offences, as determined by the domestic law of Ruritania (including some offences the suppression of which is mandated by treaties), regardless of a NIAC. When a NIAC is in progress, all acts of violence committed by insurgents (unlike those performed by members of governmental armed forces and law enforcement agencies in the discharge of their domestic legal duty to put down the insurrection) will be deemed ordinary crimes by the Ruritanian executive and judicial authorities. LONIAC pays much heed to the question of whether acts of violence (and ancillary activities) can be subsumed under the heading of hostilities, as distinct from war crimes (see *infra* 42). By contrast, the Ruritanian domestic legal system casts aside any distinction between hostilities and other acts of violence, stripping away the trappings of a NIAC and inquiring only whether the conduct under review has been in breach of the domestic penal code.

38. Needless to say, the outbreak of a NIAC does not entail the cessation of those criminal activities in Ruritania that are extraneous to the conduct of hostilities. Indeed, ordinary crimes may be on the rise once a NIAC is in full swing. There are a host of possible reasons, e.g., (i) psychological impulses associated with uncertain times; (ii) the omnipresence of weapons during a NIAC; and even (iii) a shift in the attention of law enforcement agencies from run-of-the-mill transgressions to the more vicious atrocities widespread in a civil strife.

39. Ordinary crimes, which are perpetrated without a connection to the NIAC *per se*, are spurred by personal stimuli (anger, revenge, fear, greed, lust, etc.), and not by the impetus to vanquish the foe in the NIAC. For the most part, ordinary crimes are offences committed by 'civilians' (see *infra* 185) against one another.[43] But, exceptionally, (i) at one end of the spectrum, certain acts by civilians directed at fellow civilians may also be tantamount to war crimes (see *infra* 198); and (ii) at the other end, acts by insurgent fighters will be deemed by the domestic law to be ordinary crimes despite their connection to the NIAC (see *supra* 37).

---

[43] See A. Cassese, *International Criminal Law* 83 (2nd edn, 2008).

40. The Ruritanian domestic legal system is the sole arbiter of the prosecution and punishment of ordinary crimes (pursuant to the Ruritanian penal code), whether or not they take place during a NIAC. In this respect, Ruritania is subordinated only to international human rights law. As for LONIAC, it is not interested in ordinary crimes – as defined by the domestic law of Ruritania – and it does not apply to them at all, unless they constitute acts of hostilities in the NIAC.[44]

41. Should foreign troops belonging to Utopia take part in the NIAC in Ruritania at the invitation of the incumbent Government (see *infra* 238 *et seq.*), the legal frame of reference will be similar. From the viewpoint of Utopia, any insurgent attack against its armed forces will be considered a crime (whether or not it is also a war crime).[45]

C. War crimes

42. NIAC war crimes are serious violations of LONIAC for which there is individual accountability. In Chapter 10, we shall review what particular acts are labelled by international criminal law as NIAC war crimes. The domestic legal system of Ruritania may opt to incorporate these illicit acts in its penal code, commingling them with ordinary crimes (without pegging them as war crimes). The unobfuscated identity of NIAC war crimes as international offences is important only for purposes of jurisdiction. Ruritania can exercise jurisdiction over any act that it chooses to penalize, as long as there exists a link of (i) territoriality (in terms of the *locus delicti*), or (ii) nationality (of either the perpetrator or the victim). However, NIAC war crimes are also subject to prosecution and punishment by international courts and tribunals (on the footing of a treaty or binding Security Council decision), as well as by foreign countries (in the exercise of universal jurisdiction; see *infra* 620 *et seq.*). The wellspring of the judicial clout of these non-domestic forums is the nature of NIAC war crimes as international crimes.

43. Ordinary crimes are ordinary because they take place – in breach of the domestic legal system of Ruritania – independently of the occurrence of a NIAC. By contrast, NIAC war crimes (as defined by international law) are committed in a manner linearly connected to the NIAC. As the ICTY

---

[44] See I *How Does Law Protect in War?* 348 (ICRC, 3rd edn, M. Sassòli, A.A. Bouvier and A. Quintin eds., 2011).

[45] See C. Greenwood, 'International Humanitarian Law and United Nations Military Operations', 1 *YIHL* 3, 26 (1998).

Trial Chamber stated in the *Delalić et al.* case of 1998: 'There must be an obvious link between the criminal act and the armed conflict'.[46] A Trial Chamber of the International Criminal Tribunal for Rwanda (ICTR), in the *Kayishema et al.* case of 1999, spoke about 'offences, which have a nexus with the armed conflict'.[47]

44. The nexus between a war crime and a NIAC goes to the heart of the matter.[48] As the *Kayishema et al.* Judgment put it, the mere fact that a crime is committed during a NIAC does not by itself establish the required nexus: the linkage has to be direct.[49] This is determined by the ambient circumstances. In the 2002 *Kunarac et al.* Judgment, the ICTY Appeals Chamber said:

> What ultimately distinguishes a war crime from a purely domestic offence is that a war crime is shaped by or dependent upon the environment – the armed conflict – in which it is committed. It need not have been planned or supported by some form of policy. The armed conflict need not have been causal to the commission of the crime, but the existence of an armed conflict must, at a minimum, have played a substantial part in the perpetrator's ability to commit it, his decision to commit it, the manner in which it was committed or the purpose for which it was committed.[50]

A NIAC must therefore lie at the root of the crime.

45. The ICTR Appeals Chamber held in 2002, in the *Akayesu* case, that the nexus to a NIAC implies – in most instances – that the perpetrator of a war crime has a 'special relationship' to a party to the conflict, although that is not a condition precedent for triggering responsibility for every war crime.[51] By applying an elastic criterion, the Appeals Judgment reversed a whole line of decisions delivered by lower-instance Trial Chambers on the same point.[52]

46. There is room for another angle of elasticity. Persons who commit NIAC war crimes while belonging to a party to the conflict do not invariably act in pursuance of the public cause which they champion. Some NIAC war crimes are perpetrated by such persons for strictly private

---

[46] *Prosecutor* v. *Delalić et al., supra* note 37, at para. 193.

[47] *Prosecutor* v. *Kayishema et al.* (ICTR, Trial Chamber, 1999), para. 185.

[48] See C. Meindersma, 'Violations of Common Article 3 of the Geneva Conventions as Violations of the Laws or Customs of War under Article 3 of the Statute of the International Criminal Tribunal for the Former Yugoslavia', 42 *NILR* 375, 386 (1995).

[49] *Prosecutor* v. *Kayishema et al., supra* note 47, at para. 600.

[50] *Prosecutor* v. *Kunarac et al.* (ICTY, Appeals Chamber, 2002), para. 58.

[51] *Prosecutor* v. *Akayesu* (ICTR, Appeals Chamber, 2001), para. 444.

[52] See R. Boed, 'Individual Criminal Responsibility for Violations of Article 3 Common to the Geneva Conventions of 1949 and of Additional Protocol II Thereto in the Case Law of the International Criminal Tribunal for Rwanda', 13 *CLF* 293, 312–17 (2002).

ends. Rape in the course of hostilities (see *infra* 580) is a telling example. So is the act of pillage (see *infra* 436) or despoiling the dead (*infra* 454–5). What counts is not just the nature of the act but also the situational context, which determines whether a nexus between the war crime and the NIAC is in place.

47. No division between NIAC war crimes and ordinary crimes is as simple as it may sound. When members of the armed forces of the incumbent Government engage in violent activities, it is easier to distinguish between conduct in an official capacity – which is attributable to the State (see *infra* 360) – and exertions that are purely private. But when it comes to insurgents, borderlines may become blurred. It may task the skills of lawyers and judges to neatly compartmentalize crimes into discrete categories of those that are, and those that are not, linked to the NIAC.

48. The most egregious tableau in which ordinary crimes committed by insurgents can still have a nexus to the NIAC is that of an insurrection stoked by criminal motivations. In general, every effort must be made to draw a line between the activities of organized criminal gangs and an insurgency.[53] Still, criminal incentives (for instance, in the case of narco-traffickers or dealers in 'blood diamonds') cannot be wholly disentangled from the origins of the NIAC.[54] Criminal gangs may be 'highly organized and conduct hostilities with the government at a level of intensity consistent with the existence of a non-international armed conflict'.[55] Some commentators even believe that the current strife between the Mexican Government and drug cartels fulfils the preconditions of a NIAC.[56]

49. If insurgent criminal gangs deal with narcotics, counter-action by the Government may qualify as a part of NIAC hostilities only when launched against the rebellious narco-traffickers. Eradication of opium poppy crops or coca plants as such is a matter of law enforcement. But, since it may be ancillary to the hostilities, it may fall within the 'interstices' of the NIAC.[57]

---

[53] See P. Hauck and S. Peterke, 'Organized Crime and Gang Violence in National and International Law', 878 *IRRC* 407, 430–3 (2010).

[54] See S. Vité, 'Typology of Armed Conflicts in International Humanitarian Law: Legal Concepts and Actual Situations', 873 *IRRC* 69, 78 (2009).

[55] M.N. Schmitt, 'The Status of Opposition Fighters in a Non-International Armed Conflict', 88 *ILS* 119, 123 (*Non-International Armed Conflict in the Twenty-First Century*, K. Watkin *et al.* eds., 2012).

[56] See C. Bergal, 'The Mexican Drug War: The Case for a Non-International Armed Conflict Classification', 34 *Fo.ILJ* 1042–88 (2010–11).

[57] Cf. J. Klabbers, *International Law* 217 (2013).

D. The triple classification and wilful killing

50. To better comprehend the dissonance between hostilities, ordinary crimes and war crimes, it is useful to consider the archetypical act of wilful killing. After all, the wilful killing of an adversary is the paramount manifestation of hostilities. In the form of murder, wilful killing is also a top-of-the-line ordinary domestic crime. And murder is included in the roll of NIAC war crimes (see *infra* 559).

51. The premeditated slaying of an adversary is a commonplace instance of NIAC hostilities, and it will usually be condoned by LONIAC. However, in this respect, the domestic legal system of Ruritania (the country where the NIAC is taking place) will part company with LONIAC. The Ruritanian penal system will set apart the *mise en scène* in which a member of the armed forces kills an insurgent in the line of duty and that of an insurgent killing a Government agent. The latter act will be viewed by the Ruritanian domestic legal system as plain murder. The perpetrator will not be perceived as covered by any mantle of impunity: on the contrary, given the backdrop of a rebellion, the act may be regarded as an aggravated crime punishable severely by the domestic courts.

52. The crux of the issue is that there is no built-in distinction between an act of plain murder and an act of wilful killing while fighting in a NIAC.[58] What is materially different is only the attitude of the legal system. From the Ruritanian domestic standpoint, murder is murder (regardless of the NIAC surroundings). Conversely, from a LONIAC vantage point, an act of wilful killing will not count as murder if carried out as part of the hostilities. When Common Article 3 (*infra* 409) speaks of 'murder of all kinds', the expression relates only to victims who are persons taking no active part in the hostilities.

E. The disparate perspectives of domestic and international law

53. The impression of a NIAC legal landscape completely depends on the perspective: that of the Ruritanian domestic law or of LONIAC. When observed through the lens of the Ruritanian legal system, the three prongs of the glossary of NIAC violence – (i) acts of hostilities; (ii) ordinary crimes; and (iii) war crimes – do not make a real difference in a pragmatic sense. Be the classification of the violence as it may, the perpetrator will be subject to possible prosecution and trial by Ruritanian domestic

---

[58] See *Prosecutor v. Delalić et al., supra* note 37, at para. 421.

courts. An insurgent who kills in the course of hostilities is not placed in a more advantageous position compared to an ordinary criminal or a war criminal. By turning a blind eye to the narrative of hostilities in this context, the Ruritanian domestic law thus offers a NIAC insurgent no reward for refraining from the commission of a war crime.[59] An insurgent may well ask why it behoves him to stay clear of the path of perpetrating war crimes, if he is going to languish in a Ruritanian jail whether or not he fights in compliance with LONIAC.[60]

54. The picture undergoes a kaleidoscopic change when viewed from the LONIAC perspective. As far as an international or a foreign forum is concerned – when a penal trial looms on the horizon – the exercise of jurisdiction will entirely depend on the commission of a war crime. Mere participation in hostilities, not entailing a breach of LONIAC, will be excused. Ordinary domestic crimes will be ignored (unless extradition to Ruritania is requested).

IV. Motives and goals of a NIAC

A. Motives

55. In a legal analysis, the nuts and bolts of a NIAC are not the subjective motives of an insurgency but its objective manifestations. The critical question is what is happening, and not why or wherefore. Delving into the causes driving insurgents to try to displace an incumbent Government may be of political, sociological or historical merit. However, legally speaking, this is of tangential or no interest. What ultimately counts is the reality of the NIAC.

56. As a matter of law, it is immaterial whether people feel politically oppressed; economically discontented; socially marginalized; ideologically, religiously or linguistically alienated; or are otherwise desirous of an emancipatory reform. The reasons propelling individuals and groups to engineer an uprising against the incumbent Government (or to bring about a violent confrontation between ethnic, religious or social groups

---

[59] See M. Sassòli, 'Jus ad Bellum and Jus in Bello – The Separation between the Legality of the Use of Force and Humanitarian Rules to Be Respected in Warfare: Crucial or Outdated?', *International Law and Armed Conflict: Exploring the Faultlines – Essays in Honour of Yoram Dinstein* 241, 256 (M.N. Schmitt and J. Pejic eds., 2007).

[60] See J.K. Kleffner, 'From "Belligerents" to "Fighters" and Civilians Directly Participating in Hostilities – on the Principle of Distinction in Non-International Armed Conflicts One Hundred Years after the Second Hague Peace Conference', 54 *NILR* 315, 323 (2007).

inter se, unrelated to the Government) may be obscure. As indicated (*supra* 48), an insurgency may even be riddled by ulterior criminal incentives. All that a lawyer is required to verify is that a NIAC, whatever its undercurrents, is actually taking place.

57. The irrelevance of the motives of a NIAC is especially noteworthy when they are multilayered. An insurgency may be instigated by a loose patchwork of rebellious groups whose dissensions are temporarily set aside in a joint aspiration to bring down the incumbent Government. As the NIAC in Syria since 2011 has demonstrated, insurgents of all stripes may coalesce, forming an anti-Government alliance of secularists (opposed to an authoritarian regime), Sunnis (resentful of an Alawite establishment), Muslim fundamentalists (striving to impose Sharia law) and Kurds (pining for autonomy). Given the wedge separating their short-term collaboration (actuated by a common yearning for regime change) from their long-term objectives, insurgents may slug it out with each other while doing battle with the Government.

B. Goals

58. The goals of an insurrection are of greater interest for a lawyer than its motives. As a maximum, insurgents may wish either (i) to demolish the incumbent Government and to take the helm of State into their own hands; or even (ii) to secede from the State. Yet, the horizons of a NIAC may be more limited. The insurgents may set their sights on less disruptive objectives, such as:

(i) Reorganization of the Government on the basis of a specific political blueprint;
(ii) Effectuating some radical constitutional innovations, transfer of power or land reform;
(iii) Rescinding policies which have deleterious effects on certain sections of the population;
(iv) Ensuring greater participation of peripheral groups in the political process;
(v) Securing fundamental freedoms for those feeling oppressed; or
(vi) Repealing financial decrees, gaining tax relief or obtaining monetary concessions.

59. The objectives of an insurgency may undergo reincarnation as momentum builds in the course of a NIAC. Violent outpourings of discontent – originally focused, perhaps, on minor grievances – are liable to

escalate over time, developing a wider and more ambitious agenda. Moreover, what appears at the outset to be a localized infection can metastasize into a disease potentially fatal to the body politic of the State and ending with secession.

60. The banner of secession, when hoisted by insurgents, is usually a call for total independence: the creation of a new sovereign State (Apollonia) on a portion of the territory of the local State (Ruritania). A prominent modern example of success is that of Bangladesh (which detached itself from Pakistan in 1971). Failed attempts at secession were made, e.g., by Biafra (which fought to break away from Nigeria in 1967–70) and the separatist Tamils (who stayed in the field in Sri Lanka for a quarter of a century: 1983–2009). Sometimes, there is an irredentist variant of the demand for secession. Instead of craving independent statehood, the insurgents may prefer forming a union with an existing foreign country (the way Greek Cypriot rebels wanted 'enosis' with Greece in the 1950s).

61. When secession is the goal of a NIAC, the insurgency may be consigned to a particular province, barely affecting the rest of the country. That is also the case when the goal of insurgents is regional autonomy[61] in a given district. Autonomy may either induce or solve a NIAC: it may be a coveted point of arrival as much as a rejected point of departure. When autonomy is non-existent, insurgents may insist on installing it within a portion of the Ruritanian territory. But this may be only an opening gambit. When regional autonomy is already functioning, the same or other insurgents may opt for an outright secession from Ruritania.

---

[61] On the meaning of autonomy regimes, see Y. Dinstein, 'Autonomy Regimes and International Law', 56 *Vill.LR* 437–53 (2011).

2

The preconditions of a NIAC

I. NIACs as armed conflicts

62. As we shall see (*infra* 118), the definition of NIACs appearing in AP/II establishes a rather high threshold. Yet, all NIACs are covered by the *chapeau* of Common Article 3 (*infra* 409), which adverts *tout court* to an 'armed conflict not of an international character'. This laconic language attests to the existence of the two components of (i) an armed conflict that is (ii) not of an international character. But, by themselves – even when combined – the two rudimentary ingredients do not cobble together a viable legal construct of a NIAC.

63. While a concrete determination as to whether a NIAC satisfies the demands of Common Article 3 has to be made 'on a case-by-case basis',[62] it is of the utmost importance to get a fix on the crossover point prior to which no NIAC can be recognized *in esse*. The postulate of an armed conflict is that hostilities are raging between two (or more) opposing sides (cf. *infra* 93 about parties to the conflict). We have already dwelt (*supra* 34–5) on the nature of 'hostilities'. The main challenge is to differentiate veritable NIAC hostilities from internal disturbances and IACs at both the lower and the upper ends of violence.[63] In the words of the 2004 British Manual of the Law of Armed Conflict, there is 'a spectrum of violence ranging from internal disturbances' to NIACs and IACs: each band of that spectrum is subject to another legal regime.[64]

64. The need to identify reliable gauges for determining the existence of a NIAC has been faced head-on by both the ICTY and the ICTR. In their jurisprudence, they have authoritatively established three additional criteria for NIACs: (iii) a modicum of organization of any party to the

---

[62] See *Prosecutor* v. *Rutaganda* (ICTR, Trial Chamber, 1999), 39 *ILM* 557, 575 (2000).

[63] See D. Ciobanu, 'The Concept and the Determination of the Existence of Armed Conflicts Not of an International Character', 58 *RDI* 43, 52 (1975).

[64] See *The Manual of the Law of Armed Conflict* 17 (UK Ministry of Defence, 2004).

conflict; (iv) protracted violence; and (v) intensity of fighting. All five preconditions of NIACs must be addressed.

II. NIACs distinguished from internal disturbances

A. Isolated and sporadic acts of violence

65. A NIAC raises the stakes of violence, evolving from internal disturbances that are not deemed an armed conflict. Paragraph (2) of Article 1 of AP/II[65] sets forth that it will not apply to 'situations of internal disturbances and tensions, such as riots, isolated and sporadic acts of violence and other acts of a similar nature, as not being armed conflicts'. The same formula is reprised in Article 8(2)(d) and (f) of the 1998 Rome Statute of the ICC (*infra* 570 and 605); in Paragraph (2) of Article 22 of the 1999 Second Protocol to the CPCP (cited *supra* 25); and in a 2001 Amendment to Article 1 of the 1980 Conventional Weapons Convention (CCCW)[66] (earlier, the formula was used in Article 1(3) of the 1996 Amended Protocol II to the CCCW[67]). By now, the routine treaty definition of the level of violence not amounting to a NIAC seems to be settled law.

66. Internal disturbances – not reaching the level of a NIAC – encompass disorderly demonstrations, rallies and protests. These events may be large-scale and rife with violence, perhaps inflicting incalculable human fatalities and/or colossal damage to property, but they do not become a NIAC as long as they are isolated and sporadic, i.e. they are not coordinated and sustained over a stretch of time. The mass rallies and counter-rallies in Egypt in 2011, which brought down the regime of H. Mubarak, bear testimony to this. Even the bloodbath that followed the ousting of the successor Government of M. Morsi (the Muslim Brotherhood) in 2013 did not spiral out of control beyond the verge of a NIAC (except in the Sinai Peninsula).

---

[65] AP/II, *supra* note 6, at 777.

[66] 2001 Amendment to Convention on Prohibitions or Restrictions on the Use of Certain Conventional Weapons which May be Deemed to be Excessively Injurious or to Have Indiscriminate Effects (CCCW), 1980, *Laws of Armed Conflicts* 185 n. 4. For the original text of the CCCW, see *ibid.*, 181.

[67] Amended Protocol to the CCCW on Prohibitions on Restrictions on the Use of Mines, Booby Traps and Other Devices (Protocol II), 1996, *Laws of Armed Conflicts* 196, *id.*

67. Grave internal disturbances may:

(i) Be the portents of an incipient NIAC, which starts to accelerate;
(ii) Subside and lapse into non-violent activities; or
(iii) Lead to the fall of the incumbent Government without a NIAC.

B. The law enforcement paradigm

68. The paradigm applicable to isolated and sporadic internal disturbances is that of law enforcement, and it is associated with human rights law as distinct from LONIAC. What this means is that force will be used only as a last resort (*ultima ratio*). Law-breakers during internal disturbances are ordinarily confronted by law enforcement agencies – namely, the police, the gendarmerie and similar domestic security forces – rather than by military contingents (army, air force, navy, marines, etc.). However, the gravity of the disturbances may energize the Government to harness all available resources, summoning military detachments to lend a hand to the police in restoring law and order. By itself, the infusion of the military into the fracas does not alter the law enforcement paradigm or make LONIAC applicable to the situation.[68] The soldiers involved will presumably act more muscularly than the police, availing themselves of their superior weapons and special training. But they are still expected to conduct themselves as *ersatz* policemen: using force as a last resort, in keeping with the law enforcement paradigm.[69] Should the troops exceed the ambit of that paradigm – by using force against adversaries as a first resort, in a manner consistent with the basic tenets of LONIAC (and not with the standards of law enforcement) – they would thereby lend credibility to an assumption that a NIAC is occurring.[70]

69. As a rule, law enforcement agents enjoy less leeway – in opening fire on rioters during isolated and sporadic internal disturbances – when measured against the degree of latitude conferred on armed forces engaged in a NIAC. But there are exceptions, when more elbow room in recourse to certain weapons is given to law enforcement agents quelling an ordinary internal disturbance, compared to military contingents in a NIAC. Preeminently, in Article I(5) of the 1993 Chemical

---

[68] See *Prosecutor* v. *Musema* (ICTR, Trial Chamber, 2000), para. 248.
[69] See C. von der Groeben, 'The Conflict in Colombia and the Relationship between Humanitarian Law and Human Rights Law in Practice: Analysis of the New Operational Law of the Colombian Armed Forces', 16 *JCSL* 141, 154–5 (2011).
[70] See A.W. Dahl and M. Sandbu, 'The Threshold of Armed Conflict', 45 *Mil.LLWR* 369, 380 (2006).

Weapons Convention (CWC) – an instrument on the cusp of universality today – Contracting Parties undertake not to use 'as a method of warfare' any 'riot control agents' (defined in Article II(7) as producing sensory irritation or disabling physical effects that disappear in a short while); whereas Article II(9)(d) explicitly allows the employment of the same chemical agents for law enforcement purposes, including domestic riot control.[71] The prohibition of use 'as a method of warfare' applies not only to IACs but also to NIACs.[72] In riot control situations, the ability to draw on non-lethal chemical agents (such as tear gas) may prove very effective in crowd dispersal.

III. The dichotomy of NIACs and IACs

70. The underlying dichotomy in the sphere of armed conflicts is between inter-State and intra-State clashes. '[E]very armed conflict not qualified as international is perforce non-international'.[73] It follows from the incisive language of Paragraph (1) of Article 1 of AP/II (*infra* 118) that there is no undistributed middle between IACs and NIACs.

71. The intra-State attribute is the hallmark of a NIAC, which cannot be waged between States. Any armed conflict in which two States are crossing swords with each other constitutes an IAC rather than a NIAC (see *infra* 164). A NIAC may develop into an IAC and vice versa: we shall see *infra* 176–7 how that may happen. Despite occasional difficulties in drawing the line of division between them (see *infra* 178–9), intra-State and inter-State armed conflicts must be kept apart in the legal analysis.

72. It ought to be accentuated that when internal disturbances degenerate into a NIAC, an armed conflict emerges where none existed before. When a NIAC morphs into an IAC, the armed conflict subsists but it acquires different characteristics and is reclassified under the aegis of a separate legal regime. It is then regulated not by LONIAC but by IAC *jus in bello*.

73. Some scholars contend that the rigid bifurcation in armed conflicts between IACs and NIACs has become 'outmoded', and it is time

---

[71] Convention on the Prohibition of the Development, Production, Stockpiling and Use of Chemical Weapons and on Their Destruction (CWC), 1993, *Laws of Armed Conflicts* 239, 242–4.

[72] See W. Krutzsch and R. Trapp, *A Commentary on the Chemical Weapons Convention* 18 (1994).

[73] M. Sassòli, 'Use and Abuse of the Laws of War in the War on Terrorism', 22 *L&E* 195, 200 (2004).

to recognize new breeds of armed conflicts.[74] Looking for a new matrix, it is advocated that a third category of so-called 'transnational' armed conflicts should be added to the traditional binary branching into IACs and NIACs.[75] But even proponents of this thesis usually concede that the notion is 'more properly characterized as *lex ferenda* than *lex lata*'.[76] The doctrinal impulse to break with tradition may be potent, but it is not backed by the general practice of States. Whenever States have an opportunity to pore over the matter, they reaffirm the existing dual taxonomy of IACs and NIACs. We shall witness that, for example, when scrutinizing the amendment to the Rome Statute of the ICC adopted in the Kampala Review Conference as late as 2010 (see *infra* 614).

IV. The territorial dimensions of NIACs

A. A NIAC as an armed conflict within the territory of a single State

(a) The internal character of a NIAC

74. The intra-State nature of a NIAC means that the armed conflict is internal, i.e. that it is basically waged inside the borders of a single State. This focal attribute is repeatedly stressed in relevant treaty texts. Thus, the *chapeau* of Common Article 3 (*infra* 409) speaks about 'an armed conflict not of an international character occurring in the territory of one of the High Contracting Parties'. The same formula is replicated in Paragraph (1) of Article 19 of the CPCP (*supra* 25): the only change being that the preposition 'in' is replaced by 'within'. Paragraph (1) of Article 1 of AP/II (*infra* 118) also relates to armed conflicts, 'which take place in the territory of a High Contracting Party'. As well, Article 8(2)(f) of the 1998 Rome Statute mentions 'armed conflicts that take place in the territory of a State' (*infra* 605). Paragraph (1) of Article 22 of the Second Protocol of 1999 to the CPCP (cited *supra* 25) goes back to 'an armed conflict not of an international character, occurring within the territory of one of the Parties'.

75. The phrase 'within the territory of one of the Parties' is self-explanatory. But even when the text alludes only to 'the territory of a

---

[74] R.S. Schöndorf, 'Extra-State Armed Conflicts: Is There a Need for a New Legal Regime?', 37 *NYUJILP* 1, 2–6 (2004–5).

[75] See C. Kress, 'Some Reflections on the International Legal Framework Governing Transnational Armed Conflicts', 15 *JCSL* 243–74 (2010).

[76] See G. Corn and E.T. Jensen, 'Transnational Armed Conflict: A "Principled" Approach to the Regulation of Counter-Terror Combat Operations', 42 *Is.LR* 46, 50 (2009).

State' – or 'a High Contracting Party' – it should be clear enough. After all, every armed conflict (even an IAC) largely takes place within territories of States: there is no value added in the phrase 'in the territory of a State' unless it is construed as a restriction to the territory of one State.[77]

76. In the *Musema* Judgment of 2000, a Trial Chamber of the ICTR spoke expressly about 'the territory of a single State'.[78] A Pre-Trial Chamber of the ICC, in the *Gombo* Decision of 2009, similarly pointed out that a NIAC must take place 'within the confines of a State territory'.[79]

(b) Extra-territorial spillover

77. The fact that a NIAC has to take place in the territory of a single State (Ruritania) does not denote that every act of hostilities, without any exception, must be contained within that territory. In reality, there can be a cross-border spillover of the hostilities.

(i) The high seas

78. Some acts of hostilities may be waged on the high seas, viz. beyond the territorial boundaries of all States. If insurgents prey on shipping (and aviation) on (or superjacent to) the high seas, the question arises: who is the target vessel (or aircraft)? Should the insurgents attack on the high seas warships or other vessels (or aircraft) belonging to the incumbent Ruritanian Government – or to any foreign State which is militarily intervening on behalf of that Government (see *infra* 238 *et seq.*) – these maritime (or aerial) acts of violence, although occurring extra-territorially, can certainly be pigeonholed as part of the NIAC hostilities.[80]

79. If insurgent vessels (or aircraft) attack on the high seas private ships (or aircraft) for private ends, they are considered pirates (namely, the perpetrators of an international crime who are subject to universal jurisdiction; cf. *infra* 620).[81] The definition of piracy in the 1982 Law of the Sea (LOS) Convention relates to acts of violence committed on

---

[77] See K. Coombes, 'Protecting Civilians during the Fight against Transnational Terrorism: Applying International Humanitarian Law to Transnational Armed Conflicts', 46 *Can. YIL* 241, 261 (2008).

[78] *Prosecutor* v. *Musema, supra* note 68, at para. 248.

[79] *Prosecutor* v. *Gombo* (ICC, Pre-Trial Chamber, 2009), paras. 231, 246.

[80] See N. Ronzitti, 'The Crisis of the Traditional Law Regulating International Armed Conflicts at Sea and the Need for Its Revision', *The Law of Naval Warfare: A Collection of Agreements and Documents with Commentaries* 1, 11 (N. Ronzitti ed., 1988).

[81] See M. Halberstam, 'Terrorism on the High Seas: The Achille Lauro, Piracy and the IMO Convention on Maritime Safety', 82 *AJIL* 269, 288 (1988).

the high seas and carried out for private ends.[82] The LOS Convention's definition also posits that acts of piracy are directed from one ship (or aircraft) against another.[83] Acts of violence committed on the high seas on board a single ship are covered by the 1988 Convention on the Safety of Maritime Navigation.[84]

80. Insurgent vessels (or aircraft) may also launch attacks on the high seas against private ships (or aircraft) for public ends: for instance, in order to block supplies from the outside to the incumbent Government of Ruritania. In these circumstances, absent private ends, the attackers cannot be categorized as pirates under the LOS Convention's definition. All the same, a foreign flag State (Arcadia, Utopia, etc.) – whose merchant vessels are the targets – is 'entitled to take the necessary measures, including the use of armed force' against them.[85]

(ii) Cyber space

81. Cyber warfare in a NIAC raises its own issues of cross-border effects due to the peculiar dimensions of cyber space.[86] For sure, 'the transit of data through cyber infrastructure located outside a State in which a non-international armed conflict is occurring does not render the conflict international'.[87]

(iii) Cross-border hostilities on land

82. Even when carried out kinetically on land, NIAC hostilities may not be unreservedly insulated within the Ruritanian borders. Violence can creep across the land borders of Ruritania into the territory of a neighbouring country (Arcadia) in a variety of ways:

(aa) Ruritanian armed forces may pursue insurgents into the territory of Arcadia (as happened on countless occasions in the Great Lakes region of Africa), continuing the fighting across the border: this spillover would be deemed part of the NIAC.[88]

---

[82] Article 101 of the United Nations Convention on the Law of the Sea (LOS Convention), 1982, Official Text, 57.

[83] *Ibid.*

[84] Convention for the Suppression of Unlawful Acts against the Safety of Maritime Navigation, [1988] *UNJY* 248, 250 (Article 3).

[85] N. Ronzitti, *Rescuing Nationals Abroad through Military Coercion and Intervention on Grounds of Humanity* 140–1 (1985).

[86] See R. Geiss, 'Cyber Warfare and Non-International Armed Conflicts', 43 *Is.YHR* 149, 159–60 (2013).

[87] *Talinn Manual, supra* note 42, at 90.

[88] See J. Pejić, 'Status of Armed Conflicts', *Perspectives on the ICRC Study on Customary International Humanitarian Law* 77, 87 (E. Wilmshurst and S. Breau eds., 2007).

(bb) Articles 1 and 7 of the 1994 Statute of the ICTR expressly recognize the possibility that NIAC war crimes may be committed by Rwandan citizens in neighbouring States.[89] By analogy, the Rwandan model can be extrapolated to other NIACs.

(cc) Ruritania may embark on 'extra-territorial law enforcement' against insurgent bases of operations situated within the territory of Arcadia (see *infra* 170). Such action would still be considered part of the NIAC, as long as there is no clash between Ruritanian and Arcadian armed forces.

(c) The 'war' on terrorism

83. A majority of the US Supreme Court, in the *Hamdan* case of 2006, seems to have arrived at the conclusion that the post-9/11 global 'war' on terrorism should be deemed to be a NIAC.[90] From the perspective of international (as distinct from domestic US) law, this conclusion is wrong.[91] There is no armed conflict going on within the territory of the US, and occasional terrorist attacks from the outside do not instigate a NIAC. The idea that a NIAC can be global in nature is oxymoronic: an armed conflict can be a NIAC or it can be global, but it cannot be both. The so-called 'war' on terrorism (a metaphor rather than a term of art) alters neither the fundamental algorithm regarding the binary division of armed conflicts into IACs and NIACs (see *supra* 70) nor the internal character of the latter (see *supra* 74). Cross-border action against terrorists (typified by the celebrated US Navy Seals' raid that killed O. Bin Laden in Pakistan) may be carried out in self-defence against an armed attack, as an 'extra-territorial law enforcement' operation (see *infra* 170).[92] Ordinary military operations – directed at Al-Qaeda terrorists in Afghanistan – can blend into both an IAC and a NIAC waged in that country against the Taliban, but they do not create a separate global 'war' on terrorism.

(d) Divided nations

84. Disagreements as to whether an armed conflict is internal or international in character can be compounded by a complicated historical

---

[89] Statute of the ICTR, 1994, *Laws of Armed Conflicts* at 1299, 1300–1.

[90] *Hamdan* v. *Rumsfeld*, 45 *ILM* 1130, 1154 (2006) (US Supreme Court, 2006).

[91] See D.E. Graham, 'Defining Non-International Armed Conflict: A Historically Difficult Task', 88 *ILS, supra* note 55, at 43, 51.

[92] See Dinstein, *supra* note 11, at 268–77.

context. Political or military upheavals may cause the division of a country into two separate States. If an armed conflict between the two entities is sparked subsequent to that division, a controversy may crop up as to whether the hostilities ought to be designated as a NIAC (between rival regimes within the same State) or an IAC (between sovereign States). Such arguments flared up during the Korean War as well as the Vietnam War. A proper legal analysis of these armed conflicts depends on whether there were, at the time, one or two Koreas and one or two Vietnams.[93] Assuming that – at the commencement of each armed conflict – the opposing entities satisfied the international legal criteria of statehood (see *infra* 293), the violent confrontation must be viewed as an IAC. This is true irrespective of the ultimate result of the struggle. In the case of Korea, both South and North have survived the IAC and are now members of the UN. In the case of Vietnam, the South was crushed in the IAC and was brought under the fold of a single Vietnam. However, the defeat of the enemy in an IAC does not turn the armed conflict retroactively into a NIAC.

V. A clash between organized armed groups *inter se*

85. Intra-State violence may amount to a NIAC even though no Government features in the calculus of violence. That is to say, the parties to the conflict may be organized armed groups fighting exclusively among themselves. Common Article 3 (*infra* 409) – by not demarcating the exact contours of a NIAC – leaves the door open to the proposition that it applies to such clashes.[94] This becomes more vivid when Common Article 3 is silhouetted against the background of Paragraph (1) of Article 1 of AP/II (*infra* 118), which refers solely to a situation in which insurgents are fighting the armed forces of a High Contracting Party, to wit, a State. When AP/II was drafted, the International Committee of the Red Cross (ICRC) submitted an unsuccessful proposal that the instrument 'would be applicable in the case of several factions confronting each other without involvement of the government's armed forces, for example, if the

---

[93] See J.N. Moore, 'The Lawfulness of Military Assistance to the Republic of Viet-Nam', 61 *AJIL* 1, 2–7 (1967).

[94] See J. Pejic, 'The Protective Scope of Common Article 3: More than Meets the Eye', 881 *IRRC* 189, 193 (2011).

established government had disappeared or was too weak to intervene'.[95] Curiously, the initiative fell short on the ground that it was 'merely a theoretical textbook example'.[96]

86. In reality, it is by no means rare for a NIAC to be fought solely between two or more organized armed groups while the incumbent Government is unable or unwilling to play any meaningful role in the affray.[97] Governments – e.g., in the Central African Republic in 2013 – may be too weak to stop sectarian (inter-ethnic or inter-religious) fighting that causes much havoc. But even when the Government's armed forces are capable of maintaining law and order, they are liable to stay aloof (for political or other reasons) observing the fighting from afar as spectators.[98]

87. An even more drastic possibility is that an incumbent Government disintegrates and disappears from the scene as a direct result of a NIAC (as famously happened in Somalia in the 1990s). Such a process produces what is commonly called a 'failing State' (see *infra* 261), and the collapse of the Government does not necessarily put paid to the NIAC. Instead of a violent confrontation between the Government and non-State actors, there is now a melee: two or more organized armed groups fight it out *inter se*, vying for ascendance within the rudderless State. The entropy of law and order may also tempt rival criminal gangs to form their own armed groups, striving to seize control (nationally or regionally) in pursuit of their mafia-type agenda.[99]

88. Hostilities between two or more organized armed groups, subsequent to the dissolution of governmental control, cannot qualify as an insurgency. After all, who is rebelling against whom? But, whether the inter-group fighting can be deemed a direct sequel to the original insurgency – against the former Government, now defunct – or it constitutes a

---

[95] *Commentary on the Additional Protocols of 8 June 1977 to the Geneva Conventions of 12 August 1949* 1351 (ICRC, Y. Sandoz *et al.* eds., 1987) (the author of the commentaries on AP/II is S.-S. Junod).

[96] *Ibid.*

[97] See Akehurst's *Modern Introduction to International Law* 318 (7th edn, P. Malanczuk ed., 1997) (the example cited is Lebanon in 1975–6).

[98] This may also be true of a non-State entity during a period of transition. A graphic illustration is the Mandate over Palestine in the early part of 1948, when the Mandatory British Power was winding up its rule. Arabs and Jews were fighting each other (prior to the establishment of the State of Israel) with little interference from apathetic Mandatory authorities.

[99] See S. Haines, 'The Nature of War and the Character of Contemporary Armed Conflict', *International Law and the Classification of Conflicts* 9, 26 (E. Wilmshurst ed., 2012).

new struggle, the hostilities deserve recognition as a NIAC if they satisfy the preconditions to be spelt out *infra* 90 *et seq*. Admittedly, the scale of the fighting between the embattled factions may be a fraction lower than in an ordinary NIAC, if each sets its sights solely on regional control and there is no longer any incumbent Government to rein them in.[100]

89. The add-on possibility of a collision between several organized armed groups coming under the overarching concept of a NIAC has been acknowledged by the ICTY in the *Tadić* Decision on appeal, which spoke about 'protracted armed violence between governmental authorities and organized armed groups *or between such groups* within a State'.[101] Article 8(2)(f) of the Rome Statute of the ICC (*infra* 606) toes the same line. The extension of the concept of NIACs to hostilities between organized armed groups can scarcely be challenged today. Still, since the possibility is not envisaged in AP/II (see *supra* 85), that instrument will not apply when the armed forces of the State are not involved in a civil strife.[102]

VI. A modicum of organization of the insurgents

A. Insurgency distinguished from mob violence

90. Insurgents in a NIAC have to be more than a ragtag mob. Isolated mob violence, even if deadly in its repercussions, cannot be equated with an insurgency. Some measure of organization is immanent in an insurgency ranking as a NIAC.

91. In the *Akayesu* Judgment, an ICTR Trial Chamber said that '[t]he term "armed conflict" in itself suggests the existence of hostilities between armed forces organized to a greater or lesser extent'.[103] In the 2008 *Boškoski et al.* case, a Trial Chamber of the ICTY pronounced that insurgent armed groups – in all instances – must have 'some degree of organisation', it being understood that they do not have to be organized to the same extent as the armed forces of the Government.[104]

92. Paragraph (d) of Common Article 3 (*infra* 409) imposes a duty on the opposing sides in a NIAC not to pass sentences or carry out

---

[100] See R. Geiss, 'Armed Violence in Fragile States: Low-Intensity Conflicts, Spillover Conflicts, and Sporadic Law Enforcement Operations by Third Parties', 873 *IRRC* 127, 135–7 (2009).

[101] *Prosecutor* v. *Tadić*, *supra* note 33, at 54. Emphasis added.

[102] See A.P.V. Rogers, *Law on the Battlefield* 221 (2nd edn, 2004).

[103] *Prosecutor* v. *Akayesu* (ICTR, Trial Chamber, 1998), para. 620.

[104] *Prosecutor* v. *Boškoski et al.* (ICTY, Trial Chamber, 2008), para. 197.

executions without previous judgment by a 'regularly constituted court' affording all the judicial guarantees. If insurgents are able to meet the requirement of setting up such a court, this plainly implies a fairly high level of organization.[105]

B. Insurgents as a party to the conflict

93. The *chapeau* of Common Article 3 (*infra ibid.*) uses the phrase 'each Party to the conflict', which must not be confused with 'High Contracting Parties', namely, the States that are Parties to the Geneva Conventions.[106] The Parties to the conflict encompass not only the incumbent Government but also any insurgent armed group rising against it.[107] By adverting to both sides as Parties to the conflict, Common Article 3 emphasizes that it applies equally to them notwithstanding the ingrained uneven standing of the Government *vis-à-vis* the insurgents as per the domestic legal system (see *supra* 37). For that very reason, some Governments have felt that Common Article 3 goes too far in creating the wrong impression of 'two entities' facing one another.[108]

94. The dilemma of parity (in obligations) and asymmetry (in status) conjured up a subtle change in the drafting of Paragraph (1) of Article 19 of the CPCP (*supra* 25) compared to Common Article 3. The phrase in usage in the CPCP is still 'each party to the conflict', yet – not accidentally – the capital letter 'P' in the noun 'Party' has been replaced by a small 'p'. Reverting to the lower case was intended as a hint that the insurgent party is not a Party in the usual sense of a State.[109] But the hint was largely regarded by Governments as too feeble. The framers of AP/II consequently decided to eschew altogether the expression 'party to the conflict', either with a capital or with a small 'p'.[110]

95. The requirement of a modicum of organization of the insurgents in a NIAC may be said to be intrinsic in the very reference to them as a party

---

[105] See G.I.A.D. Draper, 'Humanitarian Law and Internal Armed Conflicts', 13 *Ga.JICL* 253, 270 (1983).

[106] See A. Bellal, G. Giacca and S. Casey-Maslen, 'International Law and Armed Non-State Actors in Afghanistan', 881 *IRRC* 47, 55 (2011).

[107] See *Commentary, I Geneva Convention, supra* note 5, at 51.

[108] G.H. Aldrich, 'Violations of the Laws or Customs of War', I *Substantive and Procedural Aspects of International Criminal Law: The Experience of International and National Courts* 99, 106 n. 30 (G.K. McDonald and O. Swaak-Goldman eds., 2000).

[109] See J. Toman, *The Protection of Cultural Property in the Event of Armed Conflict* 213 (1996).

[110] *Commentary on the Additional Protocols, supra* note 95, at 1339.

to the conflict (in either upper or lower case).[111] How can insurgents form a party to the conflict if they are utterly disorganized and lack any vestige of discipline? When a host of individuals (acting disjointly) raise arms against an incumbent Government – even when a massive mob is on the loose – the uncoordinated commotion is not on a par with a NIAC. Mere 'acting toward a collective goal' against the Government is not enough, and some leadership is essential.[112]

VII. Protracted violence

A. The temporal element

96. In the *Tadić* Decision on appeal, the ICTY held that – for a NIAC to exist – there must be 'protracted armed violence' (*supra* 89). The adjective 'protracted' is authoritatively repeated in Article 8(2)(f) of the Rome Statute of the ICC (*infra* 605).

97. The coinage 'protracted' is obviously the antonym of 'isolated and sporadic' (see *supra* 65). What must be inferred from 'protracted' is that:

(i) When occasional unrest haunts a country (as happens now and again, e.g., in the western provinces of China), the violence does not amount to a NIAC because of lack of a continuum.

(ii) A NIAC cannot burst in one fell swoop. It has to be preceded by a series of 'isolated and sporadic' internal disturbances, and it cannot come suddenly into existence. Only at some advanced point in the evolution of a civil strife can it be determined that the violence is no longer 'isolated' or 'sporadic', so that the stage has been set for a NIAC. In other words, the beginning of a NIAC cannot coincide with the nascence of internal disturbances within a State: there is a necessary interval of germination and sprouting of the armed conflict.

98. Since violence does not segue into a NIAC until it has become protracted, the pre-NIAC period of gestation does not come under the wings of LONIAC. Contrary to the contention of some commentators,[113] LONIAC does not become applicable retroactively to the pre-NIAC phase

---

[111] See J. Pejic, 'Terrorist Acts and Groups: A Role for International Law?', 75 *BYBIL* 71, 86 (2004).

[112] *Talinn Manual, supra* note 42, at 90.

[113] See D. Jinks, 'September 11 and the Laws of War', 28 *YJIL* 1, 28 (especially n. 191) (2003).

of violence. That phase is subject to the law enforcement paradigm (see *supra* 68).

B. *Revolutions and* coups d'Etat

99. A NIAC is not interchangeable with a revolution, which brings about a metamorphosis in the system or structure of governance in the State. Nor is it the same as a *coup d'Etat*, in which the incumbent Government is unlawfully deposed by other State agencies (typically a military *junta*).[114] A revolution or a *coup d'Etat* may occur *sans* violence. It may also come about, without a NIAC, as a result of a brief paroxysm of bloodletting (as happened in Egypt in 2011 and again in 2013).

100. A revolution or a *coup d'Etat* does not always end up successfully: the incumbent Government may overcome a temporary challenge to its authority (as happened in Ecuador in 2010). But, successful or not, a revolution or a *coup d'Etat* may be a prelude to a NIAC. Survivors of the *ancien régime* may recuperate and fight to depose the usurping Government or *junta*. Even within the new regime, efforts by rival factions to monopolize power may degenerate into a NIAC. The decisive point is that a NIAC takes a while to brew, whereas the mounting of a revolution or a *coup d'Etat* may be a cursory affair.

C. *How much time is required?*

101. Evidently, 'protracted' is a pliable term. It is not clear how much time must elapse before a determination can be made with any degree of confidence that a NIAC has commenced. There is no allotted minimum period. Does it take months of ongoing violence, or will a week or two of tumult suffice to fulfil the requirement of being protracted? Whatever the shortest admissible space of time may be, it cannot plummet down to just a few hours or even a few days.

102. The present author cannot agree with a decision rendered by the Inter-American Commission on Human Rights, in the *Abella* case of 1997 – relating to fighting in Buenos Aires that lasted 30 hours – whereby, 'despite its brief duration, the violent clash between the attackers

---

[114] A new category has been suggested, consisting of 'democratic' *coups d'Etat*, staged by the military against authoritarian regimes and leading in time to free elections. See O.O. Varol, 'The Democratic Coup d'Etat', 53 *HILJ* 292, 295 (2012). But a *coup d'Etat* is a *coup d'Etat*.

and members of the Argentine armed forces triggered application of the provisions of Common Article 3, as well as other rules relevant to the conduct of internal hostilities'.[115] Such evanescent violence by mutinous troops does not pass the test of a NIAC.

VIII. Intensity of the fighting

103. In the *Tadić* Judgment of 1997, an ICTY Trial Chamber added the precondition of the 'intensity' of the fighting in a NIAC, thereby 'distinguishing an armed conflict from banditry, unorganized and short-lived insurrections, or terrorist activities'.[116]

A. Terrorist activities

104. The allusion in the last words to 'terrorist activities' has to be perused cautiously. As we shall see (*infra* 431), 'acts of terrorism' are forbidden in a NIAC: the injunction against them implies that they are liable to be perpetrated in breach of LONIAC. In other words, 'insurrectional movements may, in the course of their struggle against a constituted government, engage in terrorist activities'.[117]

105. The *Tadić* language should, therefore, be taken as relating not to the nature of the acts but to their sporadic incidence. It is only when terrorist activities do not meet the required preconditions of a NIAC that they would move into another legal arena. Conversely, if acts of terrorism in an internal civil strife (within the boundaries of a single country) are organized, protracted and intense, they will definitely fit the mould of a NIAC.[118]

B. Intensity as an independent criterion

106. The precondition of intensity (*Tadić* 1997) comes on top of the precondition of protracted hostilities (*Tadić* 1995). It is wrong to look at

---

[115] *Abella* case (Argentina) (Inter-American Commission on Human Rights, 1997), para. 156.

[116] *Prosecutor* v. *Tadić* (Judgment) (ICTY, Trial Chamber, 1997), 36 *ILM* 908, 920 (1997). The words 'banditry, unorganized and short-lived insurrections' are borrowed from *Commentary, I Geneva Convention, supra* note 5, at 50.

[117] U. Leanza and L. Sico, 'Compensation for Victims of Maritime Terrorism', *Maritime Terrorism and International Law* 97, 100 (N. Ronzitti ed., 1990).

[118] See C. de Than and E. Shorts, *International Criminal Law and Human Rights* 162 (2003).

the intensity of the violence (as some commentators do[119]) as an alternative to protracted hostilities. Granted, in the *Haradinaj et al.* Judgment of 2008, an ICTY Trial Chamber opined that the criterion of protracted hostilities has been interpreted in practice 'as referring more to the intensity of the armed violence than to its duration'.[120] But, in the *Gombo* Decision of 2009, a Pre-Trial Chamber of the ICC neatly – and correctly – separated the requirements of the intensity of the violence and its protracted nature.[121] Violence that is protracted but not intense, or intense but not protracted, does not amount to a NIAC.

107. It has been averred that there may be some 'inverse ratio' between duration and intensity, so that either a very brief but inordinately intense or a particularly long but low-scale period of violence will count as a NIAC.[122] However, this is not borne out by general State practice. There are abundant examples of fleeting encounters between protesters and law enforcement units (sometimes beefed up by the military) that leave in their wake trails of human casualties and severe destruction of property. General State practice does not consider such episodic events as NIACs, any more than it does extended periods of peripheral violence. Cyber warfare raises the question of whether destruction of property alone (without bloodshed) can by itself satisfy the precondition of intensity,[123] but most probably the answer is negative.

C. Indicia of intensity

108. As stated by the Trial Chamber of the ICTR in the *Akayesu* case, ascertainment of the intensity of the hostilities ought to be done 'on the basis of objective criteria': it cannot be left to 'the subjective judgment of the parties to the conflict' (who may wish either to play it down or to exaggerate it).[124] In the aftermath of *Tadić*, multiple judgments of the ICTY (as summarized by a Trial Chamber, in 2008, in the *Boškoski et al.* case[125]) have come up with various indicia in order to assess the intensity of the fighting required in a NIAC. These include (not counting

---

[119] See G. Rona, 'Interesting Times for International Humanitarian Law: Challenges from the "War on Terror"', 27(2) *Fl.FWA* 55, 63 (2003).

[120] *Prosecutor* v. *Haradinaj et al.* (ICTY, Trial Chamber, 2008), para. 49.

[121] *Prosecutor* v. *Gombo*, *supra* note 79, at paras. 231, 235.

[122] E. Lieblich, *International Law and Civil Wars: Intervention and Consent* 49 (2013).

[123] See *Talinn Manual*, *supra* note 42, at 88.

[124] *Prosecutor* v. *Akayesu*, *supra* note 103, at para. 603.

[125] *Prosecutor* v. *Boškoski et al.*, *supra* note 104, at para. 177.

the time element) the numbers of casualties; the diffusion of violence over territory; the deployment of military units against the insurgents; the types of weapons (say, tanks) used; the siege of towns; and the closure of roads.[126] Where necessary, other elements of the hostilities may be thrown in for ballast.

109. The matter of the deployment of military units against the insurgents in a NIAC deserves a comment. Undeniably, such deployment may be put into action also in situations of riot-like internal disturbances (see *supra* 68). By itself, 'the involvement of military forces cannot be understood as automatically determining that an armed conflict exists'.[127] Only large-scale and prolonged (as distinct from marginal and short-term) engagements of the military in putting down a rebellion will really carry weight for purposes of assessing intensity of the fighting.[128]

---

[126] For cites of the specific judgments buttressing these and other indicia of intensity of fighting, see *ibid*.

[127] K. Watkin, 'Controlling the Use of Force: A Role for Human Rights Norms in Contemporary Armed Conflict', 98 *AJIL* 1, 26 (2004).

[128] See F. Ni Aolain, 'The Relationship between Situations of Emergency and Low-Intensity Armed Conflict', 28 *Is. YHR* 97, 103 (1998).

3

Thresholds and interaction of armed conflicts

I. The thresholds of armed conflicts

110. There are three thresholds of armed conflicts – two relating to NIACs and one to IACs – preceded by a tier of violence lying below the first threshold.

A. *Below-the-threshold violence*

111. Below-the-threshold violence relates to 'isolated and sporadic' internal disturbances (see *supra* 65). These extend to all forms of disorganized – individual or mob – violence, which do not make the grade of an armed conflict, although they may cause mayhem and provoke savage crackdowns by governmental forces. Grave internal disturbances may cause an incumbent Government to be reeling, and perhaps even force a political realignment or dissolution of the legislature, but that does not mean that a NIAC has been cut loose.

112. Internal disturbances need not be directed against an incumbent Government (see *supra* 86). Often, they give vent to sectarian – inter-ethnic or inter-religious – friction (e.g., what appears to be a perennial Hindu/Muslim tension in the Indian sub-continent). Whether or not it is the direct target, the Government may collapse as a result of the chaos produced.

113. Below-the-threshold violence lies outside the scope of application of LONIAC and is controlled by the law enforcement paradigm (see *supra* 68). As such, it is governed solely by the domestic constitutional and criminal legal system of the State, subject to the strictures of international human rights law. There have been some attempts at developing minimum humanitarian standards regulating below-the-threshold internal disturbances.[129] But these have encountered

---

[129] See T. Meron and A. Rosas, 'A Declaration of Minimum Humanitarian Standards', 85 *AJIL* 375, 377–81 (1991).

opposition,[130] and have certainly not elicited enough general support by States to become binding law.

114. The seclusion of LONIAC from below-the-threshold violence is important to keep in mind when an incumbent Government has qualms about owning up to a NIAC occurring within the State's territory (see *supra* 3). If the situation is that of below-the-threshold violence, the Government cannot rely on LONIAC and must navigate the shoals of civil unrest in consonance with human rights law standards (which may be far more stringent than those of LONIAC). A prime example is that of the 1995 *McCann et al.* Judgment, in which the European Court of Human Rights (ECHR) held against the UK in proceedings involving the use of lethal force by British soldiers against members of the Provisional Irish Republican Army (IRA), with a view to forestalling the detonation of a terrorist bomb in Gibraltar.[131] Had LONIAC been applied to the case, such action would have been entirely lawful, since military units are allowed to use force against adversaries as a first resort. However, in putting the soldiers' action to the test of human rights law – which permits the use of force only as a last resort – the Court came to a different conclusion.

B. Over the first threshold

115. Whenever the preconditions of a NIAC are met, the first threshold is crossed. This threshold marks the time-slot when the bare bones of intra-State violence suffice for it to be classified as a NIAC. Once past the first threshold, Common Article 3 – given the bland formula used in its *chapeau* (*infra* 409) – is activated. It can safely be assumed that the scope of application of the CPCP, pursuant to Paragraph (1) of Article 19 (*supra* 25), matches that of Common Article 3.[132]

116. Although there are two thresholds of NIACs (see *infra* 118), it must be understood that all NIACs (whatever their threshold) have to satisfy the elementary preconditions set out in Chapter 2. The higher threshold does not replace these preconditions: it supplements them with further requirements.

117. Curiously, the authoritative ICRC Commentary on the Geneva Conventions offers additional criteria (which are 'not obligatory and are only mentioned as an indication') to the lower threshold of NIACs,

---

[130]   See T. Meron, *The Humanization of International Law* 60 (2006).
[131]   *McCann et al.* v. *UK* (ECHR, 1995), paras. 213–14.
[132]   See Toman, *supra* note 109, at 209.

and these include control over territory and even 'recognition of belligerency'.[133] The proposed criteria 'can be seriously misleading'.[134] Control over territory belongs to the second – rather than the first – threshold of NIACs (see *infra* 141), and 'recognition of belligerency' transforms a NIAC to the legal regime applicable in an IAC (see *infra* 338).

C. Over the second threshold

118. The second threshold is laid down in Paragraph (1) of Article 1 of AP/II (cited *supra* 65):

> This Protocol, which develops and supplements Article 3 common to the Geneva Conventions of 12 August 1949 without modifying its existing conditions of application, shall apply to all armed conflicts which are not covered by Article 1 of the Protocol Additional to the Geneva Conventions of 12 August 1949, and relating to the Protection of Victims of International Armed Conflicts (Protocol I) and which take place in the territory of a High Contracting Party between its armed forces and dissident armed forces or other organized armed groups which, under responsible command, exercise such control over a part of its territory as to enable them to carry out sustained and concerted military operations and to implement this Protocol.

119. As a matter of historical record, the second threshold does not correspond with the first because in 1977 (when AP/II was concluded) there were still governmental misgivings about adopting a new set of intricate provisions concerning the application of LONIAC.[135] AP/II was the best text that could be attained at the time, and acceptance of the instrument was contingent on limiting its framework to NIACs narrowly defined by Paragraph (1) of Article 1.

120. Since 1977, there have been many voices clamouring for a reform in NIAC law by eliminating the disparity in application of Common Article 3 and AP/II, ratcheting the second threshold down to the first.[136] However, the Rome Statute of the ICC, concluded more than two decades after AP/II, has retained in principle the two thresholds approach (see

---

[133] *Commentary, I Geneva Convention, supra* note 5, at 49–50.

[134] R. Provost, *International Human Rights and Humanitarian Law* 266 (2002).

[135] See *Commentary on the Additional Protocols, supra* note 95, at 1335.

[136] See C. Greenwood, 'International Humanitarian Law (Laws of War)', *The Centennial of the First International Peace Conference: Reports and Conclusions* 161, 228–33 (F. Kalshoven ed., 2000).

infra 570, 605), and there is not even a faint signal indicating that States desire to relinquish it any time soon.

121. Before proceeding to dissect the prerequisites devised by the authors of AP/II for NIACs to be past the post of the second threshold, it is imperative to point out that – just as the preconditions of a NIAC under Common Article 3 are supplemented and not replaced by AP/II (see *supra* 116) – the substantive norms activated at the point of crossing the first threshold remain in force in every NIAC. These norms (generated by Common Article 3) apply alongside any new substantive rules set in motion (by AP/II) when a NIAC climbs over the fence of the second threshold (see *supra* 23).

(a) Government armed forces

122. A vital ingredient of a NIAC above the second threshold, as posited by Paragraph (1) of Article 1 of AP/II, is the participation in the hostilities of Government armed forces. This narrows the field, considering that NIACs can – and often do – take place between organized armed groups *inter se* (see *supra* 87). Hence, as indicated (*supra* 89), AP/II will not be applicable to hostilities devoid of Government armed forces.

123. There is no international yardstick determining the make-up of the Government armed forces deployed against insurgents in a NIAC.[137] These armed forces will ordinarily be comprised of military units. But, despite contrary views, there is no reason to circumscribe them to the military.[138] Just as military contingents may be called upon for assistance in below-the-threshold internal disturbances (see *supra* 68), police and other law enforcement cohorts may be mobilized by the Government – together with, or in lieu of, the military – to quash an insurgency.

(b) Dissident armed forces

124. Insurgents may be members of 'dissident armed forces', belonging to breakaway military units that have mutinied against the incumbent Government. In many NIACs, 'dissident armed forces' constitute the backbone of the insurgency, since they are relatively well-organized, well-led, well-trained and well-equipped.

---

[137] See S. Watts, 'Present and Future Conceptions of the Status of Government Forces in Non-International Armed Conflict', 88 *ILS, supra* note 55, at 145, 149.

[138] See K.J. Partsch, 'Scope of This Protocol', *New Rules for Victims of Armed Conflicts: Commentary on the Two 1977 Protocols Additional to the Geneva Conventions of 1949* 622, 626 (M. Bothe, K.J. Partsch and W.A. Solf eds., 1982).

125. Not every mutiny within the armed forces of a State necessarily leads to a NIAC. An episodic mutiny hatched up by some disgruntled officers is not a rare event, but it falls below the first threshold of a NIAC. Even when entire units defect (sometimes against their own officers) – as happened in Bangladesh in 2009 – the mutiny may not earn the appellation of a NIAC if it is smothered swiftly (see *supra* 102). Regardless of numbers, mutineers may also turn into banditry – or even piracy[139] – without triggering a NIAC. Yet, when mutineers are lifting arms against the Government as 'dissident armed forces' – and the violence meets other preconditions – a NIAC, even above the second threshold, will be in progress whether or not anybody else joins the uprising.

(c) Other organized armed groups under responsible command

126. A country may be convulsed by a NIAC over the second threshold even if no 'dissident armed forces' have split from the main body of the military. When 'dissident armed forces' do exist, their ranks may be swollen by volunteers who – taking umbrage at the incumbent Government – join the fight against it. Insurgents may also hoist the banner of insurrection separately from any 'dissident armed forces'. They may consist of paramilitary militias, formerly serving the State outside the framework of its armed forces. They may be composed of regional (rather than national) paramilitary units, especially if they fight for secession of an autonomous province from the State. However formed, insurrectionists over the second threshold must have organized armed groups, and these must fulfil certain conditions in compliance with Paragraph (1) of Article 1 of AP/II.

(i) The constituent elements

127. The three-word expression 'organized armed group' has as many constituent elements. There has to be (i) a 'group', which needs to be (ii) 'armed', as well as (iii) 'organized'. Each of these three elements has to be separately dwelt on.

128. A 'group' is a cluster of individual human beings. There is no acid test for determining exactly who is a member of an insurgent organized armed group in a NIAC. Given the precarious conditions of an insurrection, it is hard to conceive of any formal conditions of membership (such

---

[139] On piracy by a warship, government ship or government aircraft whose crew has mutinied, see Article 102 of the LOS Convention, *supra* note 82, at 58.

as registration).[140] Accordingly, it may be difficult to produce hard evidence that an individual belongs to an organized armed group.[141] Absent formal attestations of affiliation, what usually counts – in the words of the ICRC – is 'taking up a certain function for the group'.[142] But what function are we talking about? Do only combat roles count (see *infra* 194) or are ancillary tasks germane as well? 'International law has provided no criteria that can be applied to identify members of armed groups'.[143] Circumstances may vary from one group to another and from one NIAC to another.

129. The insistence on organized groups being 'armed' is principally designed to distinguish them from non-violent opposition factions that are striving to replace the incumbent Government without resorting to force. At times, insurgent groups create composite structures consisting of a 'political wing' and a 'military wing'. Some scholars attach great significance to this profiling,[144] but in many instances telling the two wings apart may be a chimera. The military/political dual labelling can work as long as members are not intermingled, each discrete wing pursuing its own separate agenda (especially when the political leadership operates from abroad). But should a stronghold of the 'military wing' be stormed by Government forces, claims by persons present on site to be members of a so-called 'political wing' would not guarantee them immunity from attack.

130. For sure, being 'armed' does not imply that the weapons employed by insurgents have to be sophisticated. All the same, some armament is a *condicio sine qua non*. A capacity to launch lethal or destructive cyber attacks may count as being 'armed'.[145]

131. An armed group participating in a NIAC above the second threshold must be 'organized'. Dissident military forces mutinying against the incumbent Government (see *supra* 124) will naturally possess a built-in structure and hierarchy. A relatively high level of organization – and even tight discipline – may also be displayed in other instances, e.g., (aa) when paramilitary militias join the insurgency (see *supra* 126); or

---

[140] See N. Melzer, *Targeted Killing in International Law* 320–1 (2008).

[141] See Otto, *supra* note 41, at 240–1.

[142] ICRC, *Interpretive Guidance on the Notion of Direct Participation in Hostilities under International Humanitarian Law* 33 (N. Melzer ed., 2009).

[143] L. Zegveld, 'Accountability of Organized Armed Groups', *Non-State Actors and International Humanitarian Law: Organized Armed Groups: A Challenge for the 21st Century* 109, 112 (32nd Round Table, San Remo, 2000; M. Odello and G.L. Beruto eds.).

[144] S. Sivakumaran, *The Law of Non-International Armed Conflict* 367 (2012).

[145] See *Talinn Manual*, *supra* note 42, at 88.

(bb) when private military contractors contribute to the formation of an insurgent group.[146] Other – improvised – groups of civilians, combining their resources in rebelling against the Government, are likely to be more loosely knit (at least in the early stage of the insurgency).

132. As noted (*supra* 90 *et seq.*), a smidgeon of organization is a precondition of all NIACs. However, the level of organization required of the insurgents by Paragraph (1) of Article 1 of AP/II is more advanced than that implied by Common Article 3.[147] The words 'under responsible command' are particularly emphatic. In the *Hadžihasanović et al.* Decision of 2003, the Appeals Chamber of the ICTY pronounced: 'It is evident that there cannot be an organized military force save on the basis of responsible command'.[148] Although a 'rigid military hierarchy' is not demanded of insurgent armed groups,[149] there must be some structural authority capable of imposing a measure of internal discipline.[150] When divested of any command structure, an armed group will not count as organized. It may still fight the incumbent Government, but then the violence will not cross the second threshold of a NIAC (and conceivably not even the first).

(ii) The five factors of organization

133. The higher degree of organization required by the second threshold of NIACs – compared to the first – invites elaboration. In the *Tadić* Judgment of 1999, the Appeals Chamber of the ICTY held:

> Plainly, an organised group differs from an individual in that the former normally has a structure, a chain of command and a set of rules as well as the outward symbols of authority. Normally a member of the group does not act on his own but conforms to the standards prevailing in the group and is subject to the authority of the head of the group.[151]

134. The degree of organization of armed groups need not have a fixed pattern, but the ICTY – after *Tadić* – persisted in searching for specific indicia fleshing out required components, and the case law is replete with

---

[146] See L. Vierucci, 'Private Military and Security Companies in Non-International Armed Conflicts: *Jus ad Bellum* and *Jus in Bello*', *War by Contract: Human Rights, Humanitarian Law, and Private Contractors* 235, 252 (F. Francioni and N. Ronzitti eds., 2011).

[147] See *Prosecutor* v. *Boškoski et al., supra* note 104, at para. 197.

[148] *Prosecutor* v. *Hadžihasanović et al.* (Decision) (ICTY, Appeals Chamber, 2003), para. 16.

[149] S. Junod, 'Additional Protocol II: History and Scope', 33 *AULR* 29, 37 (1983–4).

[150] See A. Carrillo-Suárez, '*Hors de Logique*: Contemporary Issues in International Humanitarian Law as Applied to Internal Armed Conflict', 15 *AUILR* 1, 96 (1999–2000).

[151] *Prosecutor* v. *Tadić* (Judgment) (ICTY, Appeals Chamber, 1999), 38 *ILM* 1518, 1541 (1999).

precedents on this topic. In the *Boškoski et al.* case of 2008, the Trial Chamber summed up the legal position (as it emerges from the previous jurisprudence) by itemizing five factors.[152]

135. The first factor is the existence of a chain of command. Such structure can be displayed in diverse ways: the setting up of a headquarters; the emergence of a military hierarchy; the issuance of directives to commanders in the field; the dissemination of internal regulations; the marshalling of weapon supplies, and so forth.[153]

136. The second factor relates mostly to capacities. Organization is suggested by the capacity of the armed group to devise strategy; to undertake large-scale military operations; to coordinate the activities of discrete units, etc.[154] A further capacity – to control territory, to carry out sustained and concerted military operations, and to implement LONIAC – is expressly laid down in AP/II and will be discussed *infra* 141 *et seq.*

137. The third factor pertains to the level of logistical abilities. An organized armed group will be able to recruit new members; to provide military training; to organize supplies; to establish communications linking headquarters with units in the field, etc.[155]

138. The fourth factor brings to the fore the possession by the armed group of a certain level of discipline, enabling it to implement LONIAC obligations.[156]

139. The fifth and last factor consists of evidence that the armed group is able to speak with one voice.[157]

140. Patently, all these factors represent only indicia. There are remaining quandaries not resolved by the five factors, and the *Boškoski et al.* Judgment broached one of them: can an armed group be deemed organized when its members frequently violate LONIAC? The Trial Chamber arrived at the conclusion that it all depends on whether these violations 'were primarily the result of a military strategy ordered by those leading the group or whether they were perpetrated by members deciding to commit attacks of their own accord'.[158] A policy of resorting to unlawful means and methods of hostilities – if adopted by an armed group – does not negate the organized character of the operations.[159] It is when

---

[152] *Prosecutor* v. *Boškoski et al.*, *supra* note 104, at paras. 199–203.

[153] These and other elements are enumerated especially in *Prosecutor* v. *Limaj et al.* (ICTY, Trial Chamber, 2005), paras. 46, 94–103, 111.

[154] See especially *ibid.*, paras. 108, 129, 158.   [155] See especially *ibid.*, paras. 118–23.

[156] See especially *ibid.*, paras. 113–17.   [157] See especially *ibid.*, paras. 125–9.

[158] *Prosecutor* v. *Boškoski et al.*, *supra* note 104, at para. 205.

[159] See A. Bianchi and Y. Naqvi, *International Humanitarian Law and Terrorism* 163 (2011).

individual members act entirely on their own initiative, in total disregard of a countervailing policy espoused by the armed group, that one may question whether the group is genuinely organized.

(d) Control over territory

141. A new element in the second threshold of NIACs is that the insurgent organized armed group must exercise control over part of the territory of the State. For AP/II to apply, the insurgents can neither (i) be completely scattered and constantly on the move, nor (ii) operate solely from bases outside the national territory.[160]

142. In any country raked by insurrection, control over swathes of territory may pass from the incumbent Government to organized armed groups of insurgents and vice versa. In the ebb and flow of a NIAC, the insurrectionist armed group may lose control over a particular area earlier captured, and the tranche of land that it has seized may shrink in size. By itself, that is inconsequential. What is indispensable for the crossing of the second threshold NIAC is that the rebels retain control over some territory at any given time.

143. The size of the region over which the insurgents have carved out their control is not defined, and efforts to add to the AP/II phrase 'part of its territory' an adjective such as 'substantial' or 'non-negligible' failed.[161] No doubt, the zone taken hold of by those rising against the incumbent Government must be large enough to enable them to abide by the remaining two conditions (see *infra* 148 *et seq.*).

144. Control over territory is admittedly an imprecise expression. The degree of mastery of an area by the insurgents is subject to fluctuations, and it need not exceed the ability to satisfy the remaining conditions. Much depends on vagaries of terrain, density of population, and so on. Control ought to be adjudged in comparison to any competing powers exercised by the incumbent Government within the same space. When the Government's armed forces have been thoroughly evicted, the insurgents' control can scarcely be denied even if their presence on the ground is light.

145. Insurgent control over territory raises immense difficulties from the angle of the domestic legal system.[162] What laws, enacted by whom, are going to apply there? On the one hand, the insurgents are likely to be

---

[160] See L.C. Green, *The Contemporary Law of Armed Conflict* 321 (2nd edn, 2000).

[161] See *Commentary on the Additional Protocols, supra* note 95, at 1352.

[162] See P. Rowe, 'Liability for "War Crimes" during a Non-International Armed Conflict', 34 *Mil.LLWR* 149, 154 (1995).

indignant at the continued application of laws passed by an incumbent regime which they are seeking to replace. On the other hand, the insurgents may prefer to leave intact some legislation, reaping the benefits of preexisting statutes, for instance in the sphere of taxation.

146. The question marks about the domestic laws in force in the rebel-controlled districts do not affect the status of LONIAC. The applicability of AP/II is contingent on the second threshold of a NIAC being crossed. Once it is, AP/II will be applicable throughout the land: not only in the zones controlled by the insurgents but also in those under the sway of the incumbent Government. In other words, Government-run areas – which insurgents have not wrested from its armed forces – will be subject to AP/II, as much as insurgent-controlled territory. AP/II thus filters into the whole territory of the country in consequence of control by the insurgents over some areas (and the fulfilment of the other conditions set in the instrument).

147. From the outlook of LONIAC, there is a dual practical benefit derived from the control of some territory by the insurgents. First, such territorial control enables the insurgents to comply with their LONIAC obligations, which otherwise might not lend themselves to straightforward execution (see *infra* 149). Second, the very emergence of a NIAC is apt to be murky, and it is easy to err on the side of caution by not detecting its inception. Exercise of control by the insurgents over part of the State's territory is a very simple litmus test for the existence of a NIAC. There have been more than a few instances in which an insurgency was organized, protracted and intense – e.g., the struggles by the IRA in Northern Ireland or the Basque Separatists in Spain – yet absence of insurgents' control over territory excluded the violence from crossing the second threshold (thereby disenabling AP/II to come into play).[163]

(e) Sustained and concerted military operations

148. In a NIAC over the second threshold, the insurgent organized armed group must be able to carry out 'sustained and concerted military operations'. There are two ingredients here:

(i) 'Sustained' means that military operations have to be kept up more or less continuously, although intermittent pauses in the trail of violence

---

[163] See G.D. Solis, *The Law of Armed Conflict: International Humanitarian Law in War* 131 (2010).

are almost bound to transpire.[164] In the *Limaj et al.* Judgment of 2005, the ICTY Trial Chamber held that occasional intervals of several days in the fighting cannot be ruled out.[165]

(ii) 'Concerted' signals that the military operations are executed according to some plan of action.[166]

Together the two ingredients form rather rigorous strictures, and they will scarcely be satisfied at an early part of a NIAC. That is why an insurgency will usually go through two stages correlative to the two tiers of Common Article 3 and AP/II.[167]

(f) Capacity to implement AP/II

149. Insurgent organized armed groups over the second threshold must have the capacity to implement AP/II. Control over a part of the State's territory creates for them the opportunity for meeting their obligations. For instance, such control will enable the insurgents to build 'the minimum infrastructure required' to care for the wounded and sick.[168]

150. Since NIAC hostilities are usually in a state of flux, the competence to implement AP/II may be acquired by insurgent organized armed groups and then lost. When insurgent presence on the ground is receding, a NIAC – which has already crossed the second threshold – may slide back below it (so that only Common Article 3, and not AP/II, will be applicable).[169]

151. The insurgents' ability to comply with AP/II is a matter of potentiality, which need not coincide with the overall record of their performance. To the extent that reciprocity between the parties to the conflict is an issue,[170] it is reciprocity in capabilities and not in actual conduct. As long as an organized armed group possesses the means to implement AP/II, the crossing of the second threshold is not linked to the insurgents making overt use of their latent powers.

(g) Permutations

152. An insurgency may wax and wane. It may rise from the first threshold of a NIAC to the second, and it may drop from the second to the first. More significantly, an insurgency may falter – winding down

---

[164] See S. Boelaert-Suominen, 'The Yugoslavia Tribunal and the Common Core of Humanitarian Law Applicable to All Armed Conflicts', 13 *LJIL* 619, 635 (2000).

[165] *Prosecutor* v. *Limaj et al.*, *supra* note 153, at para. 168.

[166] See *Commentary on the Additional Protocols, supra* note 95, at 1353.

[167] See *ibid.*   [168] See *ibid.*, 1352–3.   [169] See Schindler, *supra* note 25, at 148.

[170] See L. Moir, *The Law of Internal Armed Conflict* 107–8 (2002).

below the first threshold – with violence relegated to sporadic internal disturbances (see *supra* 65). In that case, although the violence is not halted, the NIAC *per se* is over.

153. Whenever ongoing violence does not meet the two preconditions of minimum organization and intensity (the third precondition of being protracted is an issue that arises at the outset of the NIAC but not at its tail end), it ceases being a NIAC. Undeniably, continued violence may consign the country to an unstable future, and the embers of the NIAC may be rekindled at any time. But meanwhile, LONIAC is dormant.

D. The end of a NIAC

154. A NIAC need not linger inconclusively. It may come to an unequivocal end in several basic scenarios:

(i) The insurgents are roundly beaten and the incumbent Government finds itself, again, securely in the saddle.

(ii) The insurgent cause triumphs, bringing about one of the following outcomes:

    (aa) The incumbent Government is dismantled.

    (bb) The territorial integrity of the country is impaired by secession, preceded perhaps by interim measures (e.g., international territorial administration).[171]

    (cc) Regional autonomy is introduced.

    (dd) Other mechanisms of structural reform in the way the country is run are adopted.

(iii) A compromise scheme between the conflicting positions of the parties to the NIAC is agreed upon and implemented. An agreement by itself may be the light of a false dawn, so it is implementation that ultimately counts.

(iv) The incumbent Government crumbles, but the result is endemic chaos leading to a 'failing State' imbroglio (see *infra* 261).

(v) The NIAC evolves into an IAC (across the third threshold; see *infra* 161).

---

[171] In the case of East Timor, a referendum was held in 1999 on whether the territory should have special autonomy within Indonesia or gain independence. When the latter option gained the upper hand, East Timor was administered by the UN until the attainment of statehood in 2002. See R. Wilde, *International Territorial Administration: How Trusteeship and the Civilizing Mission Never Went Away* 182–8 (2008).

155. A NIAC may be terminated in a peace accord (however designated) between the incumbent Government and the insurgents, crafting agreed-upon terms for the cessation of hostilities. The need for such an accord – as an alternative to one-sided victory – will be particularly acute when there is a stalemate in the fighting or battle fatigue is caused by distressing numbers of casualties and woeful devastation.

156. In extreme instances, a peace accord may pave the way for secession entailing the creation of a new State (Apollonia) on part of the territory of the State where the NIAC was raging (Ruritania). When Ruritania survives the NIAC intact, the purpose of the peace accord will be to set terms for post-conflict national reconstruction. The accord will then commonly include stipulations covering, e.g., restructure of the Government with a view to power-sharing; free elections; future referendums; constitutional amendments; disbanding and disarmament of militias; securing human rights; prosecution of criminals; amnesties; agrarian reform; the release of detainees; and/or the return of displaced persons.

157. A peace accord between an incumbent Government and non-State actors, however important, does not constitute a treaty (see *supra* 19). It is often propounded that such an accord is meant to be binding on the international legal plane, and that the non-State signatories will thereby become subjects of international law.[172] But, unless a peace accord leads to secession, this is not the case. It would be rather odd for the insurgents to be endowed with an international legal standing only in order to sign an agreement, which prompts their disappearance from the scene (as a result of the end of the insurrection). If Ruritania continues to exist within its original borders, the instrument ought to be categorized as domestic in nature. The proposition was confirmed by the Appeals Chamber of the Special Court for Sierra Leone (SCSL) in the *Kallon et al.* case (see *infra* 224).

158. Sometimes, a peace accord writing *finis* to a NIAC is concluded in the presence of foreign dignitaries as 'witnesses' (who may even co-sign the instrument). That does not alter the legal nature of the accord. 'The signature of a witness, however distinguished or powerful, has no legal significance'.[173] It is no more than an expression of external political support for an agreement patching up the intra-State feud.

159. The termination of a NIAC, with or without a peace accord, does not necessarily mean that Ruritania returns to tranquillity. The

---

[172] See C. Bell, 'Peace Agreements: Their Nature and Legal Status', 100 *AJIL* 373, 381 (2006).
[173] A. Aust, *Modern Treaty Law and Practice* 93 (3rd edn, 2013).

convulsion of the insurrection may leave behind a surge of violence, and some rogue militias may continue to operate sporadically on a sub-NIAC level of intensity (below-the-threshold). This activity can still cause serious trouble, as happened in Libya in 2012. Both local and foreign targets were struck by terrorists, culminating in a deadly attack against the US Consulate in Benghazi (where the Ambassador was killed). The violence against foreign installations and personnel did not engage State responsibility on the part of Libya, inasmuch as the (new) Government in Tripoli was not capable of thwarting the attack committed by private persons (see *infra* 366 about the concept of due diligence).

160. Some aspects remaining on the agenda in a post-NIAC period can be the subject of specific LONIAC treaty provisions, as illustrated by Paragraph (2) of Article 2 of AP/II:[174]

> At the end of the armed conflict, all the persons who have been deprived of their liberty or whose liberty has been restricted for reasons related to such conflict, as well as those deprived of their liberty or whose liberty is restricted after the conflict for the same reasons, shall enjoy the protection of Articles 5 and 6 until the end of such deprivation or restriction of liberty.

Post-conflict issues can go far and wide. Thus, the Remnants of War Protocol (Protocol V) to the CCCW (cited *infra* 494) is concerned with abandoned explosives.

E. Over the third threshold

161. Whereas the gap between the first and the second thresholds is quantitative (the second threshold providing weightier evidence that a NIAC is actually occurring, although narrowing the field in terms of the applicability of treaty LONIAC), the leap over the third threshold is qualitative. Crossing the third threshold does not mean 'more of the same'. It represents a whole new paradigm: a move from one species of armed conflict (NIAC) to another (IAC), and from one legal regime (LONIAC) to another (the *jus in bello*). An armed conflict originally pegged as intra-State becomes inter-State in character.

162. The impression is sometimes gained that the boundaries between IACs and NIACs are porous. This is explicable in view of the growing convergence between LONIAC and IAC *jus in bello* (see *infra* 671 *et seq.*). In the *Tadić* Decision on appeal, the conclusion reached by the ICTY was

---

[174] AP/II, *supra* note 6, at 777.

that 'it does not matter' whether a serious violation of the law of armed conflict occurred in an IAC or in a NIAC, as long as the act forms an infringement of customary international law.[175] Similarly, in the *Halilović* case of 2005, a Trial Chamber of the ICTY observed that – by virtue of the general applicability of the provisions of Common Article 3 in both IACs and NIACs (as per *Nicaragua*; *supra* 30) – 'it is immaterial whether the armed conflict was international or non-international in nature'.[176] The observation is accurate as far as certain war crimes are concerned. But, in other contexts, it is far from 'immaterial' whether an armed conflict constitutes an IAC or a NIAC.

163. A misplaced sense that it does not matter whether an armed conflict is an IAC or a NIAC can lead to missteps. For instance, in 2010, a Committee of the International Law Association lumped together IACs and NIACs in applying to both the preconditions of organization and intensity of fighting.[177] These are two of the three preconditions governing NIACs (the precondition of protracted violence was not mentioned). But, albeit indispensable in all NIACs, the two preconditions of organization and intensity cannot be simply transplanted to IACs. Organization is a redundant precondition where only States are concerned: how can their armed forces not be organized? More significantly, the requirement of intensity of fighting is by no means a *sine qua non* in IAC practice.[178]

164. The third threshold of armed conflict is crossed automatically once two or more States conduct hostilities against each other, irrespective of the intensity of the fighting.[179] As the ICTY Appeals Chamber in *Tadić* pronounced, 'an armed conflict exists whenever there is resort to armed force between States'.[180] The ICRC Commentary on Common Article 2 of the Geneva Conventions (regulating IACs) is adamant that it does not matter 'how much slaughter takes place' in an IAC; and, even if there is 'only a single wounded person as a result of the conflict', IAC *jus in bello*

---

[175] *Prosecutor* v. *Tadić, supra* note 33, at 62.

[176] *Prosecutor* v. *Halilović* (ICTY, Trial Chamber, 2005), para. 25.

[177] International Law Association, Committee on Use of Force, Final Report on the Meaning of Armed Conflicts in International Law, *Report of the Seventy-Fourth Conference* 676, 713 (The Hague, 2010).

[178] See D. Akande, 'Classification of Armed Conflicts: Relevant Legal Concepts', *International Law and the Classification of Conflicts, supra* note 99, at 32, 41.

[179] See C. Hellestveit, 'The Geneva Conventions and the Dichotomy between International and Non-International Armed Conflict: Curse or Blessing for the "Principle of Human-ity"?', *Searching for a 'Principle of Humanity' in International Humanitarian Law* 85, 100–1 (K.M. Larsen, C.G. Cooper and G. Nystuen eds., 2013).

[180] *Prosecutor* v. *Tadić, supra* note 33, at 54.

will apply.[181] Depending on its dimensions, an IAC may make the grade of a full-scale war or it may amount to a 'short of war' incident, but either way the clash of arms between States invites the application of IAC *jus in bello*.

165. There are two exceptional contingencies in which a NIAC is treated as if it had crossed the third threshold:

(i) When 'recognition of belligerency' is granted. This eventuality, which is predicated on customary international law, will be tackled *infra* 338.

(ii) Under Article 1(4) of AP/I,[182] armed conflicts in the exercise of the right of self-determination are subject to the application of AP/I and the Geneva Conventions in their amplitude (not only Common Article 3), although they do not involve two opposing States. It must be noted, however, that Article 1(4) is a polemical provision that does not bind non-Contracting Parties to AP/I.

II. Interaction between armed conflicts

A. Two or more NIACs

166. Two or more NIACs may be going on – usually in distinct parts of a large territory – within a single country. The situation crops up when an incumbent Government has to grapple with assorted insurrections having diverse, and perhaps even contradictory, aims. The leading example is that of the Philippines, plagued for long stretches of time by several unconnected insurgencies in different islands.[183] Each NIAC is suffused with its own special colours, and has to be analyzed independently of the other(s).

167. A NIAC in Ruritania may have staggering spin-off effects in adjacent lands. Waves of refugees may flee into Arcadian territory; commercial ties may be frayed or severed, thereby causing serious economic hardships in both countries; smuggling of arms may lead to cross-border incidents; artillery fire or air strikes directed at adversaries in the NIAC may inadvertently stray across the Arcadian frontier, etc. As long as the armed

---

[181] *Commentary, I Geneva Convention, supra* note 5, at 32.

[182] AP/I, *supra* note 21, at 715.

[183] See R.B. Ferrer and R.G. Cabanbang, 'Non-International Armed Conflicts in the Philippines', 88 *ILS, supra* note 55, at 263, 265–71.

conflict retains its basic intra-State character, and the protrusion of violence abroad is a marginal extension of the civil strife within Ruritania, the hostilities remain in a NIAC matrix. The offshoots of violence into an adjacent territory do not deprive a NIAC of its inherently internal character (see *supra* 82).

168. Even when NIAC hostilities in Ruritania are confined to its territory, they may indirectly stimulate internal violence within Arcadia. That would be the case, in particular, when the same ethnic or religious groups straddle the Ruritanian–Arcadian border, and the NIAC in Ruritania has ripple effects in the trans-boundary vicinity. The NIAC in Ruritania may serve as a catalyst for a fully-fledged new NIAC directed against the incumbent Government of Arcadia. The two simultaneous NIACs in Ruritania and Arcadia do not need to proceed in lockstep although they may intermingle. For example, in 2013, dozens of Syrian soldiers – under pressure from Syrian insurgents – sought a haven on the Iraqi side of the frontier, at which point they were ambushed and killed by Iraqi insurgents. No matter how connected the underlying causes of the two NIACs are, they must be considered individually in a legal review of the violence.

169. When the incumbent Governments of Ruritania and Arcadia wage hostilities against insurgents within their respective territories, the two simultaneous armed conflicts – while appearing to be intertwined – remain separate NIACs. The pair of Governments may collaborate with each other if the insurgents that they face act in unison. However, unauthorized incursions by Ruritanian armed forces into Arcadia – in pursuit of Ruritanian insurgents (see *supra* 82) – may cause inter-State friction. Such incursions can become a furnace stoking a confrontation between the two Governments. Should Ruritanian and Arcadian military units engage in combat, their countries will plunge into an IAC. That is to say, a new armed conflict crossing the third threshold will break out.

170. There is a possibility that Ruritania will be the target of armed attacks launched by an organized armed group from within the territory of Arcadia, there being no complicity on the part of the Arcadian Government. If Arcadia is unable or unwilling to put an end to the raids, Ruritania may take direct action against the group. Should this be done without the consent of Arcadia, as an exercise of 'extra-territorial law enforcement', it becomes a self-defence issue falling under the rubric of *jus ad bellum*.[184] As long as recourse to 'extra-territorial law enforcement' does not lead to a clash between the military forces of Ruritania and Arcadia, there is no

---

[184] On 'extra-territorial law enforcement', see Dinstein, *supra* note 11, at 268–77.

IAC between these two countries. When there is a NIAC in Ruritania, the incursion into Arcadian territory has to be deemed an extension of that internal conflagration (see *supra* 82), regulated by LONIAC. In essence, the legal status of the operation depends on its context.[185]

B. Combinations of NIACs and IACs

171. There are multiple potential combinations of NIACs and IACs, which are linked to one another geographically and are waged either simultaneously or consecutively.

(a) Simultaneous combinations

172. The territory of a single State may be mired in disparate sets of hostilities that can be categorized, respectively, as an IAC (between two or more States) and a NIAC (between the incumbent Government and an insurgent armed group, or between two or more rival organized armed groups vying for power within a 'failing State'; see *infra* 261). These armed conflicts, one inter-State and the other intra-State, may commence simultaneously or consecutively (the IAC may be preceded by the NIAC or vice versa). But, whether synchronized or unsynchronized, the legal strands of the inter-State and the intra-State hostilities must be kept apart.[186]

173. The possibility of an IAC being prosecuted side by side with a NIAC was expressly recognized by the ICJ in the *Nicaragua* case: the Judgment classified the conflict between the *contras* and the armed forces of the Government of Nicaragua as a NIAC, whereas a related conflict between the US and the Nicaraguan Government was pronounced to be an IAC.[187]

174. Two more recent illustrations of the confluence of a NIAC and an IAC in the same country are Afghanistan and Libya. In Afghanistan, the Taliban regime – having been embroiled in a long-standing NIAC with the Northern Alliance – became a Belligerent Party in an IAC with the US (and its allies) in 2001, by dint of providing shelter and steadfast support to the Al-Qaeda terrorists who had launched the notorious armed attack against the US on 9/11. The IAC and NIAC in Afghanistan were

---

[185] On the importance of context in this respect, see Schöndorf, *supra* note 74, at 58.

[186] See C. Greenwood, 'The Development of International Humanitarian Law by the International Tribunal for the Former Yugoslavia', 2 *MPYUNL* 97, 117 (1998).

[187] *Nicaragua* case, *supra* note 36, at 114.

subject to different legal regimes, although running simultaneously and connectively.

175. In Libya, sporadic violence against the Qaddafi Government turned into a full-blown NIAC in 2011. Later that year, an IAC broke out between some NATO (North Atlantic Treaty Organization) countries – as well as others – and the Qaddafi regime, on the heels of Security Council resolutions (see *infra* 280–2).[188] The two discrete armed conflicts went on separately – albeit concurrently – and ended only following the death of M. Qaddafi and the utter disappearance of his regime.[189]

(b) Consecutive combinations

176. Diverse armed conflicts may have consecutive combinations. First, an armed conflict may commence as a NIAC but later segue into – or bring about – an IAC. We shall see how a military intervention by Arcadia on the side of insurgents against the incumbent Government of Ruritania will trigger an IAC (see *infra* 264). By contrast, when a military intervention by Utopia is undertaken at the request of the Ruritanian Government against the insurgents (see *infra* 238 *et seq.*), the armed conflict remains a NIAC. But, if the insurgents defeat and replace the Ruritanian Government, continuation of the hostilities by Utopia against the erstwhile insurgents would recast the scenery. The armed conflict will convert from a NIAC into an IAC, inasmuch as the armed forces of Utopia will then be arrayed against those of the new Government of Ruritania.

177. An alternative progression of events may lead to Ruritania being shattered by the NIAC. In that crucible, new sovereign States may be forged: Apollonia, Patagonia, etc. Despite the fracture (or because of it), hostilities may persist between a diminished Ruritania and Apollonia or Patagonia. What started as a NIAC within Ruritania will then turn into an IAC between the new warring sovereign countries. As the case of Eritrea and Ethiopia shows, when a NIAC shifts into an IAC it may sever preexisting political or ideological bonds. When the Eritreans revolted against Ethiopia in a fight for secession, they collaborated with another (indigenous Ethiopian) insurgent movement bent on ousting the incumbent Government in Addis Ababa. Eventually, both parallel NIACs were crowned with success: the Eritreans gained independence (see *infra* 180)

---

[188] See E. Wilmshurst, 'Conclusions', *International Law and the Classification of Conflicts, supra* note 99, at 80, 99.

[189] See K. Mačák and N. Zamir, 'The Applicability of International Humanitarian Law to the Conflict in Libya', 14 *ICLR* 403, 413–34 (2012).

and their fellow rebels assumed power in Ethiopia. Yet, the former alliance did not last: Eritrea and Ethiopia (under the new Government) proceeded to cross swords in an IAC between the two countries.

178. The critical time for the transition from a NIAC to an IAC, consequent on the fragmentation of an existing State, is the consolidation of new sovereign States in parts of its territory. This is what occurred in Yugoslavia in the 1990s. In 1997, a Trial Chamber of the ICTY held in the *Tadić* case that – from the beginning of 1992 until May of the same year – an IAC existed between the forces of the Republic of Bosnia/Herzegovina on the one hand, and those of the Federal Republic of Yugoslavia (Serbia/Montenegro) on the other.[190] The majority of the Chamber (Judges Stephen and Vohrah) held further that, as a result of the withdrawal of Yugoslav troops announced in May 1992, the Bosnian conflict reverted to being a NIAC.[191] The Presiding Judge (McDonald) dissented on the ground that the withdrawal was a fiction and that Yugoslavia remained in effective control of the Serb forces in Bosnia.[192] The majority opinion was reversed by the ICTY Appeals Chamber in 1999.[193] The original Trial Chamber's majority opinion had elicited strident criticism from scholars;[194] and, even before the delivery of the final judgment on appeal, another Trial Chamber of the ICTY took a divergent view in the *Delalić* case of 1998.[195] Still, the essence of the disagreement must be looked at as factual in nature. Legally speaking, the fundamental character of an armed conflict as an IAC or a NIAC can metamorphose – more than once – from one time span to another.

179. Lamentably, as far as fighters in the field are concerned, it may not always be easy to detect at what exact moment a NIAC has mutated into an IAC. If the ICTY judges – with the advantage of legal expertise and hindsight – could not readily agree on a legal diagnosis of the situation in Bosnia in 1992, one can only imagine how much more bewildering the position looked from the battlefield perspective.

180. It is easier to resolve the conundrum if a distinct interval can be detected between the NIAC and the IAC. The template is Eritrea.[196] That

---

[190] *Prosecutor v. Tadić, supra* note 116, at 922.   [191] *Ibid.*, 933.
[192] *Ibid.*, 972–3.   [193] *Prosecutor v. Tadić, supra* note 151, at 1549.
[194] See, e.g., T. Meron, 'Classification of Armed Conflict in the Former Yugoslavia: Nicaragua's Fallout', 92 *AJIL* 236–42 (1998).
[195] *Prosecutor v. Delalić et al., supra* note 37, at paras. 204–34.
[196] See B. Zewde, 'The Historical Background of the 1998–2000 War: Some Salient Points', *The 1998–2000 War between Eritrea and Ethiopia: An International Legal Perspective* 21, 23 (A. de Guttry, H.H.G. Post and G. Venturini eds., 2009).

country declared its formal independence from Ethiopia – following a tenacious NIAC and a referendum – in 1993. After a while, border disputes between Eritrea and Ethiopia accelerated into a full-scale IAC in 1998–2000 (and hostilities were reignited in 2003). The dividing line between the NIAC and the IAC in the relations between Eritrea and Ethiopia, unlike the former Yugoslav provinces, is easy to trace.

181. Just as a NIAC may gravitate into an IAC, an IAC may lead to a NIAC. Iraq is a good model. After the fall of Baghdad in 2003 – in an IAC between an American-led coalition and the Baathist regime – a newly elected Government was installed, at which point a NIAC evolved between it and remnants of the Baathists backed up by other Sunni opposition groups. For years, the NIAC in Iraq was waged concomitantly with the coalition's IAC against the same foes. But while the IAC came to an end upon the termination of coalition military operations in Iraq, the NIAC was not extinguished in tandem.

4

Insurgent armed groups and individuals

I. Direct participation in hostilities

A. *The concept*

182. Participants in NIAC hostilities are either State or non-State actors. *Ex hypothesi*, insurgents – by revolting against the incumbent Government – are non-State actors. So are any members of organized armed groups fighting each other in the absence of any Government (see *supra* 87). State actors in a NIAC are those who are operating under governmental authority. They can be fighting on behalf of either (i) the Government of the State in the territory of which the conflict occurs (Ruritania); or (ii) the Government of any other country (Utopia) that militarily intervenes on behalf of the Ruritanian Government. Should there be other State actors (belonging to Arcadia) pitted in battle against the forces of Ruritania, what would ensue is an IAC, as distinct from a NIAC (see *supra* 161).

183. Common Article 3 (*infra* 409) refers to '[p]ersons taking no active part in the hostilities, including members of armed forces who have laid down their arms and those placed *hors de combat*'. The same language is used in Article 8(2)(c) of the Rome Statute (*infra* 559). The terminology here is based on the idea that 'armed forces' represent both sides, and they can therefore be either State or non-State actors.[197]

184. Paragraph (1) of Article 4 of AP/II (*infra* 431) alludes to '[a]ll persons who do not take a direct part or who have ceased to take part in hostilities'. The expression 'armed forces' is not repeated. In Paragraph (1) of Article 1 (*supra* 118), there is a distinction between 'armed forces' belonging to the State, 'dissident armed forces' (formerly belonging to it but now mutinous) and 'other organized armed groups' (of insurgents). This is a more calibrated approach. The common denominator of all the members of the armed forces or groups mentioned is that, whether

---

[197] See *Interpretive Guidance*, *supra* note 142, at 28.

they are State actors or non-State actors, they are taking a direct part in hostilities.

185. Direct participation in hostilities is a construct that excludes genuine civilians. 'Civilians' (individually) and 'the civilian population' (collectively) can be defined as those persons who do not belong to the armed forces (or armed groups) of either side in the NIAC. In principle, civilians are protected by LONIAC from attack. But LONIAC cannot ignore the fact that some people who profess to be civilians occasionally take a direct part in hostilities. Paragraph (3) of Article 13 of AP/II (*infra* 462) denies protection from attack to civilians 'for such time as they take a direct part in hostilities'. In other words, persons who take a direct part in hostilities – for such time as they do so – remove themselves from the umbrella of civilian exemption from attack in a NIAC.

186. The ICRC 2009 Interpretive Guidance on the Notion of Direct Participation in Hostilities under IHL contends that, although a person directly participating in NIAC hostilities loses civilian protection from attack, there are still limitations on the degree of force that can be used against him, and – if circumstances permit – he should be captured rather than be subjected to lethal force.[198] This exceedingly controversial position confuses NIACs with the law enforcement paradigm governing below-the-threshold violence (see *supra* 68). It is 'unsupported by any positive or customary' norm of LONIAC,[199] and was adopted against stalwart advice tendered by many experts in the field.[200] There may be extraneous reasons (primarily, the need to avoid 'excessive' collateral damage to genuine civilians who happen to be nearby; see *infra* 694) for averting recourse to deadly force against lawful targets. Nevertheless, under LONIAC as it stands, losing civilian protection means full exposure to the risks of hostilities in which a person chooses to engage.

187. Common Article 3 speaks about 'active', whereas both Paragraph (1) of Article 4 and Paragraph (3) of Article 13 of AP/II advert to 'direct', participation in hostilities. It is generally agreed that where participation in hostilities is concerned, there is no substantive difference between the adjectives 'active' and 'direct'.[201] Admittedly, in the 2012 *Lubanga* Judgment, an ICC Trial Chamber maintained that the phrase

---

[198] *Ibid.*, 77–82.

[199] G. Corn and C. Jenks, 'Two Sides of the Combatant Coin: Untangling Direct Participation in Hostilities from Belligerent Status in Non-International Armed Conflicts', 33 *UPenn.JIL* 313, 348 (2011–12).

[200] See H. Parks, 'Part IX of the ICRC "Direct Participation in Hostilities" Study: No Mandate, No Expertise and Legally Incorrect', 42 *NYUJILP* 769, 828 (2009–10).

[201] See *Interpretive Guidance, supra* note 142, at 43–4.

'to participate actively in hostilities' (appearing, in the context of child-soldiers, in Article 8(2)(e)(vii) of the Rome Statute; *infra* 572) is broader in scope than 'direct' participation in hostilities.[202] But there is not even slender evidence in practice for such an assertion.[203]

188. The significance of either the adjective 'active' or 'direct' is that it sets those who are participating in hostilities – those who can be deemed fighters – apart from genuine civilians who are entitled to protection from attack. Civilians do not lose their status of exemption from attack only because they sympathize with an insurgency, verbally express support for its goals or even contribute financially to the cause. What counts for loss of civilian protection from attack is a more specific involvement in the armed conflict.[204] This will take place in one of two ways: (i) belonging to an organized armed group; or (ii) individually being engaged in the hostilities (on the gamut of the germane activities, see *infra* 190–1). Engagement in hostilities must be construed broadly, spreading over preparatory measures as well as deployment to – or disengagement/return from – the venue of the execution of the act.[205]

189. Common Article 3 sees the protection extended to '[p]ersons taking no active part in the hostilities' as including also 'members of armed forces who have laid down their arms and those placed *hors de combat*' (*infra* 409).[206] Paragraph (1) of Article 4 of AP/II is somewhat more nuanced by using the conjunction 'or' in order to differentiate between persons 'who do not take a direct part' in hostilities and those 'who have ceased to take part in hostilities' (*infra* 431).

B. The meaning

(a) Activities

190. Direct participation in hostilities is embedded in the actor's conduct in a NIAC. The concept must not be seen as confined to open

---

[202] *Prosecutor* v. *Lubanga* (ICC, Trial Chamber, 2012), 51 *ILM* 1021, 1068 (2012).

[203] See N. Wagner, 'A Critical Assessment of Using Children to Participate Actively in Hostilities in *Lubanga*: Child Soldiers and Direct Participation', 24 *CLF* 145, 165–6 (2013).

[204] See D. Akande, 'Clearing the Fog of War? The ICRC's Interpretive Guidance on Direct Participation in Hostilities', 59 *ICLQ* 180, 188 (2010).

[205] See *Interpretive Guidance, supra* note 142, at 65.

[206] Attention should be paid to the deliberate use of the pronoun 'who' rather than 'which': arms must be laid down by the specific members of the armed forces, and not by the entire armed forces to which they belong. See S. Wills, 'The Legal Characterization of the Armed Conflicts in Afghanistan and Iraq: Implications for Protection', 58 *NILR* 173, 184–5 (2011).

fighting or to acts of violence. The pivotal question is whether the activities engaged in 'by their nature or purpose, are likely to cause actual harm to the personnel or matériel' of the opposing side.[207]

191. This definition includes an ensemble of non-violent activities ancillary to fighting, such as delivering ammunition to fighters or collating sensitive military information.[208] By the same token, any person undertaking to serve as a scout, guide or courier for fighters loses his civilian protection under LONIAC (as for couriers, see also *infra* 585).

(b) Members of organized armed groups

192. Most commonly, insurgents will be affiliated with an organized armed group (for a definition of the term, see *supra* 127 *et seq.*). In the words of an ICTY Trial Chamber in the *Galić* Judgment of 2003, '[f]or the purpose of the protection of victims of armed conflict, the term "civilian" is defined negatively as anyone who is not a member of the armed forces or of an organized military group belonging to a party to the conflict'.[209]

193. Membership in an insurgent organized armed group is a salient issue. The premise is that for such time as a person is a member of an organized insurgent group, he is directly participating in the hostilities. In consequence, he will forfeit his civilian protection from attack owing to mere belonging to the group, irrespective of any engagement in actual fighting on his part.[210] As the ICTY Appeals Chamber in the *Blaškić* Judgment of 2004 observed: 'If he is indeed a member of an armed organization, the fact that he is not armed or in combat at the time of the commission of crimes, does not accord him civilian status'.[211]

194. The ICRC Interpretive Guidance argues that, in a NIAC, 'the concept of organized armed group refers to non-State armed forces in a strictly functional sense', and 'the decisive criterion for individual membership in an organized armed group' is 'continuous combat function'.[212] It must be appreciated that this 'is not a restatement of the law as it stands today'.[213] An insurgent organized armed group consists not only of persons fulfilling a 'continuous combat function' but also of support

---

[207] The quotation is from *Prosecutor* v. *Dragomir Milošević* (ICTY, Appeals Chamber, 2007), para. 947. The Judgment deals with IACs, but the issue is the same in NIACs.

[208] See *San Remo Manual on the Law of Non-International Armed Conflict* 4–5 (M.N. Schmitt, C.H.B. Garraway and Y. Dinstein eds., 2006).

[209] *Prosecutor* v. *Galić* (ICTY, Trial Chamber, 2003), para. 47.

[210] See Otto, *supra* note 41, at 239–42.

[211] *Prosecutor* v. *Blaškić* (ICTY, Appeals Chamber, 2004), para. 114.

[212] *Interpretive Guidance, supra* note 142, at 33.

[213] C. de Cocq, 'Counter-Insurgency Operations in Afghanistan. What about the "*Jus ad Bellum*" and the "*Jus in Bello*": Is the Law Still Accurate?', 13 *YIHL* 97, 118 (2010).

staff (technicians, drivers, secretaries and the like). A peculiar element of inequality between the opposing sides in a NIAC is symptomatic of the ICRC position.[214] After all, why should 'the cook, the cleaner, the lawyer and others without a combat function' in an insurgent organized armed group not be susceptible to attack (on the ground that they perform a non-combat function), while their peers serving in the armed forces of the State do not enjoy a similar exemption?[215]

195. Of course, there is a chronic problem of establishing that a person belongs to an insurgent armed group, which is not likely to issue membership cards (see *supra* 128). In many instances, an extensive grey area of doubt obscures the exact standing of a person who has no combat function in an insurgent armed group. Yet, a similar doubt may also affect those who have a combat function in the group but do not advertise it. As put forward by a Trial Chamber of the ICTY in the 2011 Đorđević Judgment, it makes sense to apply in NIACs the IAC *jus in bello* principle that – in cases of doubt as to whether a person is a civilian – the presumption will be that he is so.[216] But not every situation is shrouded by a veil of doubt. When doubts are stirred, they can be weeded out in several ways, either through skilful intelligence gathering or as a result of an in-depth investigation of the individual's past record.

(c) Individuals

196. Persons taking a direct part in NIAC hostilities may be acting under their own steam. They may be vigilantes fighting on the incumbent Government's side. More commonly, they may form an unwieldy assemblage of unaffiliated malcontents who join the fighting against the Government without belonging to any organized insurgent group.

197. If all those who rebel against the Government are *francs-tireurs*, no party to the conflict is formed, and – in the absence of minimum organization – there is no NIAC (see *supra* 90 *et seq.*). However, if an organized insurgent 'party to the conflict' is formed, LONIAC will also cover fighting waged at its fringes by *francs-tireurs*[217] (who will be categorized as persons directly participating in the hostilities).

198. It has already been mentioned (*supra* 45) that the ICTR *Akayesu* Judgment on appeal did not insist on a 'special relationship' between perpetrators of NIAC war crimes and a party to the conflict.

---

[214] See Schmitt, *supra* note 55, at 133.   [215] Akande, *supra* note 204, at 186.

[216] *Prosecutor* v. Đorđević (ICTY, Trial Chamber, 2003), para. 2066.

[217] Provost, *supra* note 134, at 161.

Francs-tireurs directly participating in hostilities are demonstrably apt to commit war crimes. An example would be the killing of a wounded fighter by a so-called civilian (who would thereby become a *franc-tireur*).

199. There might be some hesitation before an individual – who is not a member of an organized armed group – is tagged as taking a direct part in hostilities (cf. *supra* 195). But there should be no ambivalence about those who do so in a recurring manner. When a cycle of active contributions to military operations is punctuated by time frames of plying civilian trades (what is known as a farmer-by-day fighter-by-night syndrome), the individual recidivist can be regarded as directly participating in hostilities on a continuous basis. Being involved in 'revolving door' activities, he loses his civilian protection on a 24/7 basis: he can be targeted in any location, even during respites when he is engaged in innocent chores.[218] The present author is unable to agree with the ICRC's Interpretive Guidance claim that civilian protection is restored each time that a segment of participation in hostilities is ended.[219] If followed in practice, the ICRC approach – aimed at providing 'uninvolved civilians' with greater protection – would actually create 'a form of immunity for insurgents'.[220]

II. Why are insurgent armed groups bound by LONIAC?

A. The axiom

200. There is a generally accepted axiom that insurgent armed groups are bound by LONIAC. The postulate is already reflected in the language of Common Article 3 (*infra* 409): the Article 'purports to impose obligations on any party to a non-international armed conflict, not just on governments'.[221] These obligations are occasionally underlined by the Security Council, for instance in Resolution 1564 (2004) – a Chapter VII binding resolution on the situation in Darfur – where the Council demanded that 'all armed groups, including rebel forces, . . . ensure that their members comply with international humanitarian law'.[222]

---

[218] See Schmitt, *supra* note 55, at 136–7.

[219] *Interpretive Guidance, supra* note 142, at 70–1.

[220] See K. Watkin, 'Opportunity Lost: Organized Armed Groups and the ICRC "Direct Participation in Hostilities" Interpretive Guidance', 42 *NYUJILP* 641, 689 (2009–10).

[221] C. Lysaght, 'The Scope of Protocol II and Its Relation to Common Article 3 of the Geneva Conventions of 1949 and Other Human Rights Instruments', 33 *AULR* 9, 12 (1983–4).

[222] Security Council Resolution 1564 (2004), para. 10.

201. The Appeals Chamber of the SCSL struck the right chord when it pronounced in the *Norman* case of 2004:

> it is well-settled that *all* parties to an armed conflict, whether states or non-state actors, are bound by international humanitarian law, even though only states may become parties to international treaties. Customary international law represents the common standard of behavior within the international community, thus even armed groups hostile to a particular government have to abide by those laws.[223]

The *Institut de Droit International*, in a Resolution of 1999, also subscribed to the view that '[a]ll parties in armed conflicts in which non-State entities [defined as 'parties to internal armed conflicts'] are parties, irrespective of their legal status . . . have the obligation to respect international humanitarian law as well as fundamental human rights'.[224]

B. The rationale

202. The conceptual underpinning for the proposition that insurgent armed groups are bound by LONIAC has riveted much scholarly attention, fuelling considerable controversy. Even the most superficial discussion of the subject must draw a distinction between treaty law and customary law, although the significance of the distinction is tempered by the fact that many treaty provisions (chiefly, Common Article 3) are currently deemed declaratory of customary international law.

(a) Treaty law

203. When LONIAC treaties (such as AP/II) are concluded, the framers' intention is normally that the new stipulations – however innovative – will apply equally to both sides of the NIAC: insurgent armed groups as much as the incumbent Government's armed forces.[225] That intention is expressed in no uncertain terms in the Preamble of the 2008 Dublin Convention on Cluster Munitions:

---

[223] *Prosecutor v. Norman* (Decision on Jurisdiction) (SCSL, Appeals Chamber, 2004), 43 *ILM* 1129, 1137 (2004). Emphasis in the original.

[224] *Institut de Droit International*, Resolution on 'The Application of International Humanitarian Law and Fundamental Human Rights, in Armed Conflicts in which Non-State Entities Are Parties', 68-II *AIDI* 387, 393 (Berlin Session, 1999).

[225] See F. Kalshoven and L. Zegveld, *Constraints on the Waging of War: An Introduction to International Humanitarian Law* 144 (4th edn, 2011).

> *Resolved* also that armed groups distinct from the armed forces of a State shall not, under any circumstances, be permitted to engage in any activity prohibited to a State Party to this Convention.[226]

204. Even when the authors of a NIAC treaty are pellucidly determined that their text must be obeyed by non-State actors, the implementation of their wishes is fraught with a perplexing problem. Two inter-related queries arise here: (i) on whom do treaty obligations (and any corollary rights) devolve when they relate to an insurgent armed group? and (ii) how can these obligations (with the attendant rights) be created by treaty?

(i) Non-State bearers of obligations and rights

205. An insurgent armed group – even when fully organized – is not vested by international law (and obviously not by domestic law) with a legal personality. Some scholars contend that a legal personality of a 'limited nature' emanates for insurgent armed groups from Common Article 3 and kindred instruments.[227] At times, they call it a 'functional personality'.[228] But the thesis has no support in the general practice of States.

206. Attention must be paid to the last sentence of Common Article 3 (*infra* 409): 'The application of the preceding provisions shall not affect the legal status of the Parties to the conflict'. The formula is repeated word-for-word in Paragraph (4) of Article 19 of the CPCP and in Paragraph (6) of Article 22 of its Second Protocol (both cited *supra* 25). We have already referred (*supra* 93–4) to the associated issue of the insertion of the phrase 'Party to the conflict' in Common Article 3 and its deletion from AP/II.

207. The ICRC Commentary on the Geneva Conventions states in this context:

> the fact of applying article 3 does not in itself constitute any recognition by the *de jure* Government that the adverse Party has authority of any kind.[229]

The Appeals Chamber of the SCSL pronounced in the *Kallon et al.* Decision of 2004 that 'there is now no doubt' that Common Article 3 is binding on States and insurgents alike, and that insurgents are subject to

---

[226] Dublin Convention on Cluster Munitions, 2008, 48 *ILM* 357, *id.* (2009).

[227] L. Zegveld, *Accountability of Armed Opposition Groups in International Law* 151–2 (2002).

[228] M. Pedrazzi, 'The Status of Organized Armed Groups in Contemporary Armed Conflicts', *Non-State Actors and International Humanitarian Law, supra* note 143, at 67, 76.

[229] *Commentary, I Geneva Convention, supra* note 5, at 61.

LONIAC: that fact, however, does not by itself vest an insurgent group 'with international personality under international law'.[230]

208. The proposition that insurgent armed groups lack a legal personality (even one that is not fully grown) does not preclude the creation of rights or obligations for individual insurgents by treaty. As early as 1928, the PCIJ held, in the Advisory Opinion on the *Jurisdiction of the Courts of Danzig*:

> it cannot be disputed that the very object of an international agreement, according to the intention of the contracting Parties, may be the adoption by the Parties of some definite rules creating individual rights and obligations and enforceable by the national courts.[231]

A prodigious body of law that has mushroomed since World War II demonstrates that modern treaties frequently bestow rights on individuals (human rights) and impose obligations on them (as part of an expanding international criminal law). Many of these rights and obligations are now enforceable not only by domestic courts but also by international courts and tribunals.

209. It is in the nature of treaty human rights that they are vested in persons rather than States: indeed, the rights are generally established *vis-à-vis* the State. Similarly, the perpetrators of war crimes (acting in breach of obligations created by treaty texts of international criminal law) are also persons and not States.[232]

210. The focus on persons does not mean that human beings have to be considered in isolation from each other. After all, NIACs turn on minimum organization of insurgent groups (see *supra* 90 *et seq.*), and individuals who act solitarily are incapable of implementing sundry obligations set out by LONIAC treaties (e.g., the obligation of collecting and caring for the wounded and sick, pursuant to Paragraph 2 of Common Article 3; *infra* 409). Organized insurgent groups are the cynosure of such treaties. Denied legal personality, the groups must be seen for what they really are: clusters of individuals. In the course of a NIAC, individual insurgents (belonging to an organized armed group) exercise jointly the rights and obligations crafted by LONIAC treaties.

---

[230] *Prosecutor v. Kallon et al.* (Decision on Jurisdiction) (SCSL, Appeals Chamber, 2004), para. 45.

[231] Advisory Opinion on the *Jurisdiction of the Courts of Danzig* (Pecuniary Claims of Danzig Railway Officials Transferred to the Polish Service) (1928), II *WCR* 237, 246–7.

[232] See D. Matas, 'Armed Opposition Groups', 24 *Man.LJ* 621, 633 (1996–7).

211. There is a clear-cut precedent for conferring – by treaty – collective human rights without the tool of an international legal personality. The precedent is to be found in the twin 1966 International Covenants on human rights: one devoted to Economic, Social and Cultural Rights and the other to Civil and Political Rights. While most of the provisions of these instruments grant human rights to individuals, it is of singular significance that:

(aa) Both Covenants, in Common Article 1, confer on all 'peoples' (an expression not defined in scope) the right of self-determination.[233]
(bb) Article 27 of the Civil and Political Rights Covenant also establishes rights to be enjoyed by persons belonging to ethnic, religious or linguistic minorities, 'in community with the other members of their group'.[234]

Neither peoples nor minorities possess an international legal personality, and the correct analysis of their respective entitlements is that they constitute collective human rights (or human rights exercised communally, i.e. jointly rather than severally).[235] The collective dimension of these human rights manifests itself in their being 'premised on the existence of a community'.[236]

212. The rights of minorities[237] and of peoples[238] can be regarded as group rights. In addition, 'national, ethnical, racial or religious' groups are expressly protected from genocide under the 1948 Genocide Convention[239] and Article 6 of the Rome Statute of the ICC.[240] There is no exigent reason to reject the possibility that additional groups – specifically, insurgent groups in NIACs – may also benefit from collective rights set up by treaty.

---

[233] International Covenant on Economic, Social and Cultural Rights, [1966] *UNJY* 170, 171; International Covenant on Civil and Political Rights, *ibid.*, 178, 179.
[234] International Covenant on Civil and Political Rights, *ibid.*, 186.
[235] See Y. Dinstein, 'Collective Human Rights of Peoples and Minorities', 25 *ICLQ* 102, 102–3 (1976).
[236] P. Thornberry, 'Images of Autonomy and Individual and Collective Rights in International Instruments on the Rights of Minorities', *Autonomy: Applications and Implications* 97, 106 (M. Suksi ed., 1998).
[237] See N. Lerner, *Group Rights and Discrimination in International Law* 34 (2003).
[238] See J. Crawford, 'The Rights of Peoples: Some Conclusions', *The Rights of Peoples* 160, 165 (J. Crawford ed., 1988).
[239] Convention on the Prevention and Punishment of the Crime of Genocide, 1948, *Laws of Armed Conflicts* 839, 840 (Article 2).
[240] Rome Statute of the ICC, *supra* note 7, at 1315.

213. No similar illustration exists of obligations (as distinct from rights) imposed collectively on groups by treaty. In the 1946 Nuremberg Judgment, the International Military Tribunal (IMT) dealt with the issue of 'group criminality' and found it 'analogous to a criminal conspiracy'.[241] Article 25(1) of the Rome Statute of the ICC restricts the Court's jurisdiction over war crimes (and other crimes) to 'natural persons'.[242] Still, Article 25(3) recognizes the possibility of the joint commission of crimes.[243] This is tied in with the construct of a 'joint criminal enterprise' developed in the case law of the ICTY.[244] It must be perceived, however, that membership of a group does not by itself suffice for criminal conviction.[245]

(ii) Non-State actors and treaties

214. Article 11 of the VCLT prescribes that the consent of a State to be bound by a treaty – namely, to become a Contracting Party – may be expressed in several ways (principally, signature, ratification and accession).[246] Whatever its form, the State's consent is indispensable. Who expresses that consent? Pursuant to Article 7, only a person endowed with full powers to represent the State.[247]

215. By definition, an insurgent armed group in a NIAC does not represent the State: after all, it rises in revolt against those who do (the incumbent Government). Consisting of unauthorized non-State actors, the armed group – albeit organized – is incompetent to participate in the process of the conclusion of treaties, since this privilege is reserved exclusively to States (see *supra* 19). The question then is as follows: if the armed group is unable to be a Contracting Party to a treaty, why would it be affected by any consent to be bound by the instrument, as expressed by the existing Government (which the group repudiates) or by any previous Government?

216. The facile answer is that the binding force of a treaty on Contracting Parties is not diminished by a change of Governments in a State, and any new regime must perform the State's duties as prescribed in the treaty.[248] The rule therefore is that, should an insurgency be crowned with success and the incumbent Government is ousted, the new Government would be obligated to observe any treaty (including any LONIAC treaty) to which the State is a Contracting Party.

---

[241] Nuremberg Judgment (IMT, 1946), 41 *AJIL* 172, 251 (1947).
[242] Rome Statute of the ICC, *supra* note 7, at 1327. [243] *Ibid.*
[244] See G. Werle, *Principles of International Criminal Law* 172–3 (2nd edn, 2009).
[245] See R. Cryer, H. Friman, D. Robinson and E. Wilmshurst, *An Introduction to International Criminal Law and Procedure* 369 (2nd edn, 2010).
[246] VCLT, *supra* note 19, at 143. [247] *Ibid.* [248] See Aust, *supra* note 173, at 55, 161–2.

217. A complementary rule appears in Article 10(1) of the Draft Articles on the Responsibility of States for Internationally Wrongful Acts – as formulated by the International Law Commission (ILC) in 2001 – whereby '[t]he conduct of an insurrectional movement which becomes the new Government of a State shall be considered an act of that State under international law'.[249] By the same token, under Article 10(2) of the text, the conduct of an insurrectional movement that succeeds in establishing a new State in part of the territory of a preexisting State is considered an act of the new State under international law.[250]

218. When all this is stitched together, it ensues that successful insurgents (who either form the new Government of an existing State or secede and create a new State) bear responsibility for their own conduct in breach of a LONIAC treaty during the insurrection. That being the case, it would make no sense to regard the insurgents as absolved from complying with the treaty provisions pending their successful takeover of the Government's seat of power. One may proceed another step arguing that, whether or not the insurgents are ultimately successful, treaties already in force for a State when an insurrection erupts ought to remain binding on the insurgent armed group once the fighting is under way.[251]

219. Withal, it is necessary to concede the existence of two fragile links in the logical chain. First, this line of thought makes full sense only with respect to treaties to which the State – through the Government – has expressed its consent prior to the outbreak of the insurgency. If the incumbent Government assumes obligations under a treaty subsequent to the onset of the insurgency – i.e. after the Government's ostensible authority to represent the State has been challenged by the insurgents – it is no longer possible to hew to that line. The insurgents can be expected to refuse to apply the treaty on the ground that it has been adopted when they were already in open revolt and they have not been afforded an opportunity to make up their minds on whether or not they are willing to subscribe to its provisions.[252]

220. Second, the insurgents' antagonism to treaties concluded by the incumbent Government may be aggravated when they are fighting not merely to bring about regime change within the compass of an existing

---

[249] Draft Articles on Responsibility of States for Internationally Wrongful Acts, Report of the ILC, 53rd Session, [2001] II (2) *ILC Ybk* 1, 26.

[250] *Ibid.*   [251] See Lord McNair, *The Law of Treaties* 676 (1961).

[252] See R.R. Baxter, 'Ius in Bello Interno: The Present and Future Law', *Law and Civil War in the Modern World* 518, 528 (J.N. Moore ed., 1974).

State, but to secede from that State. Considering that they would like to alienate themselves from the State as structured for the nonce, the insurgents are likely to refuse to be bound by any undertaking entered into by the State after they have rebuffed its authority to speak on their behalf.

221. The proposition that insurgents can be bound by a LONIAC treaty is often deemed to be bolstered by 'the competence of the governments to legislate for all its nationals' and the transformation of the treaty provisions into the domestic legislation in a manner binding on everyone within the jurisdiction.[253] But this conceptual scaffolding is not particularly sturdy.[254] Insurgents anyhow reject the established order, acting in defiance of the domestic legal *status quo*. Why would an insurgent armed group respect the specific part of the legislative corpus that incorporates LONIAC obligations?[255] Moreover, not every State goes through the process of transforming treaties into the law of the land, and at times there is no need to take any legislative action since the treaties are self-executing.[256] There are also other questions, related to the philosophical interface of international and domestic law (dualism versus monism) and the status of non-nationals who are members of the insurgent groups.[257]

(iii) Agreements between Governments and insurgents

222. An insurgent organized armed group may pledge to apply the provisions of a LONIAC treaty. Article 34 of the VCLT deals with the issue of *pacta tertiis* proclaiming:

> A treaty does not create either obligations or rights for a third State without its consent.[258]

Although there is no counterpart clause in the VCLT concerning the acceptance of treaty obligations or rights by a third party that is not a State, it is uncontested that insurgents may accept rights and obligations engendered by a LONIAC treaty.[259] Some commentators stress the status

---

[253] S. Sivakumaran, 'Binding Armed Opposition Groups', 55 *ICLQ* 369, 381 (2006).
[254] The thesis has apparently been abandoned by the previously cited author in Sivakumaran, *supra* note 144, at 241 n. 43.
[255] See La Haye, *supra* note 2, at 120.
[256] See T. Meron, *Human Rights in Internal Strife: Their International Protection* 39 (1987).
[257] See J.K. Kleffner, 'The Applicability of International Humanitarian Law to Organized Armed Groups', 882 *IRRC* 443, 447–9 (2011).
[258] VCLT, *supra* note 19, at 150.
[259] See A. Cassese, 'The Status of Rebels under the 1977 Geneva Protocol on Non-International Armed Conflicts', 30 *ICLQ* 416, 428 (1981).

of the insurgents as a party to the conflict (*supra* 93), adding that their consent to the operation of the treaty may be explicit or implicit.[260]

223. We have already considered the status of a peace accord between the incumbent Government and the insurgents terminating hostilities (see *supra* 155 *et seq.*). A peace process may entail a series of confidence-building interim agreements between the parties (as seems to have been the case in Colombia in 2012–13). But agreements between the Government and the insurgents may also be concluded – in the course of the fighting – for an assortment of more limited purposes, principally bringing about a temporary cease-fire.[261] Common Article 3 (*infra* 409) encourages 'special agreements' that the Parties to the conflict should endeavour to conclude, with a view to taking their pick of other provisions of the Geneva Conventions (namely, IAC *jus in bello*).

224. Agreements between the incumbent Government and the insurgents, signed during a NIAC, may lead to the consolidation of international custom by displaying State practice. However, poles apart from what is argued by some commentators,[262] these agreements cannot rank as treaties because they are not concluded between States (see *supra* 19). In the *Kallon et al.* case of 2004, the Appeals Chamber of the SCSL – which held that Common Article 3 is 'binding on States and insurgents alike' (*supra* 206) – pronounced that an agreement between the insurgents and the Government is 'neither a treaty nor an agreement in the nature of a treaty'; consequently, while it may create obligations under the domestic law of the State, the agreement does not establish obligations under international law.[263]

225. The experience gained in the course of many a NIAC reveals that the path of reaching an agreement between an incumbent Government and the insurgents is 'strewn with obstacles' and often stalled, due to governmental fears that it might confer on insurgents a new legal status or (at least) some 'political respectability'.[264] Empirically, it is not easy to prod reluctant Governments into formal agreements with insurgents,

---

[260] See M. Bothe, 'War Crimes in Non-International Armed Conflicts', *War Crimes in International Law* 293, 303 (Y. Dinstein and M. Tabory eds., 1996).

[261] See C. Bell, 'Ceasefire', II *MPEPIL* 10, 13.

[262] See C. Ryngaert and A. Van de Meulebroucke, 'Enhancing and Enforcing Compliance with International Humanitarian Law by Non-State Armed Groups: An Inquiry into Some Mechanisms', 16 *JCSL* 443, 454 (2011).

[263] *Prosecutor* v. *Kallon et al.*, *supra* note 230, at para. 49.

[264] F. Bugnion, '*Jus ad Bellum, Jus in Bello* and Non-International Armed Conflicts', 6 *YIHL* 167, 193 (2003).

and fruitful coordination between the parties may have to be worked out informally through backside channels or peace-brokers.

(b) Customary international law

226. On the face of it, customary LONIAC – as reflected in Common Article 3 (see *supra* 30) and transcending that provision – may appear to suffer from the same weakness as treaty law when it comes to insurgent armed groups. But this is a misconception. Just as customary international law can bind States regardless of their consent (see *supra* 29), it is also capable of imposing obligations on all individuals and groups anywhere. Insurgent groups engaged in a NIAC against the incumbent Government do not form an exception to the rule. Customary LONIAC, like other sets of rules of customary international law, is binding on everyone.

227. Jurisprudentially, it does not matter whether insurgents (or other individuals, for that matter) have given their consent to a customary norm by which they are bound. The reason is that insurgents, whether individually or collectively, do not as such contribute to the general practice that forges international custom.[265] Some scholars canvass unilateral statements and commitments of insurgent armed groups, looking upon them as a rich trove of the general practice by which international custom is shaped.[266] But these statements and commitments have no direct impact on custom-making in international law. The practice that counts for the consolidation of international custom is that of States (see *supra* 27). If agreements concluded by insurgents with Governments leave their eventual mark on customary law, this is only because the instruments reflect the practice of States.

228. Even the ICRC study of customary IHL, which consistently cites the practice of insurgent armed groups, does not attach to it any far-reaching significance:

> The practice of armed opposition groups, such as codes of conduct, commitments made to observe certain rules of international humanitarian law and other statements, does not constitute State practice as such. While such practice may contain evidence of the acceptance of certain rules in non-international armed conflicts, its legal significance is unclear.[267]

---

[265] See R. Geiss, 'Humanitarian Law Obligations of Organized Armed Groups', *Non-State Actors and International Humanitarian Law, supra* note 143, at 93, 96.

[266] For a detailed, non-exhaustive table listing such commitments, see Sivakumaran, *supra* note 144, at 144–51.

[267] I *Customary International Humanitarian Law*, Introduction, xxxvi (ICRC, J.-M. Henckaerts and L. Doswald-Beck eds., 2005).

One of the authors of the study, J.-M. Henckaerts, adds:

> Under current international law, only State practice can create customary international law. The practice of armed opposition groups formally counts only if the group is successful in its rebellion and becomes the new government.[268] [Although he thinks, *de lege ferenda*, that this legal position should change.]

All that can be said, in terms of the *lex lata*, is that (as in the laws of physics) actions of insurgent armed groups produce reactions by States. These reactions then become bricks in the edifice of customary international law.

229. There is nothing special in the perception that LONIAC customary law is developed exclusively by States, while creating rights and obligations for insurgent armed groups who do not contribute to the law-making mechanism. Customary international law across the board confers rights on individuals and groups – and imposes duties on them – without enabling the beneficiaries of the rights or the addressees of the duties to actually participate in the norm-creating process.

230. A paradox characterizes international law as a whole (customary as well as treaty law) in that it is created by States, which are vested with legal personality and do not exist in reality: they are fictitious creatures of the legal system. Flesh-and-blood physical persons (human beings) do not participate in the formation of international law (except indirectly by acting as organs of States; see *infra* 360). The inability of individuals – either singly or as members of groups – to participate in custom-building does not affect the fundamental principle that, once formed (through general State practice coupled with *opinio juris*), customary international law is binding on all human beings without exception.

231. Members of insurgent groups are no different from other individuals who are bound by international custom, although they have not contributed to its formation. The wonder that is sometimes expressed, about insurgents being 'law-takers' without being 'law-makers',[269] is therefore misplaced. All human beings are 'law-takers' without being 'law-makers', as far as the international legal system is concerned.

---

[268] J.-M. Henckaerts, 'Binding Armed Opposition Groups through Humanitarian Treaty Law and Customary Law', 27 *Coll.* 123, 128–9 (2002).

[269] See Ryngaert and Van de Meulebroucke, *supra* note 262, at 443.

5

Foreign intervention in a NIAC

I. The principle of non-intervention

A. *The principle and the practice*

232. In theory, there is an overarching principle of non-intervention in NIACs by foreign States. Paragraph (2) of Article 3 of AP/II (cited *supra* 10) states:

> Nothing in this Protocol shall be invoked as a justification for intervening, directly or indirectly, for any reason whatever, in the armed conflict or in the internal or external affairs of the High Contracting Party in the territory of which that conflict occurs.

The same formula is repeated in Paragraph (5) of Article 22 (cited *supra* 25) of the Second Protocol to the CPCP.

233. As can be gleaned from the wording of Paragraph (2) of Article 3 of AP/II, non-intervention is a general principle of international law, and it is not NIAC-specific. The general principle is encapsulated in the 1970 Friendly Relations Declaration adopted by consensus by the General Assembly.[270] In the 1986 *Nicaragua* Judgment, it was accentuated by the ICJ that the principle of non-intervention, involving 'the right of every sovereign State to conduct its affairs without outside interference', is 'part and parcel of customary international law'.[271]

234. In practice, although the principle of non-intervention has become 'a slogan lodged in the minds and frequently the sayings of statesmen',[272] it is not easily reconcilable with the conduct of States. Even apart from Security Council intervention on behalf of the international community at large (see *infra* 275 *et seq.*), individual States often engage in military

---

[270] Declaration on Principles of International Law Concerning Friendly Relations and Co-operation among States in accordance with the Charter of the United Nations (1970), General Assembly Resolution 2625 (XXV), 25 *RGA* 121, 123.

[271] *Nicaragua* case, *supra* note 36, at 106.

[272] R.J. Vincent, *Nonintervention and International Order* 313 (1974).

intervention in NIACs: not only in adjacent countries but across the globe. 'Foreign military interventions in civil wars have been so common in our day that the proclaimed rule of non-intervention may seem to have been stood on its head'.[273] More about State practice in this domain *infra* 244–5.

B. 'R2P'

235. The potency of the principle of non-intervention has been partly worn away by a growing consciousness of 'responsibility to protect' (widely known as 'R2P') – *inter alia*, against war crimes – notwithstanding the sovereignty of the State. The construct of 'R2P' first emerged in 2004, in a Report by a High-Level Panel on Threats, Challenges and Change (appointed by the UN Secretary-General), which stated categorically that there is a 'collective international responsibility to protect, exercisable by the Security Council authorizing military intervention as a last resort', in the event (*inter alia*) of 'serious violations of international humanitarian law which sovereign Governments have proved powerless or unwilling to prevent'.[274]

236. The 'R2P' concept was latched on to by the World Summit of Heads of States and Governments – convened in 2005 (on the sixtieth anniversary of the UN) – which emphasized that '[e]ach individual State has the responsibility to protect its populations' from (*inter alia*) war crimes; but, when 'national authorities are manifestly failing to protect their populations', collective action has to be taken 'in a timely and decisive manner' through the Security Council.[275] As we shall see (*infra* 277), the extensive powers of the Security Council are geared for the use or authorization of military force as and when necessary.

237. 'R2P' from outside the country whose population has to be protected is exclusively reserved for the Security Council. No individual foreign State, or groups of States, can arrogate to itself the power to intervene militarily in a NIAC – without the blessing of the Security Council – against any incumbent Government (in breach of the contemporary *jus ad bellum*; see *supra* 12). A different issue arises when a foreign country intervenes unilaterally in a NIAC by invitation of the local Government.

---

[273] O. Schachter, 'International Law in Theory and Practice', 178 *RCADI* 9, 160 (1982).

[274] Report of High-Level Panel on Threats, Challenges and Change Addressed to the Secretary General (2004, UN doc. A/59/565), para. 203.

[275] 2005 World Summit Outcome, General Assembly Resolution 60/1, paras. 138–9.

II. Military intervention by a foreign State in support of the incumbent Government

A. The requirement of consent

(a) Consent as a door-opener to foreign intervention

238. In the *Nicaragua* Judgment, the ICJ linked the principle of non-intervention to sovereign rights (*supra* 233). Logically, if the established Government of one State (Ruritania) invites another (Utopia) to assist it in maintaining or restoring law and order in the face of an insurrection, it is impossible to argue that by acceding to the invitation Utopia abrogates Ruritanian sovereign rights.[276] As prescribed in Article 20 of the ILC Draft Articles on State Responsibility, '[v]alid consent by a State to the commission of a given act by another State precludes the wrongfulness of that act in relation to the former State to the extent that the act remains within the limits of that consent'.[277] Article 20 'can be seen as a codification of the customary rule *volenti non fit injuria*'.[278]

239. In conformity with the general norm codified by the ILC, Ruritania – through its consent to Utopian military intervention in the ongoing NIAC – precludes any wrongfulness that may be attached to the interference in local affairs. That is to say, governmental consent is a game changer. Despite the principle of non-intervention, Ruritanian consent allows Utopia to intervene in the NIAC, subject to any specific conditions circumscribing the scope or duration of the action.

(b) The position of the *Institut de Droit International*

240. It must be recorded that Article 2 of a resolution on 'The Principle of Non-Intervention in Civil Wars', adopted by the *Institut de Droit International* in the Wiesbaden session of 1975, forbids the extension of foreign assistance (whether in the form of supply of any weapons or sending armed forces) to any party in a NIAC.[279]

241. The subject, originally designated 'Intervention by Invitation', was taken up again by the *Institut* some three decades later. In 2011, the

---

[276] See D.P. O'Connell, I *International Law* 301 (2nd edn, 1970).

[277] Draft Articles, *supra* note 249, at 27.

[278] A. Ben Mansour, 'Circumstances Precluding Wrongfulness in the ILC Articles on State Responsibility: Consent', *The Law of International Responsibility* 439, *id.* (J. Crawford, A. Pellet and S. Olleson eds., 2010).

[279] *Institut de Droit International*, Resolution, 'The Principle of Non-Intervention in Civil Wars', 56 *AIDI* 545, 547 (Wiesbaden, 1975).

Rapporteur (G. Hafner) expressed the correct view that 'the 1975 resolution did not reflect the practice at the time and thus amounted to a rule *de lege ferenda* which neither corresponded to practice at the time nor to subsequent practice'.[280] Consonant with that attitude, the Rapporteur (in Article 3 of a draft text submitted to the *Institut* in its 2009 Naples session) stated categorically that '[i]nternational law does not prohibit any State from rendering military assistance to another State in a situation that does not amount to an international armed conflict, subject, however, to the latter's prior consent' (and further legal conditions).[281] Yet, in the course of subsequent *Institut* deliberations, this provision was frittered away.

242. The final resolution – as adopted by the *Institut* in the Rhodes session in 2011 and retitled 'Military Assistance on Request' – recalls in its Preamble the Wiesbaden resolution and the need for a strict observance of the principle of non-intervention.[282] The expression 'military assistance' is defined in Article 1(a) as 'the sending of armed forces by one State to another State upon the latter's request'.[283] But the range of the resolution – which originally allowed military assistance on request in all NIACs as well as internal disturbances[284] – was diluted (in Article 2(1)) to 'situations of internal disturbances and tensions, such as riots, isolated and sporadic acts of violence and other acts of a similar nature, including acts of terrorism, below the threshold of non-international armed conflict in the sense of Article 1' of AP/II.[285]

243. The Rhodes text, as just quoted, is untenable for three reasons:

(i) As long as States have to quell riots and other below-the-threshold internal disturbances, they are prone to feel capable of handling the matter on their own. A State may issue a plea to friendly countries for (aa) procuring some scarce riot control equipment; (bb) getting assistance from troops present by prior agreement within the local territory and therefore readily available (see *infra* 258); or

---

[280] G. Hafner, 'Intervention by Invitation: New Final Report', 74 *AIDI* 183, 186 (Rhodes, 2011). In the same vein, see the present author's comments in 73 *AIDI* 437 (Naples, 2009).

[281] *Institut de Droit International*, Draft Resolution on 'Intervention by Invitation', 73 *AIDI*, ibid., at 414, 415.

[282] *Institut de Droit International*, Resolution on 'Military Assistance on Request', 74 *AIDI*, supra note 280, at 359, id.

[283] *Ibid.*

[284] See *Institut de Droit International*, Draft Resolution submitted by the Rapporteur (Article 2(1)), 74 *AIDI*, ibid., 280, 281.

[285] *Institut de Droit International*, supra note 282, at 360.

(cc) launching of missiles against terrorists in a secluded region (as happened with US missiles targeting objectives in Yemen). As for sending 'boots on the ground' from abroad (as happened in Bahrain in 2011), this will generally be sought only when the local State acutely feels the gathering storm of a NIAC or – more commonly – after the NIAC has already started. A deployment of armed forces by a foreign country is not undertaken lightly, and it is not likely to take place in response to merely 'isolated and sporadic acts of violence'.

(ii) The outright exclusion of NIACs above the second threshold of AP/II clearly does not jibe with the *lex lata*, as combed in the Rapporteur's report and as will be outlined *infra* 244–5.

(iii) When the initial proposals of the Rapporteur were overturned, it was not noticed that the all-important category of NIACs above the first threshold (of Common Article 3) had been completely lost in the shuffle. In practice, the forgotten category of NIACs – in between below-the-threshold 'internal disturbances and tensions, such as riots' and NIACs above the second threshold of AP/II – is the one that is most likely to induce an invitation of armed forces from abroad.

(c) The general practice of States

244. Even in the past, the dominant opinion was that '[t]here is no rule of international law which forbids the government of one state from rendering assistance to the established legitimate government of another state with a view of enabling it to suppress an insurrection against its authority'.[286] More recently, in the *Nicaragua* Judgment, the ICJ held that intervention is 'allowable at the request of the government of a State'.[287] This statement of the law has been generally accepted as consistent with the contemporary practice of States,[288] and the practice is confirmed in detail by the *Institut*'s Rapporteur.[289] As he pointed out, in the *Armed Activities* case of 2005 (cited *infra* 250), the ICJ did not question the right of Uganda to send troops to the Congo – during a NIAC – as long as the deployment was done with the consent of the Congolese Government.[290]

---

[286] See J.W. Garner, 'Questions of International Law in the Spanish Civil War', 31 *AJIL* 66, 68 (1937).

[287] *Nicaragua* case, *supra* note 36, at 126.

[288] Cf. L. Doswald-Beck, 'The Legal Validity of Military Intervention by Invitation of the Government', 56 *BYBIL* 189–252 (1985).

[289] Hafner, *supra* note 280, at 187–95.   [290] *Ibid.*, 190.

245. Nowhere has the practice of furnishing military assistance from the outside to Governments imperilled by insurgency been so much in evidence as in the African continent. Some of the foreign interventions were made by other African countries. But recent – widely acclaimed – French military interventions by invitation, in the Ivory Coast (2010) and in Mali (2013), are probably the ones that catch the eye. The timing of the military intervention on behalf of the incumbent Government in Mali demonstrates that the foreign armed forces may be deployed in the nick of time, when the insurgents seem to be poised on the verge of victory. The last-minute intervention contradicts the assertion that 'in the case of civil war, the assistance to the government is lawful so long as the government exercises effective control over the territory or most part of it'.[291] Yet, brinkmanship is not a precondition: at times, foreign intervention in Africa has been procured at a much earlier phase of a NIAC.

(d) The validity and parameters of consent

246. The ILC underscored that a State's consent must be 'valid' (*supra* 238). Certain modalities may have to be followed by the incumbent Government, in accordance with relevant provisions of the domestic law.[292] But, above all, the host country must exercise free will when expressing its consent to foreign military intervention in a NIAC. One State cannot be helped by another against its true wishes. An incumbent Government, impaled on the horns of an internal insurrection and fear of foreign intervention, cannot be compelled to accept unrequited attentions from abroad.[293]

247. As explained by J. Crawford (the final Special Rapporteur of the ILC on State responsibility), 'Article 20 excludes cases where consent is ostensibly given after the act has occurred, which are more properly treated as a form of waiver or acquiescence (Article 45[294])'.[295] The validity of the request made by a Government, inviting intervention by foreign State, may therefore be blighted by its *ex post facto* character. The Soviet military intervention in Hungary in 1956 is a notorious illustration of a situation in which the existence of the Government issuing the invitation 'seemed to be

---

[291] J.-Y. de Cara, 'The Arab Uprisings under the Light of Intervention', 55 *GYIL* 11, 24–5 (2012).

[292] See Draft Articles, *supra* note 249, at 73.

[293] See G. Fitzmaurice, 'The General Principles of International Law Considered from the Standpoint of the Rule of Law', 92 *RCADI* 1, 178 (1957).

[294] Draft Articles, *supra* note 249, at 29.

[295] J. Crawford, *State Responsibility: The General Part* 287 (2013).

connected with the intervention it had requested'.[296] Retroactive consent by a compliant Government – installed thanks to the foreign military intervention – is irredeemably flawed, since in such a case the foreign State actually invites itself.[297] We shall address separately the question of foreign recognition of an insurgent regime as a new Government in a move that is a precursor to military intervention in the NIAC (see the example of Libya *infra* 280–2).

248. In its Rhodes resolution on 'Military Assistance on Request' (*supra* 242), the *Institut de Droit International* admonished that assistance of this nature is prohibited 'when its object is to support an established government against its own population' (Article 3(1)).[298] But, at bottom, this is pure lip-service. Broadly speaking, it cannot be gauged with any degree of confidence whether an 'established government' is in a confrontation with 'its own population'. Civil strife is normally brought about by a deep-seated cleavage in a nation, with some segments of the population repudiating the incumbent Government while others are upholding it. The massive rallies and counter-rallies in Egypt in 2013 are emblematic of the difficulty of determining what the population really wants.

249. Ruritanian consent to Utopian intervention in a local NIAC may be limited in time, in which case military operations by the Utopian forces deployed on Ruritanian soil may not continue beyond the deadline without further agreement.[299] Subject to practical considerations (see *infra* 256), should Utopian armed forces overstay their welcome in Ruritanian territory, this would spawn an IAC between Utopia and Ruritania.

250. As held by the ICJ in the *Armed Activities* Judgment of 2005, Ruritanian consent demarcates the contours of the Utopian military operations: Utopia is restricted by 'the parameters of that consent, in terms of geographic location and objectives'.[300]

251. Article 3(e) of the 1974 General Assembly Definition of Aggression encompasses '[t]he use of armed forces of one State which are within the territory of another State with the agreement of the receiving State, in contravention of the conditions provided for in the agreement or any extension of their presence in such territory beyond the termination of the

---

[296] See I. Brownlie, *International Law and the Use of Force by States* 318 (1963).

[297] See N. Ronzitti, 'Use of Force, *Jus Cogens* and State Consent', *The Current Legal Regulation of the Use of Force* 147, 152, 160–1 (A. Cassese ed., 1986).

[298] *Institut de Droit International, supra* note 282, at 360.

[299] Cf. *ibid.*, 361 (Article 6(2)).

[300] *Case Concerning Armed Activities on the Territory of the Congo* (Congo v. Uganda), [2005] *ICJ Rep.* 168, 198–9.

agreement'.[301] Aggression, as defined here, is a crime under a 2010 Kampala amendment to the Rome Statute of the ICC.[302]

(e) Consent by treaty

252. Article 4(2)–(3) of the Rhodes resolution of the *Institut de Droit International* rightly lays down that, if the prior consent of the Ruritanian Government to Utopian military assistance is based on a treaty, an additional *ad hoc* request is still required in the specific case.[303] Although the resolution is inapplicable to NIACs (see *supra* 242), this is certainly the law in every instance of intervention by invitation.

253. The prerequisite of double consent in the case of a treaty should be fully understood. When prospective in nature, the treaty necessarily relates to hypothetical insurgencies rather than to concrete events. Once the NIAC materializes, the incumbent Government of Ruritania may believe that foreign intervention is superfluous or inimical to its image in the eyes of its own population (whose hearts and minds must be won over), or it may think that the timing is wrong. Whatever the reason for such second thoughts, a further *ad hoc* consent by Ruritania is indispensable. The issue is not, as surmised by some scholars, the legal validity of the treaty.[304] Rather, it is the right of Ruritania to revoke its consent when the moment of truth arrives[305] (for revocation of consent, see *infra* 255).

254. Treaties allowing foreign military intervention – designed to assist an incumbent Government to overcome an insurrection – may be bilateral, regional or global. A prototype regional arrangement, in which Contracting Parties confer on each other the right to intervene in future NIACs, can be found in the 2002 Durban Protocol of the African Union.[306]

(f) Revocation of consent

255. As attested by the ICJ – in its Judgment in the *Armed Activities* case – Ruritanian consent to Utopian military intervention in a NIAC can always

---

[301] Definition of Aggression, General Assembly Resolution 3314 (XXIX), 29(1) *RGA* 142, 143 (1974).
[302] Article 8 *bis* (2) of the Rome Statute of the ICC, as added in Kampala in 2010 (First Review Conference, Resolution 6, Annex I, 49 *ILM* 1334, 1335 (2010)).
[303] *Institut de Droit International, supra* note 282, at 360.
[304] See D. Wippman, 'Treaty-Based Intervention: Who Can Say No?', 62 *UChi.LR* 607, 630–1 (1995).
[305] See Lieblich, *supra* note 122, at 192–7.
[306] Durban Protocol Relating to the Establishment of the Peace and Security Council of the African Union, 2002, *Africa: Selected Documents on Constitutive, Conflict and Security, Humanitarian, and Judicial Issues* 161, 163 (J.I. Levitt ed., 2003).

be revoked.[307] Once consent to the presence of the foreign troops in Ruritanian territory is revoked, the rug is pulled from under the legality of any further foreign intervention: Utopia's entitlement to deploy armed forces in Ruritania expires, and it must recall them. The revocation may occur at any time, notwithstanding an inconsistent treaty provision lying at the root of the intervention (see *supra* 253).[308]

256. Withdrawal of Utopian troops from the territory of Ruritania as a result of revocation of consent to their continued presence cannot ordinarily be accomplished overnight. The process may consume some time (depending on numbers of troops; the stationing of military units in relatively remote outposts; logistical handicaps spawned by the type of equipment used; road conditions and availability of transport; terrain and weather), but there must be no arbitrary procrastination.

(g) Constraints

257. Foreign military intervention by consent in a NIAC usually requires serious coordination by Utopia and Ruritania. Planning and preparation are indispensable to ensure agreed timing, place and form of deployment of the Utopian troops. Field operations must then be combined with those of the Ruritanian armed forces, for it is imperative to preempt 'friendly fire'. The intervention from abroad may be further complicated when it is orchestrated by an alignment of States (Utopia, Numidia, etc.) acting in a concerted manner.

258. Military intervention by Utopia in the Ruritanian NIAC need not come strictly from the outside, inasmuch as Utopian troops may already be stationed by consent within the borders of Ruritania (as part of a military alliance) and may be called upon to assist in maintaining or restoring law and order.[309] However, the fact that these troops are stationed within Ruritanian territory by consent does not mean that they have a blanket invitation to spring into unbidden action against insurgents. They are not allowed to intervene in the NIAC with a view to putting down the insurrection, unless overtly invited to do so by the Ruritanian Government.

259. Consensual foreign military intervention may have multiple incarnations in the course of a long NIAC. Utopia may first limit its intervention to the shipment of armaments with military trainers or advisers. It may

---

[307] *Case Concerning Armed Activities on the Territory of the Congo, supra* note 300, at 197.
[308] Cf. *Institut de Droit International, supra* note 282, at 360 (Article 5).
[309] See D.W. Greig, *International Law* 901 (2nd edn, 1976).

then launch cross-border drones and/or missiles against rebel targets. But when the fighting escalates, Utopia may step up the scale of the consensual intervention, fielding combat units in Ruritania.

260. Any military intervention by Utopia in the Ruritanian NIAC – even if lawful *per se* – must comply with general rules of international law. When armaments are supplied for subduing the insurgency, Utopia has to abide by a number of treaty provisions proscribing the transfer of certain weapons to any recipient whatsoever. That is true, pre-eminently, of weapons of mass destruction: such transfer is prohibited in Article III of the 1972 Convention on Bacteriological (Biological) and Toxin Weapons (BWC),[310] and in Article I(1) of the CWC (see *infra* 506). In 2013, an Arms Trade Treaty (ATT) was adopted by the General Assembly, whereby Contracting Parties undertake (in Article 6(3)) not to transfer conventional arms (e.g., combat aircraft or tanks) if those arms would be exploited in the commission of war crimes.[311]

B. 'Failing States'

261. In recent times, the phenomenon of 'failing States' has vexed the international community.[312] In this constellation of events, the incumbent Government of an existing State – battered by a NIAC – vanishes without being replaced by any new Government. Only organized armed groups (or warlords) are left to do battle with each other in the 'failing State'. As we have seen (*supra* 87), such a violent struggle will still qualify as a NIAC.

262. The power vacuum in a 'failing State' means that nobody is left to express authoritative consent to foreign military intervention in a NIAC. Correspondingly, no organized armed group in the 'failing State' can revoke a previous invitation extended to a foreign State (Utopia) to enter the fray. As a result, the military operations of a Utopian expeditionary force within the local territory – based on an invitation issued by the now defunct Government – may proceed uninterrupted, without catapulting the NIAC into an IAC.

---

[310] Convention on the Prohibition of the Development, Production and Stockpiling of Bacteriological (Biological) and Toxin Weapons and on Their Destruction (BWC), 1972, *Laws of Armed Conflicts* 136, 137.

[311] Arms Trade Treaty (ATT), 2013, 52 *ILM* 988, 991 (2013).

[312] See D. Thürer, 'Failing States', III *MPEPIL* 1084–94.

III. Military intervention by a foreign State against the incumbent Government

A. *Use of* de facto *organs*

263. The thrust of the principle of non-intervention in a NIAC relates to military action taken by Arcadia against the incumbent Government of Ruritania. Arcadia is liable to intervene in Ruritanian affairs by clandestinely fomenting an insurgency against the Government. If Arcadia has effective control over the insurgents, their acts may be attributed to it as acts of State (see *infra* 360) – i.e. the insurgents may be regarded as *de facto* organs of Arcadia – although there exists a controversy between the ICJ and the ICTY as to the degree of subordination to Arcadia required for such attribution.[313] There is no need to go into the details of the controversy here. Suffice it to say that, at some point, the armed conflict may be internationalized.[314] What appears on the face of it to be a NIAC in Ruritania would consequently constitute an IAC between Ruritania and Arcadia.

B. *Military assistance to insurgents*

264. In most instances, the issue of military intervention by Arcadia in a Ruritanian NIAC relates to a less flagrant scenario. The presupposition is that a genuine NIAC – not stoked or controlled by Arcadia – is ablaze in Ruritania, but Arcadia lends military assistance to the insurgents against the Ruritanian Government. The Arcadian military intervention may also elicit a counter-intervention by Utopia on behalf of the Ruritanian Government.[315] This is what happened in Vietnam, when the North invaded the South in support of the Vietcong rebellion, and the US dispatched a large expeditionary force to prop up the South Vietnamese Government against both the Vietcong (in a NIAC) and the North Vietnamese (in an IAC). There are other illustrations of intervention and counter-intervention.[316]

265. When Arcadia militarily intervenes in the Ruritanian NIAC – against the incumbent Government and in support of the insurgents – the

---

[313] On this entire issue, see Dinstein, *supra* note 11, at 219–24.

[314] See C. Byron, 'Armed Conflicts: International or Non-International?', 6 *JCSL* 63, 81 (2001).

[315] See R. Higgins, 'International Law and Civil Conflict', *The International Regulation of Civil Wars* 169, 176–7 (E. Luard ed., 1972).

[316] For an example, see C. Gray, *International Law and the Use of Force* 96 (3rd edn, 2008).

action crosses the third threshold and brings about an IAC between Arcadia and Ruritania.[317] If Utopia counter-intervenes militarily at the request of the Ruritanian Government, the result will be an IAC between both Ruritania and Utopia on the one hand, against Arcadia on the other.

266. Irrefutably, Arcadian military intervention in support of Ruritanian insurgents against the incumbent Government is a breach of international law. The breach is of both the *jus ad bellum* principle of non-use of inter-State force (see *supra* 12) and the principle of non-intervention.[318] As for the latter principle, the ICJ held – in the *Nicaragua* Judgment – that 'no such general right of intervention, in support of the opposition within another State, exists in contemporary international law'.[319] The Judgment stressed that it is the 'element of coercion' – in a military action against a Government – which 'defines, and indeed forms the very essence of, prohibited intervention'.[320] The ICJ also made it clear that only a Government (as distinct from an opposition group) can validly issue an invitation for assistance from a foreign State that would be consistent with the principle of non-intervention (see *supra* 244).[321]

267. The question is: how much legal elbow room is available to Arcadia before its assistance to insurgents in Ruritania is considered to have crossed the third threshold? The majority of the ICJ in *Nicaragua* did not believe that mere 'assistance to rebels in the form of the provision of weapons or logistical or other support' amounts to illicit intervention.[322] Nevertheless, the Court conceded in the subsequent *Armed Activities* case that 'training and military support', given by Uganda to insurgents in the Congo, violated international legal obligations.[323] It is also necessary to recall the prohibition of funnelling certain types of weapons either to the insurgents or to the incumbent Government (see *supra* 260).

268. When assistance to insurgents does not *per se* amount to a breach of international law, it may still prove to be a slippery slope for Arcadia. By strengthening and emboldening the insurgents – to the dismay of the incumbent Government of Ruritania – Arcadia may find itself on a collision course with Ruritania, which eventually may produce a full-blown IAC.

---

[317] See L. Arimatsu, 'Territory, Boundaries and the Law of Armed Conflict', 12 *YIHL* 157, 184 (2009).

[318] In the *Nicaragua* case, *supra* note 36, the ICJ dealt with the two principles separately: non-use of force mainly on pp. 98–106 and non-intervention chiefly on pp. 106–9.

[319] *Ibid.*, 109.   [320] *Ibid.*, 108.   [321] *Ibid.*, 126.   [322] *Ibid.*,104.

[323] *Case Concerning Armed Activities on the Territory of the Congo, supra* note 300, at 226.

269. The international legal norms about foreign intervention in support of insurgents in a NIAC are yoked to official action. Arcadian nationals may individually choose to enlist on either side in the Ruritanian NIAC. There may be an issue of mercenaries (see *infra* 771–2). But when individual Arcadian volunteers join the Ruritanian insurgents – on religious, ethnic, ideological or other grounds – the act cannot be attributed to Arcadia, and the principle of non-intervention is not contravened. Plainly, if the numbers involved soar, Ruritania may be wary of the spectacle of Arcadian 'collusion in the export of volunteers to further national policy'.[324] To avoid potential disputes, neighbouring States may undertake by treaty to take all possible measures to prevent their respective nationals from extending any help to present or future insurgents in the other country.[325]

IV. The applicable law

A. *LONIAC or IAC* jus in bello?

270. There are three possible scripts in case of foreign military intervention in a NIAC, and it is important to discern which legal regime of armed conflict is operative in each instance. The primary setting is that of Utopia militarily intervening by invitation of the incumbent Government of Ruritania against the insurgents. In such circumstances, the Utopian armed forces 'are taking part on the side of the [Ruritanian] government in what is, legally speaking, a purely non-international conflict'.[326] The law applicable to all parties to the conflict (Ruritania, Utopia and the insurgents) is LONIAC.[327] This is the legal position not merely when Utopian military units just skirmish with the Ruritanian insurgents. Utopia may deploy in Ruritania a large expeditionary force engaged in intense hostilities against the insurgents, inflicting and sustaining heavy casualties. However, considering that the Utopian troops are not battling the armed forces of another State but are fighting shoulder to shoulder with the Ruritanian military to snuff out the flames of insurrection, the armed conflict is not an IAC.

---

[324] I. Brownlie, 'Volunteers and the Law of War and Neutrality', 5 *ICLQ* 570, 574 (1956).

[325] See, e.g., Article 6(a) of a bilateral Treaty of Brotherhood and Alliance between Iraq and Transjordan, 1947, 23 *UNTS* 154, 158.

[326] W. Kälin and J. Künzli, *The Law of International Human Rights Protection* 155 (2009).

[327] See R. Kolb and R. Hyde, *An Introduction to the International Law of Armed Conflicts* 80 (2008).

271. The second storyline is that Arcadia militarily intervenes in Ruritania on behalf of the insurgents and against the incumbent Government. Here the legal situation changes dramatically, producing an IAC between Ruritania and Arcadia. As a result, two armed conflicts will be running parallel: the Ruritanian/Arcadian IAC (regulated by the *jus in bello*) and the Ruritanian NIAC (administered by LONIAC). On simultaneous IACs and NIACs, see *supra* 172 *et seq.*

272. The third strand of the narrative consists of foreign intervention and counter-intervention in the Ruritanian NIAC by both Utopia (on the side of the incumbent Government) and Arcadia (on the side of the insurgents). If the Arcadian and Utopian armed forces pound at each other, there will be an IAC between them. This armed conflict will be waged jointly with another IAC (between Arcadia and Ruritania) and side by side with a NIAC (involving the insurgents and the Ruritanian Government plus Utopia). The NIAC will be governed by LONIAC, but the law applicable to both IACs will be the *jus in bello*.

B. Some outstanding problems

273. Utopian intervention in the Ruritanian NIAC, when put in motion in support of the incumbent Government and against the insurgents, raises certain questions with regard to the application of LONIAC. The first is whether AP/II (as distinct from Common Article 3 and customary international law) can be operative in these hostilities. After all, Paragraph (1) of Article 1 of AP/II (*supra* 118) counts on a NIAC occurring 'in the territory of a High Contracting Party between its armed forces' and the insurgents. Strictly speaking, the combination of the requirements that the NIAC will take place within the State's own territory and that the fighting will be carried out by 'its armed forces' invites the conclusion that AP/II is inapplicable.[328] A more lenient deciphering of Paragraph (1) of Article 1, based on the spirit rather than the letter of the text, is that 'the expression "its armed forces" should in this case cover not only the troops of the territorial State, but also those of any other State intervening on behalf of the government' (although they are not within their territory).[329]

274. Ruritanian consent to the use of force by Utopia within its territory does not leave Utopia free to decide how to handle captured insurgents in the NIAC. Generally speaking, after a short-term period of detention, Utopia ought to hand them over to the competent authorities of Ruritania

---

[328] See Akande, *supra* note 178, at 55.   [329] See Vité, *supra* note 54, at 80.

for treatment in compliance with Ruritanian domestic law.[330] But there are some practical issues that have not been settled:

(i) Utopia may have concerns – which cannot be easily dissipated – about 'refoulement' of detainees to Ruritania, in view of tangible risks of their mistreatment by the Ruritanian judicial system. General State practice does not resolve the uncertainty of whether apprehensions about 'refoulement' are relevant only where rendition is effected by crossing an international frontier, or also when this is done within the same territory[331] (on 'refoulement' of refugees, see *infra* 781).

(ii) Utopia may opt for rendition of insurgent captives to a third State (Numidia). Such rendition is contingent on obtaining Ruritanian consent (separate from the consent to the use of force by Utopia). Yet, complex problems arise when the consent given – by the incumbent Ruritanian Government – is not consistent with the domestic law of Ruritania.[332]

V. Intervention by the Security Council in a NIAC

A. *The UN Charter*

275. Pursuant to Article 39 of the UN Charter, having determined the existence of any threat to the peace (as well as breach of the peace or act of aggression), the Security Council may recommend or decide what measures shall be taken to maintain or restore international peace and security.[333] Whereas recommendations are hortatory in nature, Security Council decisions have a binding character under Article 25 of the Charter.[334] This binding character is not limited to, but positively covers, decisions adopted under Chapter VII of the Charter (a chapter opened by Article 39).[335] Binding decisions of the Council (under Chapter VII) may impose – or authorize the imposition of – a

---

[330] See P. Rowe, 'Is There a Right to Detain Civilians by Foreign Armed Forces during a Non-International Armed Conflict?', 61 *ICLQ* 607, 710 (2012).

[331] See J. Pejic, 'Conflict Classification and the Law Applicable to Detention and the Use of Force', *International Law and the Classification of Conflicts, supra* note 99, at 80, 99.

[332] See A.S. Deeks, 'Consent to the Use of Force and International Law Supremacy', 54 *HILJ* 1, 27–30 (2013).

[333] Charter of the United Nations, *supra* note 10, at 343.   [334] *Ibid.*, 339.

[335] See Advisory Opinion on the *Legal Consequences for States of the Continued Presence of South Africa in Namibia (South West Africa) notwithstanding Security Council Resolution 276 (1970)*, [1971] *ICJ Rep.* 16, 52–3.

whole panoply of sanctions against those who do not comply with its bidding.

276. Although the expression 'threat to the peace' may appear at first sight to be inextricably linked to inter-State relations, the freedom of action vested by the Charter in the Security Council is unfettered.[336] In practice, the Council has interpreted its powers in such a way that it can stigmatize intra-State violence as a threat to either international or regional peace (for an illustration, see *infra* 280–1). In the *Tadić* Decision on appeal, the ICTY observed that 'the practice of the Security Council is rich with cases of civil war or internal strife which is classified as a "threat to the peace" and dealt with under Chapter VII'.[337]

277. The principle of non-intervention does not curtail the wide powers conferred on the Security Council under Chapter VII. Article 2(7) of the Charter, in precluding intervention by the UN 'in matters which are essentially within the domestic jurisdiction of any state', unequivocally adds a proviso that 'this principle shall not prejudice the application of enforcement measures under Chapter VII'.[338] It is agreed that the proviso 'includes all binding decisions which the SC makes under Chapter VII'.[339] Thus, the authority of the Council under the Charter overrides – as and when necessary – the prerogatives of sovereignty of any UN Member.[340] Consent to intervention from the outside in a NIAC, which is of crucial importance where individual (or even groups of) foreign States are concerned (see *supra* 238), is irrelevant to enforcement measures under Chapter VII taken by the Council.[341]

278. An intervention by the Security Council in a NIAC, beside having a direct impact on the parties to the conflict in the country involved, may have knock-on effects on foreign States. The Council may impose an embargo on the supply of arms to the Government and/or the insurgents (see *infra* 280, 286). The Council may also instruct foreign States not to unilaterally intervene in the conflict. In its Rhodes resolution on 'Military

---

[336] See Dinstein, *supra* note 11, at 308–14.   [337] *Prosecutor* v. *Tadić*, *supra* note 33, at 43.

[338] Charter of the United Nations, *supra* note 10, at 332.

[339] G. Nolte, 'Article 2(7)', I *The Charter of the United Nations: A Commentary*, *supra* note 12, at 280, 308.

[340] Strangely, in Resolution 688 (1991), condemning the repression of the Iraqi civilian population, especially the Kurds – 'the consequences of which threaten international peace and security in the region' (para. 1) – the Council added a Preambular clause expressly '[r]ecalling' Article 2(7) of the Charter. Security Council Resolution 688 (1991), 30 *ILM* 858, 858–9 (1991).

[341] See E. Lieblich, 'Intervention and Consent: Consensual Forcible Interventions in Internal Armed Conflicts as International Agreements', 29 *BUILJ* 337, 373 (2011).

Assistance on Request', the *Institut de Droit International* rightly stated that such assistance 'shall not be provided' when it is inconsistent with a Chapter VII decision of the Security Council 'relating to the specific situation' (Article 3(2)).[342]

279. All Security Council resolutions have to be adopted in accordance with the Charter, and here is the rub: under Article 27 of the Charter,[343] each of the five Permanent Members (the US, the UK, France, Russia and China) may veto a resolution by casting a negative vote. In too many instances, lack of unanimity among the Permanent Members has staved off a Council resolution. Thus, in the case of the NIAC in Syria, no meaningful resolution[344] could be adopted between 2011 and 2013 until the use of chemical weapons drove the Council into action (see *infra* 507). When paralyzed by the exercise of the veto power, the Council cannot be supplanted by any other UN organ.

B. *The case of Libya*

280. A prototypical exercise of the powers of the Security Council, in the face of escalating internal violence, relates to Libya in 2011. First, in February of that year, in Resolution 1970, the Council (acting under Chapter VII) dubbed the situation a threat to the peace, demanding 'an immediate end to the violence' and calling for 'steps to fulfil the legitimate demands of the population'.[345] The resolution relied, *inter alia*, on the use of violence by Government forces against civilians; widespread and systematic attacks against the civilian population that might amount to crimes against humanity; gross and systematic violations of human rights and international humanitarian law; the plight of refugees forced to flee the violence; and concern for the safety of foreign nationals.[346] Operatively, the Council decided to refer the situation to the Prosecutor of the ICC and to order an arms embargo on Libya, as well as a travel ban on certain individuals and an assets freeze.[347]

281. When conditions did not improve, the Security Council adopted – a few weeks later – Resolution 1973, in which (acting again under Chapter VII) it determined that the situation in Libya continued to constitute a

---

[342] *Institut de Droit International, supra* note 282, at 360.

[343] Charter of the United Nations, *supra* note 10, at 340 (as amended in Protocol of Entry into Force of Amendments to the Charter, [1965] *UNJY* 159, 160).

[344] A United Nations Supervision Mission in Syria (UNSMIS) was established in Security Council Resolution 2043 (2012), para. 5, but the consequences were trivial.

[345] Security Council Resolution 1970 (2011), para. 1.

[346] *Ibid.* (Preamble).   [347] *Ibid.*, paras. 4, 9, 15, 17.

threat to the peace; but this time (apart from demanding an immediate cease-fire), it authorized Member States 'to take all necessary measures' (a well-established euphemism for the use of force) to protect civilians – without proceeding to a foreign occupation of the country – and, with that in mind, to establish a no-fly zone in Libyan airspace.[348] The implementation of the resolution was left to a 'coalition of the willing'. NATO took operational control of enforcing Resolution 1973, and the task fanned out to air strikes against ground forces belonging to the Government headed by Qaddafi.[349] Insurgents were spared. Initially, this might have been connected to the difficulty of telling them apart from civilians from high altitude (cf. *infra* 680).[350] But later the anti-Government dimensions of the intervention became more evident. Ultimately, the forcible action by the coalition facilitated a regime change, thereby exceeding the scope of the mandate under Resolution 1973.[351]

282. The coalition's military intervention beyond the mandate of Resolution 1973 is anchored in an invitation issued by an insurgent Government in Benghazi – the National Transitional Council (NTC) – which was recognized as the new Government of Libya (see *infra* 320). The coalition's unabashed contribution to regime change in Libya has been subjected to abounding critiques by those who discountenance the admissibility of foreign intervention by invitation in NIACs.[352] Yet, as has been shown (*supra* 244–5), trepidations on this ground are not shared by States in their general practice.

C. The range of the Security Council's intervention

283. By intervening in a NIAC, the Security Council may tip the scales of victory or defeat for the insurgents. Of course, the Security Council's intervention in a NIAC need not be directed (as in Libya) against the incumbent Government. Largely speaking, the Council would be more disposed to intervene against insurgents.

---

[348] Security Council Resolution 1973 (2011), paras. 1, 4, 6.

[349] See J.R. Crook, 'Contemporary Practice of the United States Relating to International Law', 105 *AJIL* 569, 571–3 (2011).

[350] See M. Payandeh, 'The United Nations, Military Intervention, and Regime Change in Libya', 52 *Vir.JIL* 355, 386–7 (2011–12).

[351] See J. Cerone, 'International Enforcement in Non-International Armed Conflict: Searching for Synergy among Legal Regimes in the Case of Libya', 88 *ILS, supra* note 55, at 369, 386.

[352] See G. Ulfstein and H.F. Christiansen, 'The Legality of the NATO Bombing in Libya', 62 *ICLQ* 159, 169 (2013).

284. Angola is a case in point, where the Security Council intervened forthrightly against insurgents. In Resolution 1127 (1997), the Council – having determined that the situation in Angola constituted a threat to international peace and security in the region, and acting under Chapter VII – imposed sundry sanctions on the insurgents armed group UNITA (Union for the Total Independence of Angola).[353]

285. The most extreme instances of intervention, undertaken by the Security Council (acting under Chapter VII) in order to back the authority of distressed Governments, are three resolutions adopted in 2013. Two of these resolutions do this directly:

(i) Resolution 2098 (2013), in which the Council set up an unprecedented 'Intervention Brigade' of the United Nations Organization Stabilization Mission in the Congo (MONUSCO), empowering it to 'take all necessary measures' to neutralize armed groups in Eastern Congo (thus safeguarding Congolese governmental authority in the region).[354]

(ii) Resolution 2100 (2013), where the Council established the United Nations Multidimensional Integrated Stabilization Mission in Mali (MINUSMA), the mandate of which is principally to shore up the Government of Mali so as to extend its administration throughout the country and to prevent the return of armed elements.[355] The resolution expressly authorizes MINUSMA 'to use all necessary means' for carrying out its mandate.[356]

In the third instance, intervention is indirect:

(iii) In Resolution 2127 (2013) on Central African Republic, the Council authorized a non-UN force – an African-led International Support Mission in the Central African Republic (MISCA), supported by French troops – to take 'all necessary measures' for the protection of civilians and the restoration of security and public order; the stabilization of the country and the restoration of State authority over the whole of its territory; as well as the creation of conditions conducive to the provision of humanitarian assistance to the population in need.[357]

---

[353] Security Council Resolution 1127 (1997), para. 4.
[354] Security Council Resolution 2098 (2013), paras. 9, 12.
[355] Security Council Resolution 2100 (2013), paras. 7, 16.   [356] *Ibid.*, para. 17.
[357] Security Council Resolution 2127 (2013), para. 28.

286. The Security Council may also intervene in a NIAC in an impartial manner, which does not favour either the incumbent Government or the insurgents. Obvious examples would be a Chapter VII demand of a cease-fire between the opposing sides or the imposition of a general arms embargo. For instance, in Somalia in two Chapter VII resolutions of 1992–3, a general arms embargo was ordained (Resolution 733[358]), and a cease-fire demand was addressed to 'all Somali parties, including movements and factions' (Resolution 814[359]). A caveat is called for in this context. While such resolutions are even-handed in theory, their practical implementation may give an edge to that party to the conflict (i) which has gained the upper hand on the ground on the eve of the cease-fire, or (ii) is already possessed of enough weapons and ordnance to continue the fighting once it resumes.

287. The Security Council (acting under Chapter VII) may create 'safe areas' in a country ravaged by a NIAC, deploy UN peacekeeping forces and authorize them to use force in protecting these 'safe areas', as well as insist on freedom of movement of humanitarian assistance convoys.[360] Evidently, maintaining bubbles of security within the chaos of a NIAC is not a simple undertaking.

288. Elevating the level of its intervention, the Security Council established both the ICTY (in 1993)[361] and the ICTR (in 1994)[362] for the prosecution (*inter alia*) of persons responsible for serious violations of LONIAC in the former Yugoslavia and in Rwanda.

D. Peacekeeping forces

289. The Security Council often decides to deploy (with the consent of the host State) a peacekeeping force in a country in the throes of a NIAC. The mandates of such forces are becoming increasingly 'robust' (a poignant example is that of MINUSMA; see *supra* 285). But it is important to press the point that, as long as a UN peacekeeping force is not actively participating in NIAC hostilities, its personnel have to be regarded as ordinary civilians.[363]

---

[358] Security Council Resolution 733 (1992), para. 5.
[359] Security Council Resolution 814 (1993), para. 8.
[360] For an illustration, see Security Council Resolution 836 (1993), para. 9, re Bosnia/Herzegovina.
[361] Security Council Resolution 827 (1993), para. 2.
[362] Security Council Resolution 955 (1994), para. 1.
[363] See C. Greenwood, 'Protection of Peacekeepers: The Legal Regime', 7 *DukeJCIL* 185, 191 (1996–7).

290. Should a UN peacekeeping force be dragged into actual fighting in a NIAC, the conduct of hostilities will be governed by the law of armed conflict. The UN Secretary-General published in 1999 a Bulletin, whereby fundamental rules of IHL – set out in the Bulletin – will apply 'in situations of armed conflict', when UN forces 'are actively engaged therein as combatants'.[364] The phrase 'situations of armed conflict' certainly covers both IACs and NIACs, although the Secretary-General did not find it necessary to distinguish between them in the application of the legal standards listed in the Bulletin.[365]

291. There is some debate whether the mere involvement of UN forces in a NIAC should turn the conflict into an IAC (so that the *jus in bello* will supersede LONIAC).[366] In the opinion of the present author, there is no difference in this respect between UN forces and the military units of a foreign State intervening unilaterally in a NIAC. The classification of an armed conflict hangs on the identity of the opponent that the UN – or foreign – forces confront in the field. If they are fighting insurgents in support of the incumbent Government the armed conflict remains a NIAC (and LONIAC will apply), whereas if they are engaged in hostilities against the Government the armed conflict converts into an IAC (subordinated to the *jus in bello*).

292. With a view to ensuring the safety of UN personnel, a Convention was concluded in 1994 criminalizing violent attacks and other acts committed against them.[367] Article 2(2) of the Convention excludes from its ambit situations in which UN personnel are engaged as combatants against organized armed forces, but only when a double condition is met: it is an enforcement action under Chapter VII of the Charter and IAC law applies.[368] When UN personnel are embroiled in fighting against organized armed forces in a NIAC, the exclusion is not activated.[369] The violence therefore comes within the scope of the Convention.

---

[364] UN Secretary-General's Bulletin on the Observance by United Nations Forces of International Humanitarian Law, 38 *ILM* 1656, *id.* (1999).

[365] See D. Shraga, 'The Secretary-General's Bulletin on the Observance by United Nations Forces of International Humanitarian Law: A Decade Later', 39 *Is.YHR* 357, 372 (2009).

[366] See O. Engdahl, 'The Status of Peace Operation Personnel under International Humanitarian Law', 11 *YIHL* 109, 120 (2008).

[367] Convention on the Safety of United Nations and Associated Personnel, [1994] *UNJY* 237, 241. See also Optional Protocol, 2010, 49 *ILM* 1661 (2010).

[368] *Ibid.* (Convention), 239.   [369] See Greenwood, *supra* note 363, at 199.

6

Recognition

I. Recognition of an insurgent Government

A. Conditions for the existence of a State and a Government

293. Every State must have a Government. Possessing a Government is one of four conditions requisite of statehood, conjointly with (i) territory, (ii) nation, i.e. population, and (iii) sovereignty, viz. independence.[370] '[T]he existence of an effective and independent government is the essence of statehood'.[371] The Government is the instrumentality through which the State – a legal personality – acts and functions (both internally and externally), exercising its rights and discharging its duties.

294. The powers of governance in a State are usually divided between a central authority – with jurisdiction over the entire national territory – and multiple regional (in a federal State, provincial-cantonal) as well as local authorities vested with competence within prescribed areas. Whichever way powers are allocated, the Government of a State (in the comprehensive sense of the term) must fulfil two cumulative conditions under international law: (i) independence from any other Government; and (ii) effective control over the State's territory.[372]

295. The independence of Government is an extrapolation of sovereignty as a condition of statehood. If a given Government is not independent – if it is a 'puppet Government' with the strings manipulated by a foreign State – either there is another (genuine) Government of the same State or the entity in question is not (or no longer) a State.

296. While a Government is supposed to have effective control over the territory of the State, the degree to which the Government actually

---

[370] The four conditions of statehood are presented in different forms. For a classical illustration, see Montevideo Convention on the Rights and Duties of States, 1933, 28 *AJIL*, Supp., 75, *id.* (1934) (Article 1).

[371] I. Brownlie, *Principles of Public International Law* 90 (7th edn, 2008).

[372] See J. Crawford, *The Creation of States in International Law* 55 (2nd edn, 2006).

exerts that control is not fixed. It depends on topography as much as demography, and it has to be adjusted to changing circumstances.

297. An exceptional situation arises in the anarchical conditions of a 'failing State' (see *supra* 261), when law and order collapse and the Government disappears (although fragments of authority may survive regionally). Were this to happen in an entity still striving to become a State, the absence of a Government would indubitably make it unfit for statehood. By contrast, existing States benefit from a built-in resilience, enabling them to spring back into shape after an *interregnum* of disorder during which two, or even more, organized armed groups wrangle with each other over power in the land (without a Government to bridle them).

298. Differently put, the criterion of having a Government as a condition of statehood (see *supra* 293) is applied more scrupulously with respect to the creation of new States than their later perseverance.[373] What prods the more favourable treatment of existing States is an animus on the part of the international community against a hasty acknowledgement of their demise, and a proclivity for considering the meltdown of effective governance as no more than an ephemeral malady. It is clear, however, that the phase of being a 'failing State' must be transitory, even if it lasts for years.[374]

B. Recognition of a new Government

299. Governments in every existing State come and go. A smooth transition from one Government to another happens more rapidly in a democratic society and more slowly under authoritarian regimes. Yet, eventually, even the most despotic Governments run their course. A change of Governments in Ruritania does not require recognition by other States (Arcadia, Utopia, etc.), as long as the new Government comes into power in a constitutional manner (as per the domestic legal system of Ruritania). Foreign recognition of a new Ruritanian Government becomes an issue only when that Government assumes power as a result of a break in (domestic) legal continuity, following a revolution, a *coup d'Etat* or a NIAC.[375]

---

[373] See *ibid.*, 59.

[374] See P. Pustorino, 'Failed States and International Law: The Impact of UN Practice on Somalia in Respect of Fundamental Rules of International Law', 53 *Ger.YIL* 727, 728 (2010).

[375] See Oppenheim's *International Law*, I, 148 (9th edn, R. Jennings and A. Watts eds., 1992).

300. Foreign recognition (or non-recognition) of a Government may have a far-reaching impact on its standing, rights and immunities on the internal plane – especially before the domestic courts – of the recognizing (or non-recognizing) State. However, on the international plane, foreign States use recognition (or non-recognition) of a new Government mainly as a political and ideological tool. Non-recognition does not negate the reality of a new Government. One problem for foreign States is to de-link two disparate matters: objective status (of the new regime as a Government) and subjective approval or disapproval of it.[376]

301. Support for the proposition that a Government may exist in reality, even if it is denied general recognition, can already be found in an influential Arbitral Award delivered in 1923. In the *Aguilar-Amory* case, the sole Arbitrator (US Chief Justice W.H. Taft) held that non-recognition of a particular Government – in this instance, the Tinoco Government in Costa Rica – cannot outweigh the evidence that the Government has attained independence and effective control, 'entitling it by international law to be classed as such'.[377]

302. General foreign recognition of a Government does not constitute a third condition for its existence, in addition to effectiveness and independence. Foreign recognition by itself does not create a Government (absent effectiveness and independence), just as non-recognition cannot obliterate it (assuming that the two conditions are met). Although deprived of access to assets located abroad and divested of diplomatic ties, a new Government denied recognition is still the Government of the State, provided that it meets the two conditions of effectiveness and independence.[378]

303. The subject is pregnant with controversy. A contemporary illustration is that of the Taliban Government in Afghanistan in 2001, which failed to gain general recognition by the international community. It has been alleged that, absent recognition, the Taliban were not the 'legitimate government of Afghanistan'.[379] But the better view is that – since the Taliban were independent from foreign domination and wielded effective control over most of the territory of Afghanistan – their regime had to be

---

[376] See M.J. Peterson, 'Recognition of Governments Should Not Be Abolished', 77 *AJIL* 31, 47 (1983).

[377] *Aguilar-Amory and Royal Bank of Canada Claims* (Great Britain *v.* Costa Rica), 1923, I *RIAA* 369, 381.

[378] See Restatement of the Law Third, I *The Foreign Relations Law of the United States* 85 (1987).

[379] R. Wolfrum and C.E. Philipp, 'The Status of the Taliban: Their Obligations and Rights under International Law', 6 *MPYUNL* 559, 577 (2002).

considered the actual Afghan Government.[380] The Taliban Government was ousted from Kabul by the end of 2001 not by words (non-recognition) but by deeds (combat), as an outcome of an IAC with the US and its allies (see *supra* 174). At the time of writing, the Taliban are still fighting tenaciously to regain their lost position.

C. Issues related to recognition of Governments

(a) The three main scenarios

304. When an insurgency in Ruritania erupts, it may lead to three main scenarios raising diverse issues germane to recognition of Governments. First, the insurgents may gain effective control over some – or even most – of the territory of Ruritania, purporting to create their own Government. If the incumbent Government does not yield, doing its utmost to regroup and bring the insurgents to heel, foreign Governments may be faced with a choice of continuing to recognize the incumbent Government or bestowing recognition on the insurgent regime as the new Government of Ruritania.

305. Second, the incumbent Government of Ruritania may collapse and vanish. This does not necessarily mean that the NIAC is over, inasmuch as there may be several rival authorities set up by (former) insurgent armed groups, each seeking recognition as the sole new Government of Ruritania. In such circumstances, Arcadia, Utopia, etc., will (sooner or later) have to determine which – if any – of these authorities they prefer to recognize and deal with.

306. Third, although the insurgents drive the incumbent Government away from the territory of Ruritania, it (or remnants of it) may operate as a Government-in-exile from a base in Utopia, while the territory of Ruritania is dominated by the insurgents.

(b) Formation of an insurgent Government

307. No option of recognition of a new insurgent Government of Ruritania presents itself for foreign States (Arcadia, Utopia, etc.) unless the insurgents have actually forged and proclaimed a Government. This appears to be a truism, but forming a Government is not always as simple as it may sound. When diverse insurgent groups are at loggerheads with each other, they may be unable to cement a cohesive front despite their

---

[380] See C. Greenwood, 'International Law and the "War against Terrorism"', 78 *Int.Aff.* 301, 312–13 (2002).

joint desire to displace the incumbent regime. As long as the insurgents are incapable of getting their act together, no foreign recognition can be forthcoming. Differently phrased, foreign recognition cannot be offered antecedent to the formation of an insurgent Government.

(c) Only one Government can be recognized at any given time

308. The fundamental concept underlying any discourse of recognition is that no State can have more than one Government at any given moment. In the words of the Mexico–US Claims Commission in the *Jansen* case of 1868, 'there can be but one government in the same state at the same time'.[381] If the insurgents in Ruritania form a new Government while the preexisting Government endures, only one of the two regimes can constitute the genuine Government of that State. The simultaneous existence of two Governments in Ruritania connotes that it has disintegrated into two new States (Apollonia and Patagonia), or that a new State (Apollonia) has seceded from Ruritania (which survives in truncated form).

309. Since only a single Government can exist within a State, not more than one Government can be recognized by any foreign State at any given time. Bestowal of recognition by Arcadia on an insurgent regime as the new Government in Ruritania implies automatic withdrawal of recognition by Arcadia from the incumbent Ruritanian Government. Similarly, continued recognition of the incumbent Ruritanian Government by Utopia implies non-recognition of any rival insurgent Government.

(d) Premature and artificially prolonged recognition

310. In principle, international law allows each foreign State unilaterally to use its discretion in determining when the tidal wave of a NIAC has reached a point justifying recognition of an insurgent regime as the new Government of Ruritania (thereby revoking recognition from the incumbent Government). This would happen without any altercations when the old Government has completely disappeared from the scene.

311. There is ample authority for the proposition that premature recognition by Arcadia of an insurgent Government in Ruritania is unlawful under international law, amounting to intervention in the internal affairs of Ruritania[382] (on the principle of non-intervention, see *supra* 232–3). It follows that Arcadia must not rush to recognize as the new Government

---

[381] *Jansen* v. *Mexico* (1868), III *History and Digest of the International Arbitrations to Which the United States Has Been a Party* 2902, 2928 (J.B. Moore ed., 1898).

[382] See J.A. Frowein, 'Recognition', VIII *MPEPIL* 656, 660.

of Ruritania an insurgent authority which has gained no more than a
foothold in terms of effective control over territory. Momentary or transitory effective control by the insurgents is also not enough.[383] Naturally,
it is not always easy to determine objectively whether recognition by Arcadia of an insurgent Government in Ruritania is premature. Practicably,
it will be the incumbent Ruritanian Government that will protest the
premature recognition of the insurgent Government as a wrongful act.
Whether or not the matter will be pressed – maturing into a full-scale
dispute between Ruritania and Arcadia – would then depend on whether
the Ruritanian Government survives the NIAC.

312. The opposite of premature recognition is non-action by foreign
States even when the incumbent Ruritanian Government is on its last
legs, tenuously holding on to waning power and scarcely reigning over
any territory at all. Arcadia may arrive at the conclusion that it must yield
to the grim reality and recognize the insurgents' regime as the genuine
Government of Ruritania. Yet, Utopia may be reluctant to follow suit.
Utopia may retain its diplomatic agents in the capital city after it has been
taken over by the insurgents, for the purpose of informal communications with the new regime. But, as long as these ties are informal and
unaccompanied by formal acts of accreditation, they will not be viewed
as transfer of recognition to the insurgent regime.[384]

313. As a rule of thumb, most foreign States confronted by a NIAC in
Ruritania prefer to await developments, and in the meantime they continue to recognize the incumbent Government. This inertia may persist
even after it has become evident that the incumbent Government is no
longer in actual command of Ruritania. Unlike premature recognition
of an insurgent Government, artificially prolonged recognition by Utopia
of a defunct Government – which has irretrievably lost effective control of
the territory of Ruritania – is not deemed a breach of international law.[385]

(e) *De facto* recognition

314. Sometimes, seeking to hedge its bets, Arcadia or Utopia will qualify its recognition of the insurgent Government of Ruritania by asserting
that it is granted only *de facto*. Yet, it is by no means perspicuous what
practical consequences separate *de facto* from *de jure* recognition of a

---

[383] See A.C. Bundu, 'Recognition of Revolutionary Authorities: Law and Practice of States',
27 *ICLQ* 18, 43 (1978).

[384] See H. Lauterpacht, *Recognition in International Law* 382–3 (1947).

[385] On this issue, see M.J. Peterson, *Recognition of Governments: Legal Doctrine and State
Practice, 1815–1995* 65–7 (1997).

new Government.[386] Whether issued *de facto* or *de jure*, recognition of an insurgent regime as the new Government of Ruritania implies withdrawal of recognition from the incumbent Government. Ergo, any form of recognition of the insurgents by Arcadia or Utopia as the new Government of Ruritania is a dramatic volte-face in the political constellation.

315. The gravity of the dilemma faced by Arcadia and Utopia, whether or not to recognize the insurgent regime (either *de facto* or *de jure*) as the new Government of Ruritania, is mitigated by the availability of two more limited forms of recognition (neither of which affects the continued recognition of the incumbent Government of Ruritania).[387] These are 'recognition of insurgency' and 'recognition of belligerency' (to be expounded *infra* 338 *et seq.*). Recognition of the insurgents as the new Government of Ruritania may be granted by Arcadia or Utopia 'prior to, in the absence of, concurrently with, or subsequent to recognition of belligerency'.[388]

(f) Implied recognition

316. Recognition of a new insurgent Government does not require a formal declaration and may be inferred from conduct. Hence, if Arcadia or Utopia wishes to avoid implied recognition of a new Government in Ruritania, it must act deftly and be circumspect in its dealings with insurgent authorities.[389]

317. The formal accreditation of diplomatic agents by Arcadia or Utopia to the insurgent authorities is proof positive of their tacit recognition as the new Government of Ruritania (in place of the previous Government).[390] But, should Arcadia or Utopia decide to discontinue diplomatic relations with the incumbent Government in Ruritania, the rupture does not by itself imply withdrawal of recognition.[391]

318. Accreditation of diplomatic agents is not the sole evidence of implied recognition of a new insurgent Government. Another indication

---

[386] See C.L. Cochran, 'De Facto and De Jure Recognition: Is There a Difference?', 62 *AJIL* 457–60 (1968).

[387] See G. Schwarzenberger, *The Law of Armed Conflict* 676 (1968).

[388] See N.J. Padelford, 'International Law and the Spanish Civil War', 31 *AJIL* 226, 228 (1937).

[389] See C. Warbrick, 'The New British Policy on Recognition of Governments', 30 *ICLQ* 568, 591 (1981).

[390] See Lauterpacht, *supra* note 384, at 381.

[391] See T.-C. Chen, *The International Law of Recognition with Particular Reference to Practice in Great Britain and the United States* 262 (1951).

would be the grant of exequatur to consular agents, which 'is generally regarded as constituting recognition of the sending Government'.[392] The conclusion of a bilateral treaty with the new insurgent Government will equivalently connote its recognition (barring an express reservation).[393]

(g) Recognition as a step towards intervention

319. The heart of the matter is that, when Ruritania is in the throes of a NIAC, recognition of a new Government transcends mundane issues of diplomatic or commercial ties and may have existential ramifications for the spurned Government. This is due to the fact that, in conformity with international law, military intervention by Arcadia, Utopia, etc. – during a NIAC in Ruritania – is permitted only at the request of the incumbent Ruritanian Government, and not against it (see *supra* 238, 264). But there is a 'causal path' from recognition of the insurgent regime by Arcadia to the legality of military intervention on its behalf in the NIAC.[394] After all, following such recognition, Arcadia is able to maintain that it is extending military assistance to the new Government – at the latter's request and invitation – against forces still loyal to the *ancien régime* (now looked upon as revolting against the reconstituted governmental authorities).

320. That is what happened in 2011 in Libya. The road to foreign military intervention was paved by Security Council Resolution 1973 (2011) (see *supra* 281). But – as indicated *ibid.* – the military intervention, spearheaded by NATO, went beyond the resolution's mandate. Legally, this was made possible by recognition of the insurgent NTC (in Benghazi) as 'the legitimate governing authority in Libya'[395] (the US version) or as 'the sole governmental authority in Libya'[396] (the UK formula). Either way, the US/UK declaration was tantamount to recognition of the NTC as the new Libyan Government. The award of such recognition entailed *eo ipso* withdrawal of recognition from the Qaddafi regime (in Tripoli).[397]

321. Withdrawal of recognition from the Qaddafi regime did not mean that the regime ceased to exist. While it lasted (namely, until the fall of Tripoli and the death of Qaddafi), the NIAC between the NTC and

---

[392] L.T. Lee, *Consular Law and Practice* 76 (2nd edn, 1991).

[393] See McNair, *supra* note 251, at 746.

[394] See C.J. Le Mon, 'Unilateral Intervention by Invitation in Civil Wars: The Effective Control Test Tested', 35 *NYUJILP* 741, 743 (2002–3).

[395] See J.R. Crook, 'Contemporary Practice of the United States Relating to International Law', 105 *AJIL* 776, 780 (2011).

[396] See K.A. Johnston, 'Transformation of Conflict Status in Libya', 17 *JCSL* 81, 109 (2012).

[397] See *ibid.*, 110.

the Qaddafi regime persisted. As for hostilities conducted between the foreign States which militarily intervened in support of the NTC (having recognized it as the new Libyan Government) and the forces loyal to Qaddafi, they must be deemed to have amounted to an IAC. The standing of the intervening States from the viewpoint of the IAC *jus ad bellum* has been impugned,[398] relying on the 1974 General Assembly consensus Definition of Aggression (where explanatory note (a) to Article 1 says that the term 'State' is used 'without prejudice to questions of recognition').[399] The issue of IAC *jus ad bellum* exceeds the bounds of this volume, but it ought to be pointed out that – in the opinion of the present author – the explanatory note pertains to recognition of States (cf. *infra* 337) and not to recognition of Governments.

322. Undeniably, the fact that Arcadia can unilaterally recognize a new insurgent regime as the Ruritanian Government – thereby conjuring up an entitlement to intervene militarily for the benefit of the insurgents – lends itself to potential abuse. The established order in Ruritania may be subverted by Arcadia through premature recognition of the insurgents' leadership as the new Government (see *supra* 311), followed by military intervention at the latter's invitation.[400] A resultant disquiet in the international community can be partly allayed when, as happened in the case of Libya, an entire group of foreign States ultimately comes to the same conclusion. But, surely, only a decisive backing of the Security Council may dispel doubts in the matter.

(h) Democracy and constitutionality

323. It has repeatedly been contended in recent years that governance has to be validated by democracy.[401] However, requiring 'democratic legitimacy' from Governments can scarcely be viewed as an established international legal norm.[402] Democracy is a political slogan that has different meanings for different people. A Government like that of Qaddafi in Libya certainly suffered from democratic deficit. But the democratic credentials of several States coming to the aid of the NTC were also imperfect.

---

[398] See O. Corten and V. Koutroulis, 'The Illegality of Military Support to Rebels in the Libyan War: Aspects of *Jus contra Bellum* and *Jus in Bello*', 18 *JCSL* 59, 65–6 (2013).

[399] Definition of Aggression, *supra* note 301, at 143.

[400] See O'Connell, *supra* note 276, at I, 301–2.

[401] See T.M. Franck, 'The Emerging Right to Democratic Government', 86 *AJIL* 46, *id.* (1992).

[402] See S.D. Murphy, 'Democratic Legitimacy and the Recognition of States and Governments', 48 *ICLQ* 545, 566–81 (1999).

324. The sole criterion which is susceptible to objective legal scrutiny – lending the incumbent Government a built-in advantage over any competing insurgent regime – is its domestic constitutionality. There has to be a presumption in favour of an incumbent Government whose credentials are founded on solid constitutional grounds (under the domestic legal system). The trouble is that the standing of a Government, like that of Qaddafi, may be fatally undercut by the fact that it is itself a progeny of a revolution or a *coup d'État* occurring at some juncture in the past. Constitutionalism is not the strong suit of those who have flouted it earlier. In such a situation, the new insurgent regime – while resorting to bullets rather than ballots – is actually shunting aside a long-standing insurgent regime. It may even purport to salvage constitutionalism in the country.

325. There is sparse support for a policy (sometimes called the Tobar Doctrine) whereby foreign recognition of a new insurgent Government in Ruritania will be deferred until that State is 'constitutionally reorganized', although in Central America the policy was embodied in two binding regional treaties: in 1907[403] and in 1923.[404] The need to put the State back on an even constitutional keel as rapidly as possible cannot be gainsaid. Regrettably, waiting until such a process is consummated in the fullness of time may not prove to be a workable option for the here and now.

(i) Avoiding recognition

326. There is no duty of foreign recognition of any new Government in Ruritania.[405] Hence, there is a distinct possibility of withdrawal of recognition from the incumbent Government without granting recognition to the new insurgent Government.[406] But if de-recognition of the incumbent Ruritanian Government is unaccompanied by recognition of a new Government, the stratagem is dysfunctional in the long term, and it casts doubt on Ruritanian statehood.

327. It is in this connection that one has to analyze the so-called Estrada Doctrine. The Doctrine is named after a Mexican Foreign Minister, G. Estrada, who argued in 1930 that the 'insulting practice' of conferring recognition on new Governments has to be discontinued and replaced by a decision whether or not to maintain diplomatic relations with a

---

[403] Additional Convention to the General Treaty of Peace and Amity, 1907, 2 *AJIL*, Supp., 219, 229–30 (1908) (Article 1).

[404] General Treaty of Peace and Amity, 1923, 17 *AJIL*, Supp., 117, 118 (1923) (Article 2).

[405] See Starke's *International Law* 122 (11th edn, I.A. Shearer ed., 1994).

[406] See M.N. Shaw, *International Law* 466 (6th edn, 2008).

Government.[407] In more recent times, other countries – including several major Powers – have also announced that they would avoid the award of recognition to new Governments and would concern themselves exclusively with the decision whether to maintain diplomatic relations with new regimes.[408] But the Estrada Doctrine – like its modern derivatives – closes its eyes to the possibility that, while there is a Government controlling the capital city, there may be a rival regime predominant in the rest of the country.[409] In any event, the Estrada Doctrine 'merely substitutes implied recognition for express recognition; recognition is not announced expressly, but can be implied from the existence of diplomatic relations or other dealings with a foreign government'.[410] Interestingly, the 'non-recognition' policy was abandoned by its most vociferous adherents in 2011, when recognition was bestowed explicitly on a new insurgent Government in Libya – the NTC – in lieu of the Qaddafi regime (see *supra* 320).[411]

(j) Government-in-exile

328. Having lost effective control of the Ruritanian territory, the incumbent Government may remove itself to Utopia and proceed to claim its authority as a Government-in-exile (see *supra* 306). The NIAC in Ruritania will then go on, although resistance to the insurgent regime – ensconced as the new Government – may be more notional than real.

329. In such circumstances, it goes without saying that Utopia (the host State) continues to recognize the Government-in-exile as the Government of Ruritania. But other foreign States (Arcadia, Numidia, etc.) may also be forced to take sides and decide whether they continue to recognize the incumbent Government (in exile) or they withdraw their recognition and grant it to the new Government established by the insurgents (and in effective control of Ruritanian territory). One way or another, as pointed out by S. Talmon, exile in this instance merely indicates the domicile of the Government: a Government, whether in exile or

---

[407] The text of the Estrada Doctrine appears in II *Digest of International Law* 85–6 (M.M. Whiteman ed., 1963).

[408] See Shaw, *supra* note 406, at 458–9.

[409] See P.C. Jessup, *A Modern Law of Nations: An Introduction* 62 (1949).

[410] Akehurst, *supra* note 97, at 88.

[411] See C. Warbrick, 'British Policy and the National Transitional Council of Libya', 61 *ICLQ* 247, 248 (2012).

in situ, is a Government.[412] Eventually, a choice between the two rival Governments has to be made (explicitly or implicitly) by virtually every foreign State. Recognition of one Government means withdrawal (or denial) of recognition as far as a contender Government is concerned.

330. Can a Government-in-exile be formed by insurgents who have not yet gained effective control of any portion of the Ruritanian territory in a NIAC? The political leadership of an insurrectionary movement often stays abroad for its own safety. But the prevailing view is that 'recognition of a revolutionary government established abroad before it has gained control over the greater part of the territory of the State concerned may well be premature and amount to an interference in the affairs of the State'.[413]

D. Action by the Security Council

331. As indicated (*supra* 322), unilateral recognition by a foreign State of a new insurgent Government may be problematic. It can also be a volatile issue, both politically and legally, by producing a chain reaction leading to the use of inter-State force. Following recognition by Arcadia of an insurgent regime in Ruritania and the deployment of Arcadian forces in the field – at the invitation of the new Government – Utopia may opt to support militarily the beleaguered incumbent Ruritanian Government (at the latter's request). The outcome will be an international conflagration. The same result will ensue if – upon the disappearance of the preexisting Ruritanian Government – Arcadia and Utopia recognize the top leaders of two different organized armed groups as the successors of that Government, muscling in militarily on opposing sides of the aisle.

332. For this and other reasons, a multilateral approach to the problem of recognition of an insurgent Government is a much preferred goal to strive for. Even in the past, efforts were often made by foreign States to act in concert in granting recognition to a new Government.[414] At present, the obvious remedy is to turn to the Security Council. If a binding decision can be adopted by the Security Council, this will determine in an authoritative fashion the true Government of the country in which a NIAC is afire. The fly in the ointment is that the necessary majority in the Council must first be obtained without a veto being cast by a Permanent Member (see *supra* 279).

---

[412] See S. Talmon, *Recognition of Governments in International Law: With Particular Reference to Governments in Exile* 14–16 (1998).

[413] A. Aust, *Handbook of International Law* 26 (2nd edn, 2010).

[414] See Lauterpacht, *supra* note 384, at 165–9.

333. The case of Sierra Leone is an outstanding example of the Security Council refusing to grant recognition to a military *junta* that had assumed the powers of Government. In the midst of a lengthy and sanguinary NIAC in Sierra Leone, the Council (acting under Chapter VII) adopted Resolution 1132 (1997), demanding that 'the military junta take immediate steps to relinquish power in Sierra Leone and make way for the restoration of the democratically elected Government and a return to constitutional order'.[415]

334. The two best illustrations of the Security Council siding with regime change relate to Afghanistan and Iraq. In Resolution 1383 (2001), the Council endorsed the Bonn Agreement (reached by the various factions opposed to the Taliban regime) on provisional arrangements in Afghanistan pending the re-establishment of permanent Government institutions.[416] Similarly, in Resolution 1546 (2004), the Council – acting under Chapter VII – endorsed the formation of a sovereign interim Government in Iraq.[417]

335. In the aftermath of a Security Council resolution of this nature, any continued fighting between the new Government's forces and the surviving forces of the *ancien régime* (like the Taliban in Afghanistan) means that the tables have been turned. The armed conflict is still a NIAC, but the previous insurgents have become the newly established Government while the previous Government has been relegated to the status of an organized armed group of (new) insurgents.

336. Although a Security Council resolution like the ones adopted in Sierra Leone, Afghanistan or Iraq affects the legal and political status of the local Government in a NIAC, it may require force to be brought to bear from the outside in order to alter the actual conditions on the ground. This is what happened in all three instances.

II. Recognition of a new State

337. Arcadia may opt to recognize an entity carved out by the Ruritanian insurgents as a new State (Apollonia). What such recognition denotes – assuming that hostilities between the insurgents and the incumbent Ruritanian Government continue – is that Arcadia no longer regards the hostilities as an intra-State NIAC, but considers them to represent an

---

[415] Security Council Resolution 1132 (1997), para. 1.
[416] Security Council Resolution 1383 (2001), para. 1.
[417] Security Council Resolution 1546 (2004), para. 1.

inter-State IAC (between Ruritania and Apollonia). That is an even more radical reshuffle of the political cards, compared to the after-effects of recognition of the insurgents as the new Government of Ruritania. Still, what the measure means is that Arcadia – in conformity with IAC *jus ad bellum* – must maintain neutrality between the two Belligerent Parties (Ruritania and Apollonia).

III. 'Recognition of belligerency'

338. The expression 'belligerency' has traditionally been used to describe the existence of an IAC between States, commonly called 'Belligerent Parties'. The terminology is clearly inapposite to a NIAC. However, an insurgency might acquire such magnitude that it may appear to warrant treatment of the opposing sides (in the NIAC) as if they were Belligerent Parties (in an IAC). While a situation like this does not flutter in a fact-free vacuum, the insurgents cannot pull themselves up to a status of 'belligerency' by their own bootstraps. Whatever the dimensions of the hostilities, the insurrectionists can acquire that status only through recognition: either by the incumbent Government or by foreign countries.[418]

A. 'Recognition of belligerency' by the incumbent Government

339. Grave setbacks in the field may compel the incumbent Government of Ruritania to come to terms with the dire consequences of the capture by insurgents of large numbers of soldiers. As we shall see (*infra* 702), in a NIAC, captured insurgents cannot expect the privileges of prisoners of war (POW). The problem is that the same rule applies symmetrically to both sides in the civil strife, so that the insurrectionists are not required to confer those privileges on captives from the governmental armed forces.[419] As long as the tally of its own captured personnel is not critically high, the Government may afford to be nonchalant about temporary triumphs by the other side. However, when droves of troops capitulate to the insurgents, public opinion will probably animate the Government to ensure that the captives benefit from POW privileges. This cannot be accomplished without guaranteeing reciprocal treatment to insurgent detainees. The only viable option, then, is for the Government to issue 'recognition of belligerency'. What such recognition means is

---

[418] See Lord McNair and A.D. Watts, *The Legal Effects of War* 33 (4th edn, 1966).
[419] See G. Blum, 'On a Differential Law of War', 52 *HILJ* 163, 170 (2011).

that the entire gamut of the *jus in bello* governing IACs (especially, albeit not exclusively, in the *materia* of the treatment of POW) will become applicable to the NIAC on condition of reciprocity.[420]

340. There is a peculiar twist here in the transposition of IAC law to NIACs. In an IAC, a Belligerent Party is not required to grant POW status to enemy combatants who are its own nationals. An enemy soldier (serving in the armed forces of Arcadia) owing allegiance to the captor State (Ruritania) – by virtue of the link of nationality or otherwise – is not regarded by IAC *jus in bello* as a lawful combatant entitled to enjoy POW privileges.[421] In a NIAC, members of the insurgent armed group fighting against the incumbent Government of Ruritania would ordinarily be nationals of that State. But, once the incumbent Government grants 'recognition of belligerency', it is obliged to treat insurgent captives as POW despite their Ruritanian nationality. What emanates is that the protection accorded to captive insurgents in a NIAC (post-'recognition of belligerency') is wider in scope than that available to captive enemy combatants in an IAC.[422]

341. When 'recognition of belligerency' is proclaimed by the incumbent Government of Ruritania, it means that IAC *jus in bello* is applied to the NIAC not only in the relations between that Government and the insurgents but also *vis-à-vis* all other States. The upshot is that the laws of neutrality will be in effect as far as Arcadia, Utopia, etc., are concerned. These States, therefore, will not be allowed to intervene militarily in the armed conflict even in support of the Government (notwithstanding the general rule; see *supra* 238 *et seq.*).

B. 'Recognition of belligerency' by foreign States

342. In case where 'recognition of belligerency' is granted by the incumbent Government of Ruritania, no further action by foreign States (Arcadia, Utopia, etc.) is required: they all become *eo ipso* neutral in the conflict.[423] However, when no such recognition comes from the Ruritanian Government, foreign States are free to act independently. Either jointly or severally, Arcadia, Utopia, etc., may issue their 'recognition of

---

[420] See S.C. Neff, *War and the Law of Nations: A General History* 258–9 (2005).
[421] See the ruling of the UK Privy Council in *Public Prosecutor* v. *Koi et al.* (1967), [1968] *AC* 829, 856–8.
[422] See Baxter, *supra* note 252, at 529.
[423] See W.L. Walker, 'Recognition of Belligerency and Grant of Belligerent Rights', 23 *TGS* 177, 199–200 (1937).

belligerency'. When this is done by Arcadia alone, the 'recognition of belligerency' does not affect the legal position of Utopia, Numidia, etc.[424] 'Recognition of belligerency' by Arcadia will alter only its own standing with respect to the NIAC in Ruritania.

343. Most significantly, 'recognition of belligerency' by Arcadia cannot impact on the status of the hostilities as far as the incumbent Government of Ruritania is concerned. The fighting with the insurgents will continue to be governed by LONIAC. What the 'recognition of belligerency' by Arcadia will do is inject the application of IAC norms into the relations between Arcadia and the armed conflict. Once IAC norms apply, Arcadia is duty bound to observe the posture of a neutral State. As expressly articulated in Article 2 of a 1957 Pan American Protocol to the Convention on Duties and Rights of States in the Event of Civil Strife, when a State 'has recognized the belligerency of the rebels', the outcome is that 'the rules of neutrality shall be applied'.[425]

344. What neutrality conveys is that Arcadia accepts the obligation of impartiality (towards both the incumbent Government of Ruritania and the insurgents) and non-participation in the armed conflict.[426] Prior to the 'recognition of belligerency', Arcadia was allowed to intervene militarily in the NIAC in favour of the incumbent Government of Ruritania (see *supra* 238 *et seq.*) and disallowed to do that in aiding and abetting the insurgents (see *supra* 264 *et seq.*). As from the turning point of the 'recognition of belligerency', Arcadia is forbidden to assist militarily any of the opposing sides. Arcadia thus loses its former right to support militarily the incumbent Government of Ruritania, without acquiring a new right to sustain militarily the insurgents' cause.

345. Since 'recognition of belligerency' by Arcadia is all about neutrality, it is more likely to be induced by insurgent takeover of Ruritanian ports and adjacent waters – affecting foreign shipping and commerce – than by the intensity of hostilities on land.[427] Considering that the onus of the obligations of neutrality far outweighs its benefits in a NIAC, 'recognition of belligerency' may be deemed burdensome for Arcadia.[428]

---

[424] See V.A. O'Rourke, 'Recognition of Belligerency and the Spanish War', 31 *AJIL* 398, 402 (1937).

[425] Pan American Protocol to the Convention on Duties and Rights of States in the Event of Civil Strife, 1957, 284 *UNTS* 201, 202.

[426] See R.P. Dhokalia, 'Civil Wars and International Law', 11 *Ind.JIL* 219, 228 (1971).

[427] See D.A. Ijalaye, 'Was "Biafra" at any Time a State in International Law?' 65 *AJIL* 551, 555 (1971).

[428] See C.G. Fenwick, *International Law* 166 (4th edn, 1865).

346. 'Recognition of belligerency' is not akin to recognition of the insurgents as a new State (see *supra* 337), even though in both instances the end result for Arcadia is an espousal of the stance of neutrality. The difference is that no inter-State relations are established between Arcadia and the insurgents as offshoots of 'recognition of belligerency'.[429]

C. Implied 'recognition of belligerency'

347. As a matter of general State practice, the grant of 'recognition of belligerency' *expressis verbis* has always been rare,[430] and it is largely[431] in disuse today.[432] Sometimes, this appears to be a matter of semantics.[433] But, in any event, it would distort the legal picture to present 'recognition of belligerency' as either dysfunctional or archaic. 'Recognition of belligerency' is as relevant today as ever, but its award is usually deduced by implication. There is no need for an express proclamation of 'recognition of belligerency', inasmuch as it may be distilled from the conduct of States.[434] Implied 'recognition of belligerency' may be inferred from the conduct or pronouncements of either the incumbent Government of Ruritania or Arcadia.

(a) By the incumbent Government

348. As far as the incumbent Government of Ruritania is concerned, implied 'recognition of belligerency' may be extracted from its conferral of the status of POW on insurgent captives. 'Recognition of belligerency' by the incumbent Government may also be implied from the imposition

---

[429] See L. Kotzsch, *The Concept of War in Contemporary History and International Law* 224 (1956).

[430] See *ibid.*, 234.

[431] There are some exceptions. See, e.g., G. von Glahn and J.L. Taulbee, *Law Among Nations: An Introduction to Public International Law* 142 (8th edn, 2007).

[432] See A. Cullen, *The Concept of Non-International Armed Conflict in International Humanitarian Law* 22–3 (2010).

[433] In the Syrian NIAC, the US announced – at the end of 2012 – that it considered the insurgent coalition as 'the legitimate representative of the Syrian people in opposition to the Assad regime' (J.R. Crook, 'Contemporary Practice of the United States Relating to International Law', 107 *AJIL* 654, 655 (2013)). This appears to be a variation of 'recognition of belligerency' (cf. the different phraseology of the US recognition of the NTC as the Government of Libya, *supra* 320). The US did not militarily intervene in the NIAC. Threats of airstrikes against Syrian targets, prior to the adoption of Security Council Resolution 2118 (2013), were strictly related to the illicit use of chemical weapons (see *infra* 507).

[434] See Y.M. Lootsteen, 'The Concept of Belligerency in International Law', 166 *Mil.LR* 109, 118–19 (2000).

of a blockade barring high seas access to or from maritime ports (or coastlines) that have been seized by the insurgents.

349. What is hanging in the balance in a blockade is not the use of force by the incumbent Government of Ruritania – within the internal or territorial waters of the country – in order to cordon off ports (or coastlines) that have fallen into the hands of insurgents. Rather, it is the entitlement of the Ruritanian Government to achieve its purpose through drawing a blockade line across the high seas, thus interfering with foreign shipping to or from the insurgent-controlled port (or coastline).[435] This is not just a matter of heralding a plan of action: a blockade line, having been demarcated, has to be effectively maintained.[436] The upside of a blockade, from the Government's frame of mind, is that it can lawfully deny foreign ships ingress to or egress from an insurgent-controlled port (or coastline). The downside is that the imposition of a blockade on such a port (or coastline) implies 'recognition of belligerency'.[437]

350. A blockade on the high seas is a means of warfare made possible by IAC *jus in bello* – subject to rigorous conditions (preeminently, that the blockade is effective and does not exist on paper only[438]) – but not by LONIAC. If the incumbent Ruritanian Government does not wish to endow an insurrectional movement (by implication) with 'recognition of belligerency', it has no choice but to avoid the imposition of a blockade on the high seas banning inbound or outbound shipping to or from an insurgent-controlled port (or coastline).[439]

351. Once the incumbent Ruritanian Government opts to impose a blockade on the high seas, sealing off a port (or coastline) controlled by the insurgents – thereby acquiescing in implied 'recognition of belligerency' and introduction of IAC *jus in bello* to the armed conflict – the result is reciprocity in the application of all belligerent rights and obligations. Hence, if they are possessed with sufficient naval or other means to maintain it effectively, the recognized insurgents are equally entitled to bring off a blockade on the high seas against ports (or coastlines) controlled by the Ruritanian Government.

---

[435] See R.W. Tucker, *The Law of War and Neutrality at Sea* 287 n. 7 (ILS, 1955).

[436] See already the Arbitral Award of 1903, between Britain and Venezuela, in the *Compagnie Générale des Asphaltes de France* case, IX *RIAA* 389, 394.

[437] See Lauterpacht, *supra* note 384, at 199–201.

[438] See *San Remo Manual on International Law Applicable to Armed Conflicts at Sea* 176–8 (L. Doswald-Beck ed., 1995).

[439] See L.H. Woolsey, 'Closure of Ports by the Chinese Nationalist Government', 44 *AJIL* 350, 353–4 (1950).

352. A blockade is a curtain drawn across the high seas. It must be distinguished from a temporary suspension of the right of innocent passage in the territorial sea of Ruritania. Such a temporary suspension – in specified areas of the territorial sea – can be announced by Ruritania, under Article 25(3) of the 1982 LOS Convention, when this is 'essential for the protection of its security'.[440] The coastal State's security may demand suspension of the right of innocent passage during a NIAC (perhaps even throughout the territorial sea, and not only in some section thereof, except straits).[441] The right of innocent passage is defined in Article 18(1) of the LOS Convention as related to traversing the territorial sea without calling on a port.[442] Hovering vessels and all those not engaged in passage may be excluded by the coastal State from its territorial sea.[443]

(b) By foreign States

353. Implied 'recognition of belligerency' with respect to the hostilities in Ruritania may flow from the conduct or the official statements of Arcadia. In particular, if neutrality in the armed conflict is promulgated by Arcadia, 'recognition of belligerency' is tacitly inferred. This is derived from the fact that 'there can be no neutrals unless there are two belligerents'.[444] Thus, instead of neutrality flowing from 'recognition of belligerency', it is the other way around.

IV. 'Recognition of insurgency'

354. 'Recognition of insurgency' in Ruritania may be issued by Arcadia. It has consequences that are less extensive than those produced by 'recognition of belligerency'. 'Recognition of insurgency' will usually come about when an organized armed group fighting the incumbent Government of Ruritania gains effective control of some territory, especially a border zone abutting the territory of Arcadia. Through 'recognition of insurgency', Arcadia signals that it will maintain some relations with the

---

[440] LOS Convention, *supra* note 82, at 29.
[441] See W. Heintchel von Heinegg, 'Methods and Means of Naval Warfare in Non-International Armed Conflicts', 88 *ILS*, *supra* note 55, at 211, 217.
[442] LOS Convention, *supra* note 82, at 26–7.
[443] See R.R. Churchill and A.V. Lowe, *The Law of the Sea* 87 (3rd edn, 1999).
[444] J.L. Brierly, *The Law of Nations: An Introduction to the International Law of Peace* 142 (6th edn, C.H.M. Waldock ed., 1963).

insurgents, in order to safeguard its own interests (and those of its nationals) in the territory actually under their sway.[445] In other words, Arcadia will be in direct contact with the insurgents (bypassing the futile channels of the Government), but that will be done strictly in matters pertaining to the area subject to their control. 'Recognition of insurgency' may also be implied from the conduct of Arcadia.

355. Unlike 'recognition of belligerency', 'recognition of insurgency' by Arcadia does not carry with it 'the technical burdens of a neutral' *vis-à-vis* the two antagonists in the armed conflict going on in Ruritania.[446]

356. Some scholars believe that 'recognition of insurgency' can also be granted by the incumbent Government of Ruritania.[447] But 'recognition of insurgency' coming from the Government can only connote that it formally concedes the existence of a NIAC and girds itself to apply LONIAC to the hostilities.

---

[445] See Oppenheim, *supra* note 375, at I, 166.
[446] C.C. Hyde, I *International Law Chiefly as Interpreted and Applied by the United States* 203 (2nd edn, 1945).
[447] See E. Castrén, 'Recognition of Insurgency', 5 *Ind.JIL* 441, 449–51 (1965).

7

State responsibility

I. The ILC Draft Articles

357. With its toxic atmosphere of defiance of law and order, a NIAC provides fertile soil for international disputes between the local State (Ruritania) and a foreign State (Arcadia). Such disputes flare up in consequence of damage caused within the territory of Ruritania, during a NIAC, to (i) Arcadian agents or installations, primarily embassies and consulates; (ii) Arcadian nationals who have entered Ruritania as tourists, businessmen, labourers, students, etc.; or (iii) the property of Arcadian nationals or corporations.

358. There is no general binding treaty regulating the international law of State responsibility. The subject was studied for decades by the ILC, and, in 2001, Draft Articles on Responsibility of States for International Wrongful Acts (cited *supra* 217) were finally presented to the General Assembly. Although the ILC Draft Articles were not (nor were they intended to be) transformed into a treaty – and therefore have no binding force – it is noteworthy that the ICJ has relied on them periodically, even before their formal adoption (see, e.g., *infra* 361). Of particular interest is Article 10 of the Draft Articles (*supra* 217), which deals with insurrectional movements. 'The wording of the article can be considered as a concise and distinct expression of international customary law.'[448]

359. The Draft Articles address the issue of an insurrection only in terms of the responsibility of the State in which a NIAC is unfolding (Ruritania) *vis-à-vis* another State (Arcadia). As the ILC noted, the final Draft Articles do not deal with the issue of direct responsibility of an insurrectional movement.[449] Earlier, the ILC had observed that, in some instances (where the insurrectional movement is in effective control of

---

[448] G. Cahin, 'Attribution of Conduct to the State: Insurrectional Movements', *The Law of International Responsibility, supra* note 279, at 247, 249.

[449] See Draft Articles, *supra* note 249, at 52.

some Ruritanian territory), Arcadia might lodge a claim directly with the movement itself during the NIAC.[450] But ordinarily Arcadia would demur, if only because at the end of the NIAC 'the movement as such is destined to disappear', and the process of settlement of the dispute (which may be convoluted and prolonged) could outlast the NIAC.[451] Under Article 10 of the Draft Articles, should the insurgents be successful, Arcadia may have a good claim – subsequent to the end of the NIAC – against the new Government (or the new State).

II. Attribution of acts to the State

A. Organs of the State

360. As pointed out in Article 2 of the ILC Draft Articles, a State incurs responsibility for conduct (an act of commission or omission) – constituting a breach of an international obligation – which is attributable to it under international law.[452] As a rule, acts attributable to the State (deemed 'acts of State') are performed by State organs (whether they exercise executive, legislative, judicial or any hybrid function) – as well as territorial units of the State – regardless of the high or low echelon to which the actors belong in the State hierarchy (Article 4).[453]

361. The expression 'State organ' covers 'all the individual or collective entities which make up the organization of the State and act on its behalf'.[454] In its Advisory Opinion of 1999 on *Immunity from Legal Process*, the ICJ (relying on a previous version of this Article) affirmed that '[a]ccording to a well-established rule of international law, the conduct of any organ of a State must be regarded as an act of that State'.[455]

362. The Iran–US Claims Tribunal held, in the *Yeager* case of 1987, that 'attributability of acts to the State is not limited to acts of organs formally recognized under internal law', adding (similarly referring to an earlier version of the ILC Draft Articles): 'It is generally accepted in international law that a State is also responsible for acts of persons, if it is established that those persons were in fact acting on behalf of the State'.[456] Frequently, in the turbulence following the collapse of a former Government in a NIAC, the new insurgent Government is still groping

---

[450] Report of the ILC, 27th Session, [1975] II *ILC Ybk* 1, 98–9.   [451] *Ibid.*, 93.

[452] Draft Articles, *supra* note 249, at 26.   [453] *Ibid.*   [454] *Ibid.*, 40.

[455] Advisory Opinion on *Difference Relating to Immunity from Legal Process of a Special Rapporteur of the Commission on Human Rights*, [1999] *ICJ Rep.* 62, 87.

[456] *Yeager (US)* v. *Iran* (Iran–US Claims Tribunal, 1987), 82 *ILR* 179, 193.

its way along the corridors of power. In default of official State authority, certain insurgent groups or persons may exercise on their own initiative elements of that authority, and the ILC acknowledged in Article 9 of the Draft Articles (citing *Yeager*[457]) that their conduct may be considered an act of the State.[458]

B. Private persons

363. There is a manifest disjuncture between State organs and private persons. The ILC emphasized that 'a corollary' to the attribution of acts of official organs to the State is that 'the conduct of private persons is not as such attributable to the State'.[459] However, Article 11 of the Draft Articles adds that non-attributable conduct by private persons may still be considered an act of State 'to the extent that the State acknowledges and adopts the conduct in question as its own'.[460] A graphic illustration is the seizure of the US Embassy in Tehran – and the detention as hostages of its diplomatic and consular staff – in 1979. The onslaught on the embassy was carried out by militants who were not organs of the Iranian State. Initially, the authorities merely failed to intervene. But, within a short while, approval of the continued seizure and detention was given by the regime. In the 1980 *Diplomatic and Consular Staff in Tehran* case, the ICJ held that the Iranian governmental approval of what was going on 'translated' the undertaking into an act of State.[461]

C. Ultra vires *acts*

364. Once empowered to act on its behalf, the conduct of State organs will be attributed to the State, even if they exceed their authority or contravene instructions (Article 7 of the Draft Articles).[462] This is of particular importance insofar as acts executed by the armed forces or law enforcement agencies of Ruritania are concerned. The rule covers not only the high command but also the rank and file.

365. State responsibility for *ultra vires* acts is well entrenched in the case law. For instance, if soldiers or policemen are sent to quell a riot but – instead of dispersing the mob – open fire on foreigners and kill or injure

---

[457] Draft Articles, *supra* note 249, at 49.   [458] *Ibid.*, 26.
[459] *Ibid.*, 38.   [460] *Ibid.*, 26.
[461] *Case Concerning United States Diplomatic and Consular Staff in Tehran* (*US* v. *Iran*), [1980] *ICJ Rep.* 3, 35.
[462] *Ibid.*

them, their action would be attributed to the State. Such was the holding of the US–Mexican General Claims Commission, in 1926, in the *Youmans* Award.[463] The ILC alluded to *Youmans*, as well as to other judicial decisions in the same vein, in support of Article 7 of the Draft Articles.[464] The most recent of these decisions is *Velásquez Rodríguez* in 1988, where the Inter-American Court of Human Rights pronounced:

> This conclusion is independent of whether the organ or official has contra-vened provisions of internal law or overstepped the limits of his authority: under international law a State is responsible for the acts of its agents undertaken in their official capacity and for their omissions, even when those agents act outside the sphere of their authority or violate internal law.[465]

III. Due diligence

A. The concept

366. State responsibility towards Arcadia may devolve on Ruritania in a finessed way. The injury to Arcadian diplomats, installations, nationals or corporations may be caused by acts committed by private persons, and – as indicated (*supra* 363) – no Ruritanian State responsibility will arise directly from them. Nevertheless, responsibility may be triggered by the fact that Ruritanian organs failed to exercise due diligence in preventing the injury or in punishing wrongdoers subsequently.[466] The attribution to Ruritania in these circumstances is not of the acts (of commission) by the private persons, but of separate acts (of omission) by State organs: what is at stake is the non-compliance by Ruritania with its own international legal obligations.[467]

B. Prevention

367. Due diligence in prevention of wrongful acts towards a foreign country is an obligation of conduct and not an obligation of result.[468]

---

463 *Youmans* case (General Claims Commission, Mexico–USA, 1926), IV *RIAA* 110, 111, 116.

464 Draft Articles, *supra* note 249, at 46.

465 *Velásquez Rodríguez* case (Inter-American Court of Human Rights, 1988), 28 *ILM* 294, 325.

466 See R. Pisillo-Mazzeschi, 'The Due Diligence Rule and the Nature of the International Responsibility of States', 35 *Ger.YIL* 9, 25–8 (1992).

467 See B. Stern, 'The Elements of an International Wrongful Act', *The Law of International Responsibility*, *supra* note 278, at 193, 208–9.

468 See T. Koivurova, 'Due Diligence', III *MPEPIL* 236, 239.

The legal obligation is to exert best efforts, rather than achieve a specific end.[469] In the words of the ILC, '[o]bligations of prevention are usually construed as best efforts obligations, requiring States to take all reasonable or necessary measures to prevent a given event from occurring, but without warranting that the event will not occur'.[470]

368. The result (successful prevention of wrongdoing by private persons) is contingent on many variables, such as what the competent State organs knew or should have known prior to the event in question. If – in spite of advance knowledge – the competent State organs failed to make more than perfunctory efforts to ward off the malfeasance, the due diligence obligation is flouted.[471]

369. The precise degree of vigilance that has to be exerted by Ruritania in the exercise of its due diligence obligation towards Arcadia is not the same in all instances: it depends on whether special precautions are required.[472] Greater vigilance is called for regarding Arcadian embassies and consulates functioning within Ruritanian territory. Article 22(2) of the 1961 Vienna Convention on Diplomatic Relations imposes on the receiving State a 'special duty to take all appropriate steps to protect the premises' of diplomatic missions.[473] A parallel provision with respect to consular premises appears in Article 31(3) of the 1963 Vienna Convention on Consular Relations.[474] The duty to protect these premises is 'special', but it is still not absolute. The steps to be taken have to be 'appropriate', and 'what is appropriate depends on the degree of threat to a particular mission and on whether the receiving State has been made aware of any unusual threat'.[475]

370. The ILC underscored that 'a receiving State is not responsible, as such, for the acts of private individuals in seizing an embassy, but it will be responsible if it fails to take all necessary steps to protect the embassy from seizure, or to regain control over it'.[476] The vivid example is that of

---

[469] See P.-M. Dupuy, 'Reviewing the Difficulties of Codification: On Ago's Classification of Obligations of Means and Obligations of Result in Relation to State Responsibility', 10 *EJIL* 371, 379 (1998).

[470] Draft Articles, *supra* note 249, at 62.

[471] See R.P. Barnidge, 'The Due Diligence Principle under International Law', 8 *ICLR* 81, 112 (2006).

[472] See A.V. Freeman, 'Responsibility of States for Unlawful Acts of Their Armed Forces', 88 *RCADI* 267, 278–9 (1955).

[473] Vienna Convention on Diplomatic Relations, 1961, 500 *UNTS* 95, 108.

[474] Vienna Convention on Consular Relations, 1963, 596 *UNTS* 261, 288.

[475] E. Denza, *Diplomatic Law: Commentary on the Vienna Convention on Diplomatic Relations* 139 (2nd edn, 1998).

[476] Draft Articles, *supra* note 249, at 39.

the initial Iranian apathy in the face of the capture of US Embassy and personnel in Tehran in 1979 (see *supra* 363).

C. Punishment

371. The obligation of due diligence in punishing wrongdoers is no more absolute than the original obligation of due diligence in prevention of the wrongful acts. This is almost self-evident, bearing in mind that condign punishment can only be meted out via a process that consists of apprehension of offenders plus prosecution, conviction and sentencing by an impartial court of law in a fair trial. The Ruritanian Government cannot guarantee the outcome of a trial by an independent and impartial court, which may end in acquittal despite strenuous prosecutorial efforts.[477] However, it is not enough for law enforcement agencies merely to lodge an indictment: if the due diligence obligation is to be implemented, the trial must be pursued to its conclusion.[478]

372. Likewise, if a convicted criminal – who committed acts harmful to the interests of Arcadia or its nationals – is released from jail or allowed to escape, Ruritania will be held responsible for a breach of its due diligence obligation to punish him.[479] A special issue is the formal grant of a pardon by Ruritania to offenders. As set forth in the Arbitral Award in the *West* case of 1927: 'There would seem no doubt but that granting amnesty for a crime has the same effect, under international law, as not punishing such a crime'.[480] All the same, see *infra* 387.

IV. Mob violence and riots

A. Reasonable precautions

373. In order to fathom the legal nuances of State responsibility in a NIAC, it is advisable to adumbrate it against the background of mob violence, riots and other sporadic internal disturbances (below-the-threshold activities; see *supra* 65, 111).

---

[477] See R.B. Lillich and J.M. Paxman, 'State Responsibility for Injuries to Aliens Occasioned by Terrorist Activities', 26 *AULR* 217, 289 (1976–7).

[478] See A.H. Feller, *The Mexican Claims Commissions 1923–1934: A Study in the Law and Procedure of International Tribunals* 151–2 (1935).

[479] See Lillich and Paxman, *supra* note 477, at 289.

[480] *West (USA) v. Mexico* (1928), IV *RIAA* 270, 271.

374. In principle, mob violence and riots in Ruritania – even when they are harmful to the interests of Arcadia – do not constitute acts of State, provided that no organs of Ruritania are involved. Yet, Ruritanian responsibility is engaged – *vis-à-vis* Arcadia – if Arcadian agents, nationals or property are harmed by riots or mob violence when Ruritanian organs have failed to take 'reasonable precautionary and preventive action' or have displayed 'inattention amounting to official indifference or connivance'.[481]

375. It is implicit in the reference to 'reasonable' precautionary action that Ruritania's obligation towards Arcadia is only to make every feasible effort. Law enforcement agents cannot be omnipresent throughout the territory of Ruritania and cannot cope with every situation in which private persons scorn law and order. It was held by the US–Panamanian General Claims Commission – in the *Noyes* case of 1933 – that the mere fact that a hypothetical presence of sufficient police force on the spot might have averted injury suffered by Arcadian nationals through mob violence does not make Ruritania liable: it must be shown concretely that Ruritanian organs failed 'to comply with their duty to maintain order, to prevent crimes or to prosecute and punish criminals'.[482]

376. As with other actions of private persons (see *supra* 363), no State responsibility will be incurred by Ruritania in relation to Arcadia as a result of the occurrence of the riot or mob violence *per se*. The internationally wrongful act triggering Ruritanian responsibility will be the failure of State organs to exercise due diligence to protect Arcadian agents, installations and nationals. As noted (*supra* 371), the exercise of due diligence goes beyond preventive measures to embrace prosecution and punishment of offenders after the event.

B. Attacks against foreigners

377. Ruritania's duty to take feasible measures within its territory to protect Arcadian interests is augmented when throngs of people are on the rampage, deliberately attacking foreigners.[483] Mob violence may be oriented at foreigners indiscriminately (owing to xenophobia) or

---

[481] Brownlie, *supra* note 371, at 454.

[482] *Noyes* case (General Claims Commission, Panama–USA, 1933), VI *RIAA* 308, 311.

[483] See *Sarropoulos c. Etat Bulgare* (Tribunal Arbitral Mixte Gréco-Bulgare, 1927), VII *Recueil des Décisions des Tribunaux Arbitraux Mixtes Institués par les Traités de Paix* 47, 50.

selectively (on account of their specific Arcadian nationality). Either way, the Ruritanian authorities have to be braced for the need to quell riots directed against foreign nationals or installations. Once more, Ruritania's responsibility in these circumstances is not spawned by the injurious acts themselves (unless they are engineered behind the scenes by the Government). The gravamen is the culpable negligence of Ruritanian organs in failing to take feasible precautions in a combustible situation.

V. Insurgency

378. Ruritanian organs (particularly the armed forces) may commit breaches of international law *vis-à-vis* Arcadia – in the course of a NIAC – even in circumstances that are totally removed, in time or space, from the hostilities against the insurgents.[484] Conversely, 'the normal consequences of suppressing the insurgents do not *as such* give rise to responsibility'.[485] Yet, it has always been acknowledged that, if Ruritanian troops perpetrate (even in defiance of explicit orders; see *supra* 364–5) acts of pillage or wanton destruction affecting Arcadian interests, this would produce Ruritanian State responsibility.[486] The same principle will apply to other violations of LONIAC committed by Ruritanian armed forces. These include acts committed by units that subsequently join the insurgents – becoming dissident armed forces (see *supra* 124) – while they still form part of the official military apparatus.[487]

379. On occasion, the overall reaction to an insurgency by the Ruritanian Government is not deemed adequate by Arcadia (whose assets, agents or nationals suffer at the hands of the insurgents). In practice, 'no arbitral tribunal has ever found a State guilty of negligence in failing to prevent a rebellion'.[488] Even when Ruritania seems to be 'accident prone' in going through a series of successive revolts, an alleged exception to the general rule of non-liability of the Government has been dismissed in the case law.[489] A claim on the ground of undue delay in the restoration of

---

[484] See M.M. Whiteman, II *Damages in International Law* 1424 (1937).

[485] I. Brownlie, *System of the Law of Nations: State Responsibility Part I* 172 (1983). Emphasis in the original.

[486] See E.M. Borchard, *The Diplomatic Protection of Citizens Abroad or the Law of International Claims* 233 (1915).

[487] See Feller, *supra* note 478, at 163.

[488] M. Akehurst, 'State Responsibility for the Wrongful Acts of Rebels – An Aspect of the Southern Rhodesian Problem', 43 *BYBIL* 49, 51 (1968–9).

[489] See *Sambiaggio* case (Mixed Claims Commission Italy–Venezuela, 1903), X *RIAA* 499, 523.

governmental power in a given district of a State – where the insurgents had remained in control by dint of ineptitude in proper law enforcement – was rebutted by the Umpire F. Plumley in the *Santa Clara Estates* case of 1903.[490]

380. Moreover, as pronounced in the *Iloilo* claims of 1925,[491] if all that is alleged by Arcadia – when its interests are harmed in a NIAC – is that military manoeuvres by Ruritania against the insurgents (run by experienced officers in good faith) might have led to more auspicious results had they been handled in a different way, this entails no State responsibility.

381. The rules of State responsibility in a NIAC are extraordinary in that Ruritania will bear responsibility towards Arcadia with respect not only to the acts of its official organs, but also to those of successful insurgents. The split between successful and unsuccessful insurgents deserves careful scrutiny.

A. Unsuccessful insurgents

(a) Non-attribution to the State of insurgent acts

382. In the words of the ILC:

> At the outset, the conduct of the members of the [insurrectional] move-
> ment presents itself purely as the conduct of private individuals. It can be
> placed on the same footing as that of persons or groups who participate
> in a riot or mass demonstrations and it is likewise not attributable to the
> State.[492]

Since injurious acts of unsuccessful insurgents in a NIAC are not attributable to Ruritania, it does not bear any responsibility for them *vis-à-vis* Arcadia.

383. It has always been settled law that a State does not incur responsibility for injuries inflicted by unsuccessful insurgents (absent some dereliction of duty on the part of State organs).[493] There are a slew of arbitral awards confirming this proposition. As an example, we may quote a

---

[490] *Santa Clara Estates Company* case (Mixed Claims Commission Great Britain–Venezuela, 1903), IX *RIAA* 455, 458.

[491] *Iloilo Claims* (Arbitral Tribunal Great Britain–United States, 1925), VI *RIAA* 158, 160.

[492] Draft Articles, *supra* note 249, at 50.

[493] See H. Silvanie, *Responsibility of States for Acts of Unsuccessful Insurgent Governments* 135 (1939).

ruling from a 1920 arbitration between the US and the UK in the *Missionary Society* case:

> It is a well-established principle of international law that no government can be held responsible for the act of rebellious bodies of men committed in violation of its authority, where it is itself guilty of no breach of good faith, or of no negligence in suppressing the insurrection.[494]

384. This is a matter not only of law but even of pure logic. As the Umpire J.H. Ralston stated in the Italian–Venezuelan Mixed Claims Commission *Sambiaggio* case of 1903, it would be difficult to maintain the proposition that a Government is responsible for wrongs done by those attempting to bring about its destruction and substitution by another regime.[495]

(b) Failure to exercise due diligence

385. The non-attribution to Ruritania of insurgent acts does not mean that Ruritania is completely absolved of State responsibility during a NIAC. Ruritania will be held responsible if it is proved that the competent authorities failed to exercise due diligence (see *supra* 366) to prevent or punish activities of insurgents harmful to the interests of Arcadia.[496] Ruritanian State responsibility is thus engaged when its own organs failed to discharge their duty to prevent insurgent wrongful acts (affecting Arcadia) or to punish them.

386. It is possible, for instance, that – in the course of a NIAC – while the incumbent Government of Ruritania brooks no direct challenge to its own authority, those in charge close their eyes to incidents of insurgent attacks against installations or nationals of Arcadia.[497] The ILC stressed that 'the failure by a State to take available steps to protect the premises of diplomatic missions, threatened from attack by an insurrectional movement, is clearly conduct attributable to the State'.[498] The duty to protect diplomatic and consular premises is special (see *supra* 369), but Ruritania also has a more general duty to protect other installations and nationals of Arcadia.

---

[494] *Home Frontier and Foreign Missionary Society of the United Brethren in Christ (United States)* v. *Great Britain* (1920), VI *RIAA* 42, 44.

[495] *Sambiaggio* case, *supra* note 489, at 512–13.   [496] See *ibid.*, 524.

[497] See *Réclamations Britanniques dans la Zone Espagnole du Maroc* (UK v. Spain, 1924), II *RIAA* 617, 642.

[498] Draft Articles, *supra* note 249, at 52.

387. The ILC noted that Ruritanian responsibility may be engaged not only as a result of failure to adopt measures of vigilance in respect of insurgent acts against Arcadian interests but also because of improper failure to punish culprits after the event.[499] Once more (see *supra* 372), an issue of pardons or amnesties given to perpetrators arises. The ILC dwelt on the topic only in an earlier Report,[500] but there is no escaping it. Much support exists for the view that no responsibility will be incurred by Ruritania towards Arcadia when a general amnesty is decreed to all former insurgents, in order to foster national reconciliation.[501] We shall come back to the theme of amnesties *infra* 633 *et seq.*

(c) *Force majeure*

388. Ruritania cannot realistically be expected 'to adopt preventive measures with respect to acts of armed groups carried out in the part of the territory over which the government does not exercise effective control'.[502]

389. Loss of governmental effective control over territory can be described as *force majeure*. Article 23 of the ILC Draft Articles precludes wrongfulness of an act owing to *force majeure*, defined as 'the occurrence of an irresistible force or the occurrence of an unforeseen event, beyond the control of the State, making it materially impossible in the circumstances to perform the obligation'.[503] The ILC expressly mentioned that material impossibility of performance of an obligation giving rise to *force majeure* may be due to 'loss of control over a portion of a State's territory as a result of an insurrection'.[504]

390. The construct of *force majeure* in case of insurrection has its roots in international arbitrations, especially the 1923 Award (by M. Huber) in the *Zone Espagnol de Maroc* case.[505] Still, *force majeure* cannot be used as an omnibus reason, relieving Ruritania of responsibility whenever an insurgency flares up.[506] There must be a link of causality between the *force majeure* and the failure to fulfil Ruritanian obligations.[507] *Force majeure* will extricate Ruritania from responsibility in a NIAC only 'in so far as it

---

[499] *Ibid.*   [500] Report of the ILC, 27th Session, *supra* note 450, at 98.

[501] See E. Jiménez de Aréchaga, 'International Responsibility', *Manual of Public International Law* 531, 563 (M. Sørensen ed., 1968).

[502] Vierucci, *supra* note 146, at 257.   [503] Draft Articles, *supra* note 249, at 27.

[504] *Ibid.*, 76.

[505] *Réclamations Britanniques dans la Zone Espagnol de Maroc, supra* note 497, at 642.

[506] See F.I. Paddeu, 'A Genealogy of *Force Majeure* in International Law', 82 *BYBIL* 381, 493 (2011).

[507] See B. Cheng, *General Principles of Law as Applied by International Courts and Tribunals* 228 (1987).

may be fitted into the rule of due diligence',[508] viz. when the Ruritanian Government is unable to maintain any semblance of law and order in areas over which it has lost effective control to the insurgents.

391. Material impossibility of carrying out an obligation, giving rise to *force majeure*, may be temporary. As soon as the *non-possumus* circumstances of *force majeure* cease to exist, the Ruritanian Government must resume the performance of its obligations (which were merely suspended).[509] Thus, if territory under the effective control of insurgents has been recovered, the *force majeure* vocabulary is no longer valid.

B. Successful insurgents

(a) A new Government

(i) Attribution of insurgent acts

392. In the event that insurgents prosper in a NIAC and crush the incumbent Government – coming to power as the new Government of Ruritania – the legal analysis is radically altered. As noted (*supra* 217), Article 10(1) of the ILC Draft Articles sets forth that the conduct of an insurrectional movement which becomes the new Government of a State 'shall be considered an act of that State under international law'. This is an unusual rule, 'since it determines the attribution of conduct not by events at the time of that conduct but by reference to later contingencies'.[510]

393. Although the ILC's text relating to successful insurgents has been subjected to some criticism,[511] it is certainly a snapshot of customary international law. In a 1928 Arbitral Award, in the *Pinson* case (between France and Mexico), the Arbitrator, J.H.W. Verzijl had already held that it is 'incontestable' that a State must assume responsibility for the acts of successful revolutionaries.[512] Indeed, given the continuity between the insurgent movement and the new Government, it 'would be anomalous' (in the words of the ILC) if that Government could avoid attribution to the State of its own actions committed during the NIAC.[513] The legal foundation of Article 10(1) is that 'the insurgents who finally succeed and become the political authority of the State are estopped from disclaiming

---

[508] C. Eagleton, *The Responsibility of States in International Law* 156 (1928).
[509] See S. Hentrei and X. Soley, 'Force Majeure', IV *MPEPIL* 151, 153.
[510] J. Crawford and S. Olleson, 'The Nature and Forms of International Responsibility', *International Law* 441, 455 (3rd edn, M.D. Evans ed., 2010).
[511] See J. D'Aspremont, 'Rebellion and State Responsibility: Wrongdoing by Democratically Elected Insurgents', 58 *ICLQ* 427–42 (2009).
[512] *Pinson (France)* v. *Mexico* (1928), V *RIAA* 327, 353.
[513] Draft Articles, *supra* note 249, at 50.

their responsibility by the plea that the injury was caused by private individuals'.[514]

(ii) Retroactivity

394. How far back does the retroactive assumption of responsibility by a successful insurrectional movement go? The ILC explained that 'the threshold for the application of the laws of armed conflict contained in Additional Protocol II of 1977 may be taken as a guide'.[515] Does this signify that the new Government incurs responsibility for the acts of the insurgents only from the moment when they crossed the second threshold, and not from the inception of the NIAC (i.e. when the first threshold had been crossed, as per Common Article 3)? Such a solution would be meretricious. There is every reason to believe that breaches of Common Article 3 by the successful insurgents, which predate the crossing of the second threshold, ought to be attributed to the new Government no less than violations of AP/II.[516] Differently put, the attribution of the insurgents' wrongdoing to the new Government must cover all their acts 'ab initio',[517] namely, from the onset of the NIAC.

(iii) Limitations

395. The ILC deliberately used the phrase 'conduct of an insurrectional movement' in Article 10(1). There are two aspects here. The first is that the retroactive qualification as acts of State 'only concerns the conduct of the movement as such and not the individual acts of members of the movement, acting in their own capacity'.[518] Admittedly, the distinction between acts of insurgents *qua* insurgents and their private acts is not easy to draw in practice (see *supra* 47). For instance, if a foreign bank is robbed by insurgents during a NIAC, it may prove impossible to verify whether the crime was committed for private ends or in order to grease the wheels of the insurgency.

396. The second aspect is that the phrase 'conduct of an insurrectional movement' does not encompass insurgents who only support the movement but do not really belong to it. In the *Short* case of 1987, the Iran–US

---

[514] See E. Jiménez de Aréchaga, 'International Law in the Past Third of a Century', 159 *RCADI* 1, 285 (1978).

[515] Draft Articles, *supra* note 249, at 51.

[516] See M. Sassòli, 'State Responsibility for Violations of International Humanitarian Law', 846 *IRRC* 401, 410 (2002).

[517] The phrase '*ab initio*' was first used by Umpire Plumley in the *Bolívar Railway Company* case (Mixed Claims Commission Great Britain–Venezuela, 1903), IX *RIAA* 445, 453. The ILC quoted the relevant sentence with approval: Draft Articles, *supra* note 249, at 51.

[518] Draft Articles, *ibid.*, 50.

Claims Tribunal distinguished between 'agents' of a revolutionary movement and mere 'supporters' of the revolution, saying:

> The acts of supporters of a revolution cannot be attributed to the government following the success of the revolution just as the acts of supporters of an existing government are not attributable to the government.[519]

(iv) Dual attribution

397. The retroactive attribution to Ruritania of the acts of a successful insurgent movement is additional to – and coexists alongside with – the attribution of the acts of the incumbent Government prior to its overthrow by the insurgents.[520] The reason is plain: at the time when the acts of the former Government were committed, they were acts of State. The subsequent collapse of that Government does not invalidate the earlier attribution of its acts to Ruritania.

398. It follows that, if insurgents in a NIAC in Ruritania attack the agents, nationals or property of Arcadia – and the incumbent Ruritanian Government fails to take feasible precautions to protect the Arcadian interests – the success of the insurrection will lead to a dual responsibility on the part of Ruritania towards Arcadia: both for the attack itself (the successful insurgents' act of commission) and for the lack of vigilance (the ousted Government's act of omission).

399. The rule that Ruritania bears responsibility simultaneously for acts committed by both sides in the NIAC – the incumbent Government (subsequently deposed) and the insurgents (ultimately victorious) – is not in contradiction to the principle that a State may have only one Government at any given time (see *supra* 308). The success of the insurgency does not annul the fact that formerly another Government was in effective control of the territory of Ruritania.

400. The dual attribution and responsibility rule has deep roots in international law. In 1903, Umpire Plumley had already pronounced in the *Puerto Cabello* case that a State may be 'liable for the acts of successful revolutionaries and for the acts of the titular government as well, the liability in either case being predicated upon the same state of evidential facts'.[521] The rule has been reconfirmed in 1987 by the Iran–US Claims Tribunal (relying on an earlier version of the ILC Draft Articles) in the *Short* case:

---

[519] *Short (US)* v. *Iran* (Iran–US Claims Tribunal, 1987), 82 *ILR* 149, 161.

[520] See Draft Articles, *supra* note 249, at 52.

[521] *Puerto Cabello and Valencia Company* case (Mixed Claims Commission Great Britain–Venezuela, 1903), IX *RIAA* 510, 513.

Where a revolution leads to the establishment of a new government the State is held responsible for the acts of the overthrown government insofar as the latter maintained control of the situation. The successor government is also held responsible for the acts imputable to the revolutionary movement which established it, even if those acts occurred prior to its establishment, as a consequence of the continuity existing between the new organization of the State and the organization of the revolutionary movement.[522]

(v) Change of Governments

401. Attribution of the acts of successful insurgents to Ruritania happens only when the insurgents actually replace the incumbent Government with their own new regime. The ILC found it necessary to remark that if the Government survives, yet – in the interest of national conciliation – is reconstructed by drawing into it some leaders of the former insurrectional movement, Ruritania does not assume retroactive responsibility for the acts of the insurgents.[523] Probably, this ought also to be the rule when the insurgents gain autonomy in part of the country.[524]

402. Should a successful insurgent Government in Ruritania be displaced after a space of time, the slate cannot be wiped clean. Even if the pre-NIAC *ancien régime* manages to return to power, there is no way to turn the clock back in terms of State responsibility. As long as it lasted, the insurgent Government (and no other) was the Government of the State and the acts attributed to it remain acts of State.

(b) A new State

403. If a NIAC precipitates an implosion of Ruritania, and a new State (Apollonia) is created by the successful insurgents on part of the original Ruritanian territory, Article 10(2) of the ILC Draft Articles provides that the conduct of the insurrectional movement will be considered an act of Apollonia (*supra* 217). Obviously, this conduct cannot be attributed to Ruritania, and its attribution to Apollonia is justified by the continuity between the insurrectional movement (in Ruritania) and the eventual new State (Apollonia).[525] In contrast to the situation of a new Government in Ruritania – established by successful insurgents – there is no dual attribution and responsibility rule (see *supra* 397 *et seq.*) in the case

---

[522] *Short (US)* v. *Iran, supra* note 519, at 160.
[523] See Draft Articles, *supra* note 249, at 51.
[524] See K. Zemanek, 'The Legal Foundations of the International System', 266 *RCADI* 9, 261 (1997) re Bosnia/Herzegovina.
[525] See Draft Articles, *supra* note 249, at 51.

of a new State. Apollonia will not assume responsibility for any acts undertaken by the Ruritanian Government to suppress the insurgency that brought about Apollonian independence.[526] Should Ruritania survive, it will bear responsibility for any wrongdoing to Arcadia by its official organs.

404. The ILC's reliance on the principle of continuity (between the insurrectional movement and Apollonia) cannot be contested, although arguably it is 'based on a logical inference rather than on established practice'.[527] There is a problem when Apollonia emerges as a new State thanks to the joint efforts of several insurgent groups, whereas only one of them actually forms its Government. The ILC has not dealt with this specific issue. There is some tepid scholarly support for the assumption of responsibility by Apollonia for the internationally wrongful acts of all the rebel groups,[528] but the idea does not sit well with the principle of continuity.

VI. Foreign intervention

A. Responsibility of the foreign State for acts of its organs

405. If Utopia intervenes militarily in the Ruritanian NIAC at the request of the Ruritanian Government, the question arises whether Ruritania incurs any responsibility (vis-à-vis Arcadia) for acts of the Utopian armed forces in suppressing the insurgency. In Article 6 of the Draft Articles, the ILC tackled the issue of organs placed at the disposal of another State.[529] The ILC was firmly of the opinion that, when Utopian armed forces are sent to assist Ruritania for any purpose, they are not placed at the latter's disposal: they remain under the authority of Utopia and do not become subject to the governmental authority of Ruritania.[530] Utopia consequently bears full responsibility (towards Arcadia) for the perpetration of internationally wrongful acts by its own armed forces in the process of quelling the insurgency within the Ruritanian territory.

---

[526] See Crawford, *supra* note 295, at 276.
[527] See M.G. Kohen, 'Succession of States in the Field of International Responsibility: The Case for Codification', *Perspectives of International Law in the 21st Century: Liber Amicorum Professor Christian Dominicé* 161, 172 (2012).
[528] See P. Dumberry, *State Succession to International Responsibility* 246 (2007).
[529] Draft Articles, *supra* note 249, at 26.   [530] *Ibid.*, 44.

B. Vicarious responsibility

406. Both Utopia and Ruritania must be careful not to shoulder what is sometimes called 'derived'[531] – or 'vicarious'[532] – responsibility for acts of organs of the other State. Article 16 of the Draft Articles lays down that '[a] State which assists another State in the commission of an internationally wrongful act by the latter is internationally responsible for doing so', provided that this is done with full knowledge of the circumstances.[533] The ILC cited the example of 'assisting in the destruction of property belonging to nationals of a third country'.[534]

407. The subject of destruction of foreign property must be treated with caution. In an armed conflict (whether an IAC or a NIAC), it is not an internationally wrongful act to cause destruction of civilian property when mounting military operations – such as shelling and bombing – against the foe, unless the destruction (i) consists of wanton acts which are unnecessary from a military standpoint[535] (see *infra* 595–6); (ii) is in breach of the principle of proportionality (see *infra* 693–4); or (iii) affects categories of property, which are the subject of special protection (e.g., hospitals or places of worship).

---

[531] See *ibid.*, 65.
[532] See O. de Frouville, 'Attribution of Conduct to the State: Private Individuals', *The Law of International Responsibility, supra* note 278, at 257, 276.
[533] Draft Articles, *supra* note 249, at 27.   [534] *Ibid.*, 66.
[535] See VIII *Digest of International Law* 825 (M.M. Whiteman ed., 1967).

8

The principal LONIAC treaty provisions

408. The present chapter will be devoted to elaborating LONIAC norms promulgated in (i) Common Article 3 and (ii) AP/II. Although these instruments go back to 1949 and 1977 respectively, they are still the principal articulations of LONIAC today. Chapters 9 and 10 will deal with other treaty texts relevant to NIACs.

I. Common Article 3

A. The text

409. The full text of Common Article 3 reads:

> In the case of armed conflict not of an international character occurring in the territory of one of the High Contracting Parties, each Party to the conflict shall be bound to apply, as a minimum, the following provisions:
> (1) Persons taking no active part in the hostilities, including members of armed forces who have laid down their arms and those placed *hors de combat* by sickness, wounds, detention, or any other cause, shall in all circumstances be treated humanely, without any adverse distinction founded on race, colour, religion or faith, sex, birth or wealth, or any other similar criteria.
> To this end the following acts are and shall remain prohibited at any time and in any place whatsoever with respect to the above-mentioned persons:
> (a) violence to life and person, in particular murder of all kinds, mutilation, cruel treatment and torture;
> (b) taking of hostages;
> (c) outrages upon personal dignity, in particular humiliating and degrading treatment;
> (d) the passing of sentences and the carrying out of executions without previous judgment pronounced by a regularly constituted court, affording all the judicial guarantees which are recognized as indispensable by civilized peoples.

(2) The wounded and sick shall be collected and cared for. An impartial humanitarian body, such as the International Committee of the Red Cross, may offer its services to the Parties to the conflict.

The Parties to the conflict should further endeavour to bring into force, by means of special agreements, all or part of the other provisions of the present Convention.

The application of the preceding provisions shall not affect the legal status of the Parties to the conflict.[536]

B. Analysis

410. As soon as a NIAC comes into existence – and as long as it lasts – LONIAC becomes operative in keeping with Common Article 3. Two preliminary comments are appropriate:

(i) Common Article 3 applies to 'each Party to the conflict' (cf. *supra* 93). That is to say that the obligations created in Common Article 3 are equal for both sides in an insurgency, notwithstanding the innate imbalance between the Parties from the vantage point of domestic law (see *supra* 37). Even scholars who are inclined to seriously mull over a proposal 'to abandon the axiom of the equality of belligerents in NIACs' do not contest that general State practice confirms that axiom.[537]

(ii) The obligations created for 'each Party to the conflict' in Common Article 3 are absolute in the sense that they apply independently of the execution of obligations by the other side, i.e. irrespective of reciprocity.[538]

411. The text of Common Article 3 has developed a vibrancy of its own, cresting with the *Nicaragua* Judgment's recognition of this clause as an epitome of 'minimum rules' applicable in any armed conflict under customary international law (*supra* 30). Whether or not originally intended

---

[536] Geneva Convention (I) for the Amelioration of the Condition of the Wounded and Sick in Armed Forces in the Field, 1949, *Laws of Armed Conflicts* 459, 461–2; Geneva Convention (II) for the Amelioration of the Condition of Wounded, Sick and Shipwrecked Members of Armed Forces at Sea, 1949, *ibid.*, 485, 487–8; Geneva Convention (III) Relative to the Treatment of Prisoners of War, 1949, *ibid.*, 507, 512–13; Geneva Convention (IV) Relative to the Protection of Civilian Persons in Time of War, 1949, *ibid.*, 575, 580–1.

[537] M. Sassòli, 'Introducing a Sliding-Scale of Obligations to Address the Fundamental Inequality between Armed Groups and States?', 882 *IRRC* 426, 427–30 (2011).

[538] *Commentary, I Geneva Convention, supra* note 5, at 51.

by the drafters to do so,[539] Common Article 3 certainly represents an irreducible bedrock of any cogent law of armed conflict. Yet, being unimpeachable does not mean that the text is immaculate.

412. The capstone of Common Article 3 is the requirement of humane treatment. This may sound all-embracing, but only two specific categories of protected persons are bracketed: (i) those who do not take an active part in the hostilities, and (ii) those who, having taken part in the fighting, are *hors de combat*. The first class of protected persons relates to persons who are true civilians (see *supra* 185), namely, non-fighters who may chance to be in the wrong place at the wrong time during a NIAC and are caught in the cross-fire of hostilities. The second class of protected persons consists of those who are *hors de combat*, a phrase defined *infra* 518. Persons who are taking an active part in the hostilities in a NIAC are not covered, and they therefore 'fall outside the protective ambit' of Common Article 3.[540]

413. Common Article 3 does not regulate the conduct of hostilities between the opposing sides in a NIAC, nor does it safeguard the civilian population against the effects of hostilities.[541] As for the protection that the clause does provide, '[t]he obligations of Article 3 are cast in such general terms and leave so many things unsaid that they cannot, even under the best of circumstances, be an adequate guide' in a NIAC.[542] There are two intrinsic drawbacks: glaring omissions[543] and the use of abstract generalities.

414. The efficacy of Common Article 3 is impaired by leaving undefined in Paragraph (1) critical expressions, principally, 'torture' and 'taking of hostages'. Along the same lines, when Paragraph (2) sets forth that the wounded and sick 'shall be collected and cared for', the wording – even if it would be an exaggeration to call it 'cryptic'[544] – is inadequate. There are no concrete guidelines as to what care for the wounded and sick entails, and there are no stipulations protecting medical personnel or facilities.

---

[539] See T. Meron, 'The Geneva Conventions as Customary Law', 81 *AJIL* 348, 356 (1987).

[540] J.E. Bond, 'Application of the Law of War to Internal Conflicts', 3 *Ga.JICL* 345, 355 (1973).

[541] See A. Cassese, 'A Tentative Appraisal of the Old and the New Humanitarian Law of Armed Conflict', *The New Humanitarian Law of Armed Conflict* 461, 492 (A. Cassese ed., 1979).

[542] Baxter, *supra* note 252, at 528–9.

[543] See A. Schlögel, 'Civil War', 108 *IRRC* 123, 132 (1970).

[544] W.A. Solf, 'Development of the Protection of the Wounded, Sick and Shipwrecked under the Protocols Additional to the 1949 Geneva Conventions', *Studies and Essays on International Humanitarian Law and Red Cross Principles in Honour of Jean Pictet* 237, 239 (C. Swinarski ed., 1984).

It is difficult to discern how the wounded and sick can be properly cared for if neither the hospital in which they are treated nor the hospital staff is free from the danger of attack.[545]

415. Common Article 3 introduces the right of an impartial humanitarian body, such as ICRC, to offer its services to the Parties to the conflict. But the entitlement is quite brittle. First, the ICRC (or its counterpart) is not authorized to determine in a binding way that a NIAC under Common Article 3 exists.[546] Second, what the ICRC's contribution will be is not open-and-shut: the tender of the offer of services is optional, just as its acceptance is not obligatory.[547] Third, the text refers to the Parties to the conflict (in the plural), but does that mean that both have to respond affirmatively to the ICRC's offer? It stands to reason that the incumbent Government's reaction has a priority in this regard compared to that of the insurgents.

416. Humane treatment of captive insurgents does not signify that they cannot be prosecuted and even sentenced to death. As already pointed out (*supra* 53), captive insurgents may be subjected to penal legal proceedings – under the domestic legal system – not only for war crimes or ordinary crimes, but even for mere participation in the hostilities (e.g., the killing of an adversary in an open encounter). The only condition is that sentence will be meted out by 'a regularly constituted court', following a fair trial 'affording all the judicial guarantees'.

417. It is not self-explanatory what 'a regularly constituted court' is within the State apparatus. An ordinary military tribunal is certainly included.[548] But does the phrase make allowance for a court established by the incumbent Government under emergency martial law adopted in response to the outbreak of the insurgency? It is also left to the reader to guess what specific judicial guarantees the framers had in mind. The only taboo that one can be confident about is that of sending an insurgent to the gallows without due process of law.

418. Common Article 3 ignores the practical complications of convening 'a regularly constituted court' – and ensuring judicial guarantees – when the boot is on the other foot, viz. when trials of Government

---

[545] See J.E. Bond, 'Internal Conflict and Article Three of the Geneva Conventions', 48 *Den.LJ* 263, 280 (1971–2).

[546] See Meron, *supra* note 256, at 50.

[547] See G. Abi-Saab, 'Non-International Armed Conflicts', *International Dimensions of Humanitarian Law* 217, 224 (UNESCO, 1988).

[548] See L.C. Green, *Essays on the Modern Law of Warfare* 400 (2nd edn, 1999).

troops or officials are held by insurgent armed groups (especially if these armed groups do not control any territory, relying on hit-and-run guerrilla tactics that lend them mobility and enable them to avoid pitched battles).[549] Judging by the unqualified manner in which the provision is couched, if the insurgents are unable to satisfy the conditions of convening 'a regularly constituted court' – and ensuring judicial guarantees – they are precluded from initiating prosecutions and trials: once trials are held by the insurgents, they must be compatible with the conditions as prescribed.[550]

II. AP/II

A. Comparisons

(a) AP/II and Common Article 3

419. AP/II complements Common Article 3, but it has a narrower scope of application, inasmuch as it comes into play solely when a NIAC crosses the second threshold. Since the two texts are not coterminous in their field of operation, AP/II cannot be regarded as a mere interpretation of Common Article 3.[551]

420. The schematic format of AP/II (within its allotted scope of application) rests on three themes: (i) humane treatment; (ii) wounded, sick and shipwrecked; and (iii) civilian population. The purpose is to leaven existing protection, as provided by Common Article 3, with additional guarantees.

421. Unlike Common Article 3, only the nucleus of AP/II is deemed declaratory of customary international law (see the *Tadić* dictum *supra* 30), and not the instrument in its entirety. To the extent that AP/II is not declaratory, it is binding only on Contracting Parties. Common Article 3 – with its wider scope of application and overall customary status – continues to be in force in every NIAC, whether or not AP/II is applicable as well (see *supra* 121).

---

[549] See A.P. Rubin, 'The Status of Rebels under the Geneva Conventions of 1949', 21 *ICLQ* 472, 485 (1972).

[550] See G.I.A.D. Draper, 'The Geneva Conventions of 1949', 114 *RCADI* 63, 90–1 (1965).

[551] See R. Abi-Saab, 'Human Rights and Humanitarian Law in Internal Conflicts', *Human Rights and Humanitarian Law: The Quest for Universality* 107, 113 (D. Warner ed., 1997).

(b) AP/II and AP/I

422. AP/II looks like a condensed version of the substance of AP/I, jointly formulated in 1977. Some IAC themes featuring in AP/I (such as civil defence[552] or medical aircraft[553]) were discarded in AP/II because of their palpable irrelevance to NIACs. But this does not account for all the dissimilarities between AP/I and AP/II. When set side by side, it becomes obvious that AP/II is flawed in five momentous respects compared to AP/I.

423. First, some rudimentary rules of IAC *jus in bello* – characteristic of AP/I – are sorely missing from the text of AP/II. Embarrassing lacunae are the prohibition of indiscriminate attacks;[554] the requirement of proportionality in collateral damage to civilians;[555] the need to take feasible precautions in attack;[556] and the prohibition of perfidy.[557] As we shall see (*infra* 689 *et seq.*), these gaps in AP/II have been filled by subsequent customary international law. Another gap, probably taken care of in evolving custom (see *infra* 679), is the ban on the use of 'human shields'.[558]

424. Second, the canopy of protection in AP/II is spread only over selected civilian objects, such as objects indispensable to the survival of the civilian population (Article 14, *infra* 466) or cultural property (Article 16, *infra* 470). Contrary to Article 52 of AP/I,[559] AP/II 'does not set out to protect civilian objects generally'.[560] This, too, has in the meantime been corrected by customary law (see *infra* 683).

425. Third, certain AP/I rules – like protection of the natural environment[561] or the prohibition of attacking persons parachuting from an aircraft in distress[562] – did not find their way into AP/II, and have not been endorsed as custom by subsequent general State practice in NIACs.

426. Fourth, there is a patent absence in AP/II of detailed definitions of pivotal expressions (such as wounded, sick and shipwrecked). As we shall see (*infra* 511), this impels turning for enlightenment in AP/I where the same phraseology is enlarged upon.

427. Fifth, AP/II often redacts elaborate provisions of AP/I, paring them down to essentials. As a sample, one can juxtapose the respective

---

[552] AP/I, *supra* note 21, at 742–6 (Articles 61–7).   [553] *Ibid.*, 725–7 (Articles 24–30).
[554] *Ibid.*, 736 (Article 51(4)).   [555] *Ibid.* (Article 51(5)(b)).
[556] *Ibid.*, 739–40 (Article 57).   [557] *Ibid.*, 730 (Article 37(1)).
[558] *Ibid.*, 736 (Article 51(7)).   [559] *Ibid.*, 737.
[560] *Commentary on the Additional Protocols, supra* note 95, at 1462.
[561] AP/I, *supra* note 21, at 730, 738 (Articles 35(3), 55).   [562] *Ibid.*, 732 (Article 42).

sections devoted to the protection of wounded, sick and shipwrecked in AP/I[563] and in AP/II (see *infra* 452 *et seq.*).

428. Paring down is not the same as toning down. It is sometimes alleged that AP/II's clauses (intended for NIACs) are necessarily less imperative in tone than their counterpart AP/I provisions (aimed at IACs).[564] However, generally speaking, when AP/II avoids unmitigated language in the regulation of NIACs, the drafting technique concerning IACs is not dissimilar. We shall take three examples that have been wrongly cited in the literature:

(i) Paragraph (3)(b) Article 4 of AP/II (cited *infra* 431) says: 'all appropriate steps shall be taken to facilitate the reunion of families temporarily separated'. The obligation is not overly rigorous, but the flexibility matches the approach of Article 74 of AP/I (where the wording is: 'shall facilitate in every possible way the reunion of families').[565]

(ii) Paragraph (2) of Article 7 of AP/II (*infra* 453) curbs its mandatory language (about the treatment of the wounded, sick and shipwrecked) by limiting it 'to the fullest extent practicable'. This opens up a possible loophole. Yet, exactly the same phraseology appears in the counterpart clause of Article 10(2) of AP/I.[566]

(iii) Article 8 of AP/II (*infra* 454) also restrains its edict (as regards search and collection of the wounded, sick and shipwrecked) with an 'all possible measures' qualifier. Still, the expression originates in Article 15 of Geneva Convention (I) of 1949.[567]

429. There are occasions on which AP/II (by being more concise than AP/I) eliminates an important saving clause, thus preserving the original obligation in a more pristine form. A singular illustration can be found in the matter of 'scorched earth' as a method of warfare. Such a policy is expressly permitted in IACs under Article 54(5) of AP/I, as a derogation from the prohibition of destruction of objects indispensable to the survival of the civilian population (provided that it is carried out as a defensive measure within the national territory of a Belligerent Party).[568] Article 14 of AP/II (*infra* 466), in following the gist of

---

[563] *Ibid.*, 718–24 (Articles 8–20).

[564] Cf. S. Sivakumaran, 'Re-Envisaging the International Law of Internal Armed Conflict', 22 *EJIL* 219, 258 (2011).

[565] AP/I, *supra* note 21, at 748.   [566] *Ibid.*, 720.

[567] Geneva Convention I, *supra* note 536, at 466.   [568] AP/I, *supra* note 21, at 737–8.

the prohibition of destruction of objects indispensable to the survival of the civilian population, pretermits the derogation clause. As a result, 'scorched earth' policy, although acceptable in certain instances in IACs, is wholly inadmissible in NIACs.[569]

430. To cap it all, AP/II may even employ more exacting language than AP/I. Thus, as we shall see in the context of child-soldiers (*infra* 443), the provision of Article 77(2) of AP/I is qualified by 'all feasible measures', while Paragraph (3)(c) of Article 4 of AP/II imposes a strict obligation.

B. Humane treatment

(a) Fundamental guarantees

431. Article 4 of AP/II[570] recites fundamental guarantees:

1. All persons who do not take a direct part or who have ceased to take part in hostilities, whether or not their liberty has been restricted, are entitled to respect for their person, honour and convictions and religious practices. They shall in all circumstances be treated humanely, without any adverse distinction. It is prohibited to order that there shall be no survivors.
2. Without prejudice to the generality of the foregoing, the following acts against the persons referred to in paragraph 1 are and shall remain prohibited at any time and in any place whatsoever:
   (a) violence to the life, health and physical or mental well-being of persons, in particular murder as well as cruel treatment such as torture, mutilation or any form of corporal punishment;
   (b) collective punishments;
   (c) taking of hostages;
   (d) acts of terrorism;
   (e) outrages upon personal dignity, in particular humiliating and degrading treatment, rape, enforced prostitution and any form of indecent assault;
   (f) slavery and the slave trade in all their forms;
   (g) pillage;
   (h) threats to commit any of the foregoing acts.

432. Paragraph (1) of Article 4 amplifies the protection of persons who are not (or no longer) fighters, which is already embedded in Common Article 3 (*supra* 409). For the first time, the need to respect convictions

---

[569] See *Commentary on the Additional Protocols, supra* note 95, at 1459.
[570] AP/II, *supra* note 6, at 777–8.

and religion is adverted to. 'Convictions' do not have to be religious, and the net of protection is also cast over agnostics and atheists.[571]

433. The last sentence of Paragraph (1) of Article 4 forbids ordering that there shall be no survivors. Here AP/II follows IAC *jus in bello*, specifically Hague Regulation 23(d) of 1899/1907 prohibiting a declaration that no quarter will be given.[572] *Au fond*, the idea is that fighters must be given an opportunity to surrender. A no-quarter repudiation gives a boost to the protection of those who are *hors de combat* (*infra* 518) in that it protects them even in advance, before they have acquired that status.[573]

434. Paragraph (2) of Article 4 reproduces some injunctions (e.g., against mutilation or the taking of hostages) appearing in Common Article 3, doing so in the same succinct language and without embellishment. That is unfortunate. Why is the sheer repetition of a norm necessary, taking into account that Common Article 3 continues anyhow to be applicable side by side with AP/II? And in what way does a duplication of the wording of Common Article 3 develop and supplement it, as AP/II is supposed to do?

435. Genuine build-up of the texture of Common Article 3 is evinced by Paragraph (2) of Article 4 in the allusion to the mental (in addition to the physical) well-being of the victims of violence, and in the interdiction of corporal punishment as an extrapolation of cruel treatment. Stark additions to Common Article 3 are the proscriptions of collective punishments; acts of terrorism; slavery and the slave trade; and pillage.

436. The meaning of slavery and acts of terrorism will be explored *infra* 525 *et seq.* and 539 *et seq.* Pillage is imported from IAC *jus in bello* (starting with Hague Regulation 28[574]), where it means looting or plundering property for private ends.[575]

(i) Collective punishments and belligerent reprisals

437. In the *Fofana et al.* case of 2008, the Appeals Chamber of the SCSL held:

---

[571] See H. McCoubrey, *International Humanitarian Law: Modern Developments in the Limitation of Warfare* 220 (2nd edn, 1998).

[572] Hague Regulations Respecting the Laws and Customs of War on Land, Annexed to Hague Convention (II) of 1899 and Hague Convention (IV) of 1907, *Laws of Armed Conflicts* 60, 66, 73.

[573] See *Commentary on the Additional Protocols, supra* note 95, at 1371.

[574] Hague Regulations Respecting the Laws and Customs of War on Land, *supra* note 572, at 74.

[575] See G. Carducci, 'Pillage', VIII *MPEPIL* 299, *id.*

The prohibition on collective punishments must be understood in its broadest sense so as to include not only penalties imposed during normal judicial processes, such as sentences rendered after due process of law, but also any other kind of sanction such as a fine, confinement or a loss of property or rights.[576]

The Chamber added that collective punishments must not be confused with targeting civilians in hostilities.[577]

438. Collective punishments should also be differentiated from belligerent reprisals. Admittedly, the ICRC maintains that the unconditional prohibition of collective punishments 'is virtually equivalent to prohibiting "reprisals" against protected persons'.[578] A specific rule against the use of belligerent reprisals in NIACs makes headway in the ICRC study of customary IHL, even separately from – and in addition to – the proscription of collective punishments.[579] However, this is a very controversial position.[580]

439. Belligerent reprisals were defined by an ICTY Trial Chamber in the 2007 *Martić* case as acts resorted to by one party to the conflict 'which would otherwise be unlawful, but which are rendered lawful by the fact that they are taken in response to a violation of that law committed by the other' party.[581] Belligerent reprisals are not forbidden as such either in Common Article 3 or in AP/II. As for AP/II, this was 'clearly not an oversight' but a result of disagreements among the framers.[582]

440. Specific prohibitions of the use of belligerent reprisals in NIACs appear in two treaty contexts:

(aa) Paragraph (4) of Article 4 of the CPCP (cited *infra* 486) disallows 'any act directed by way of reprisals against cultural property'.
(bb) Article 3(7) of Amended Protocol II to the CCCW forbids in all circumstances to direct mines, booby-traps and other devices 'by way of reprisals' against civilians or civilian objects.[583]

Absent such a concrete treaty provision, there is no evidence that belligerent reprisals are unlawful in NIACs. Even scholars stoutly opposed to

---

[576] *Prosecutor* v. *Fofana et al.* (SCSL, Appeals Chamber, 2008), para. 222.
[577] *Ibid.*, para. 230. [578] *Commentary on the Additional Protocols*, *supra* note 95, at 1374.
[579] I *Customary International Humanitarian Law*, *supra* note 267, at 374, 526.
[580] See D. Turns, 'Implementation and Compliance', *Perspectives on the ICRC Study on Customary International Humanitarian Law*, *supra* note 88, at 354, 370–1.
[581] *Prosecutor* v. *Martić* (ICTY, Trial Chamber, 2007), para. 465.
[582] S. Darcy, 'The Evolution of the Law of Belligerent Reprisals', 175 *Mil.LR* 184, 218 (2003).
[583] Amended Protocol II to the CCCW, *supra* note 67, at 196, 198.

belligerent reprisals on grounds of policy concede that the general practice of States indicates that recourse to them 'continues unabated'.[584]

(ii) The protection of children

441. Paragraph (3) of Article 4 breaks new ground as regards the special protection of children. This is a salutary addition to Common Article 3, inasmuch as children are particularly vulnerable to the concatenation of events flowing from a NIAC. The protection of children has three different dimensions.

442. The first facet of the protection of children relates to care and aid as required. The formula is flexible, correlating care to individual needs in changing circumstances.[585] The concept of care explicitly embraces children's education (including religious education), as well as steps taken to facilitate the reunion of separated families.

443. The second matter that the framers of AP/II came to grips with is that of child-soldiers. This phenomenon has been brought into relief as a result of ferocious NIACs (primarily in Africa) revealing how the manipulation of children – turning them into relentless fighters lacking mature compunction – can exponentially increase savagery in hostilities. Paragraph (3)(c) of Article 4 decrees that 'children who have not attained the age of fifteen years shall neither be recruited in the armed forces or groups nor allowed to take part in hostilities'. The reference to 'armed forces or groups' blankets both governmental units and insurgent bands. The interdiction is absolute, and it stands out when compared to the counterpart IAC stipulation adopted at the same time.[586] In Article 77(2) of AP/I, the parallel obligation imposed on Belligerent Parties is merely to take 'all feasible measures' to prevent recruitment and participation in hostilities of children under the age of fifteen.[587] We shall revisit the subject of child-soldiers *infra* 496 *et seq.*

444. The third aspect of the protection of children is that Paragraph (3)(e) of Article 4 – although permitting the temporary removal of children from a sector in which hostilities are taking place to a safer area within the country – demands that this be done, whenever possible,

---

[584] F. Kalshoven, 'Belligerent Reprisals Revisited', *Reflections on the Law of War: Collected Essays* 759, 789 (2007).

[585] See *Commentary on the Additional Protocols, supra* note 95, at 1377.

[586] See P. Tavernier, 'Combatants and Non-Combatants', *The Gulf War of 1980–1988: The Iran-Iraq War in International Legal Perspective* 129, 141 (I.F. Dekker and H.H.G. Post eds., 1992).

[587] AP/I, *supra* note 21, at 750.

with the consent of their parents and on condition that the children are accompanied by persons responsible for their safety and well-being.

(b) Internment

445. Article 5[588] establishes minimum rules for the treatment of detainees and internees. The topic, which ought to be assessed in comparison with other norms governing detainees and internees in diverse contexts (both IACs and peacetime), will not be addressed in the present volume (see Preface).

(c) Penal prosecutions

446. Article 6[589] takes up the subject of prosecution and punishment of criminal offences related to NIAC. There is no reiteration of the idiom (used in Common Article 3) 'regularly constituted court', which is ill-suited to the setting of insurgents on the run (see *supra* 418). Instead, Paragraph (2) of Article 6 requires that a conviction be pronounced by 'a court offering the essential guarantees of independence and impartiality'. The shift from a 'regularly constituted court' to an independent and impartial tribunal – an expression borrowed from Article 14(1) of the 1966 International Covenant on Civil and Political Rights (cited *infra* 450) – is commendable. Nevertheless, impartiality of judges in NIAC proceedings cannot always be guaranteed (see *infra* 618). This is particularly true of a court set up by insurgents, but – even in a court functioning on behalf of the State – it is not easy to imagine that the judges would be totally detached from what is going on around them.

447. Common Article 3 posits that the 'regularly constituted court' must afford all judicial guarantees, without itemizing them. In producing a non-exhaustive list of 'essential guarantees of independence and impartiality', Paragraph (2) of Article 6 makes great strides towards clarifying a core issue. The ICRC position is that this paragraph 'explains common Art. 3(1)(d) rather than extends it'.[590] The implication is that Paragraph (2) serves as a magnifying glass, showing in fine detail the judicial guarantees already conceptualized in Common Article 3. But a better clue to the meaning of the judicial guarantees, as listed in AP/II, would be their human rights provenance (see *infra* 450).

---

[588] AP/II, *supra* note 6, at 778–9.   [589] *Ibid.*, 779–80.

[590] See *Elements of War Crimes under the Rome Statute of the International Criminal Court: Sources and Commentary* 124, 411–12 (ICRC, K. Dörmann ed., 2003).

448. The following essential guarantees are recapitulated in Paragraph (2) of Article 6: the principle of individual penal responsibility; the presumption of innocence; the right to be informed without delay of any charges and to defend oneself against them (before and during trial); the right to trial in one's presence; freedom from self-incrimination; and the constructs of *nullum crimen sine lege* and *nulla poena sine lege*. In the latter context, the turn of phrase is 'made by law' and 'according to law'. What law is meant where the insurgents are concerned? We have already raised the general question of the legal system applied by the insurgents in the territory under their control (see *supra* 145). The judicial guarantees provided by the insurgents will depend on the law that they subscribe to: either the general State law or self-made 'insurgents' law'.[591]

449. Paragraph (4) of Article 6 further forbids (i) pronouncing the death penalty on persons who were under the age of eighteen at the time of the commission of the offence, and (ii) imposing that sentence on pregnant women or mothers of young children.

450. For the most part, the recital of essential guarantees in Article 6 of AP/II is based on Articles 14 and 15 of the Covenant on Civil and Political Rights,[592] and sometimes the language of this mother-lode text is simply cloned. For instance, the requirement in Paragraph (2)(f) of Article 6 that no one shall 'be compelled to testify against himself or to confess guilt' repeats the very words of Article 14(3)(g) of the Covenant.

451. Still, not every judicial guarantee in the Covenant has been transplanted into AP/II. Thus, the fundamental principle against double jeopardy (*ne bis in idem*) – embodied in Article 14(7) of the Covenant – has not been incorporated in Article 6 of AP/II, since 'it could not apply between the courts of the government and the courts of the rebels'.[593] Moreover, the right to have conviction and sentence reviewed by a higher tribunal – affirmed in Article 14(5) of the Covenant – was excised from AP/II, principally because insurgent armed groups cannot be expected to set up courts of appeal.[594] All that Paragraph (3) of Article 6 of AP/II requires is to advise a convicted person on any judicial and other remedies available, plus the time limits within which they may be exercised.

---

[591] See P. Gejji, 'Can Insurgent Courts Be Legitimate within International Humanitarian Law?', 91 *TLR* 1525, 1548–9 (2012–13).

[592] International Covenant on Civil and Political Rights, *supra* note 233, at 182–3.

[593] K.J. Partsch, 'Humane Treatment', *New Rules for Victims of Armed Conflicts*, *supra* note 138, at 635, 650.

[594] See *ibid.*, 652.

C. Wounded, sick and shipwrecked

(a) Protection and care

452. Paragraph (1) of Article 7[595] is innovative compared to Common Article 3, in that the protection of the wounded and sick is extended to shipwrecked. The paragraph communicates that protection embraces all persons, 'whether or not they have taken part in the armed conflict', that is to say, whether they are fighters or civilians.

453. Paragraph (2) of Article 7 fleshes out the duty of care for the wounded, sick and shipwrecked:

> In all circumstances they shall be treated humanely and shall receive, to the fullest extent practicable and with the least possible delay, the medical care and attention required by their condition. There shall be no distinction among them founded on any grounds other than medical ones.

The last sentence hammers out an important obligation of treating equally those requiring medical attention, regardless of affiliation to any of the opposing sides in the NIAC.

454. Article 8[596] expounds the theme of collection of the wounded and sick mentioned already in Common Article 3 (to whom shipwrecked are now added):

> Whenever circumstances permit, and particularly after an engagement, all possible measures shall be taken, without delay, to search for and collect the wounded, sick and shipwrecked, to protect them against pillage and ill-treatment, to ensure their adequate care, and to search for the dead, prevent their being despoiled, and decently dispose of them.

This provision is predicated on Article 15 of Geneva Convention (I) of 1949, which deals with IACs (see *supra* 428).

455. Three points deserve notice:

(i) Article 8 supplements Common Article 3 by strengthening the protection offered, but it still does not pinpoint the scope of the verb 'collect' (is there also a duty to evacuate?[597]).

(ii) As far as pillage is concerned, Article 8 does not replicate the direct prohibition appearing in Paragraph 2(g) of Article 4 (*supra* 431).

---

[595] AP/II, *supra* note 6, at 780.   [596] *Ibid.*

[597] The ICRC thinks so (see I *Customary International Humanitarian Law, supra* note 267, at 396–7). *Per contra*, see J.P. Benoit, 'Mistreatment of the Wounded, Sick and Shipwrecked by the ICRC Study on Customary International Humanitarian Law', 11 *YIHL* 175, 199 (2008).

What Article 8 does is add an obligation 'to protect' the wounded, sick and shipwrecked from pillage or ill-treatment. The parties to the conflict are therefore bound to take proactive steps against any potential looters, be they fighters or civilians.[598]

(iii) Article 8 also proceeds into a hitherto untrodden avenue. This is the important subject of search for the dead, protection from despoiling their bodies and ensuring proper burial.

(b) Medical and religious personnel

456. Article 9[599] introduces the subject of the protection of medical and religious personnel that is conspicuously missing from Common Article 3. Pursuant to Paragraph (1), such personnel must be protected and granted all available help in the performance of their duties. Oddly, there are two omissions in the text compared to Article 11 of AP/II dealing with medical units and transports (*infra* 459): Paragraph (1) of Article 9 includes neither the words 'and shall not be the object of attack' nor the rider concerning loss of protection in case of the commission of hostile acts. Yet, the lapses must not be overrated. There is every reason to assume that the range of protection afforded by Articles 9 and 11 'is in fact the same'.[600]

457. Paragraph (2) of Article 9 accentuates that, in the performance of their duties, medical personnel 'may not be required to give priority to any person except on medical grounds'. In other words, medical personnel may not be ordered to handle lightly wounded fighters of their own party to the conflict first, while deferring treatment of more seriously injured fighters of the other side.[601] This duty of impartial triage ties in with the general obligation of making no distinction between patients other than on medical grounds (see Paragraph (2) of Article 7; *supra* 453).

458. Article 10[602] states in Paragraph (1) that '[u]nder no circumstances shall any person be punished for having carried out medical activities compatible with medical ethics, regardless of the person benefiting therefrom'. The standards of 'medical ethics' are not defined here or elsewhere.[603] Other paragraphs of Article 10 deal with disclosure to the authorities of information concerning the wounded and sick under the care of medical personnel: professional obligations must be respected,

---

[598] See Condorelli, *supra* note 23, at 93.   [599] AP/II, *supra* note 6, at 780.

[600] See *Commentary on the Additional Protocols*, *supra* note 95, at 1421.

[601] See *ibid.*, 1422.   [602] AP/II, *supra* note 6, at 780–1.

[603] See D. Smith, 'New Protections for Victims of International Armed Conflicts: The Proposed Ratification of Protocol II by the United States', 120 *MLR* 59, 70–2 (1988).

but this is subordinated to national law. The requirement of compliance with national law has been subjected to disparaging scholarly comments because a physician may be obliged by that law to report to the authorities, e.g., all cases involving gun wounds.[604]

459. Article 11[605] declares, in Paragraph (1), that '[m]edical units and transports shall be respected and protected at all times and shall not be the object of attack'. Under Paragraph (2), this protection shall cease if the medical units or transports 'are used to commit hostile acts, outside their humanitarian function', provided that a warning has been given and has remained unheeded.

(c) The emblem

460. Article 12[606] instructs that the distinctive emblem of the Red Cross and its counterparts (the Red Crescent and, under the subsequent Additional Protocol III,[607] also the Red Crystal) 'shall be displayed' by medical and religious personnel, as well as by medical units and transports. The emblem must 'not be used improperly'.

461. Despite the mandatory-sounding phrase 'shall be displayed', the use of the emblem pursuant to Article 12 – as suggested by the ICRC Commentary – has to be viewed as 'optional'.[608] The legal ground is that Article 12 does not detract from Articles 9 and 11 (*supra* 456, 459), which lend protection to medical (and religious) personnel, units and transports whether or not the emblem is emblazoned. The emblem is obviously helpful in facilitating identification of those entitled to protection. But the benefit of protection accrues from the (medical or religious) function rather than flaunting the emblem.

D. The civilian population

(a) Protection from attack

462. The most striking development of LONIAC in AP/II is reflected in Article 13[609] on the protection of the civilian population:

---

[604] See Green, *supra* note 160, at 330.   [605] AP/II, *supra* note 6, at 781.

[606] *Ibid.*

[607] Protocol Additional to the Geneva Conventions of 12 August 1949, and Relating to the Adoption of an Additional Distinctive Emblem (Protocol III), 2005, 45 *ILM* 558, 559 (Article 2) (2006).

[608] See *Commentary on the Additional Protocols*, *supra* note 95, at 1440.

[609] AP/II, *supra* note 6, at 781.

1. The civilian population and individual civilians shall enjoy general protection against the dangers arising from military operations. To give effect to this protection, the following rules shall be observed in all circumstances.
2. The civilian population as such, as well as individual civilians, shall not be the object of attack. Acts or threats of violence the primary purpose of which is to spread terror among the civilian population are prohibited.
3. Civilians shall enjoy the protection afforded by this Part, unless and for such time as they take a direct part in hostilities.

463. The thrust of Article 13 is the general protection of civilians during a NIAC (Paragraph (1)). In essence, the protection is from attack (the first sentence of Paragraph (2)). Unfortunately, the term 'attack' is not defined in AP/II (but see *infra* 512–13). The language used is also rather abstract and terse, lacking vital specifics that would make it more effective.[610] What is clear is that the cloak of protection does not cover those persons who take a direct part in hostilities (on the meaning of the phrase, see *supra* 182 *et seq.*).

464. In the *Fofana et al.* case, the SCSL Appeals Chamber held that the prohibition of spreading terror among the civilian population (Paragraph (2) of Article 13) is 'a narrower derivative' of the general injunction against acts of terrorism (Paragraph (2)(d) of Article 4; *supra* 431).[611] This approach is not corroborated by general State practice, and the two AP/II edicts have to be disencumbered from each other.

465. The meaning of acts of terrorism will be probed *infra* 539 *et seq.* As for spreading terror under Paragraph (2) of Article 13, it relates to launching (or threatening) attacks against the civilian population when the primary aim is to break its spirit through intimidation (by eroding a previously unflinching determination to go on with the NIAC). The *Fofana et al.* Judgment pronounced that the forbidden acts are not limited to direct attacks against civilians, and they comprise also indiscriminate attacks (on the meaning of the phrase, see *infra* 691).[612] The additional heading of indiscriminate attacks makes sense only as long as 'the primary purpose' of the attacks is to spread terror among the civilian population. It has to be appreciated that the rule does not apply to attacks directed

---

[610] See J.G. Gardam, *Non-Combatant Immunity as a Norm of International Humanitarian Law* 128 (1993).
[611] *Prosecutor* v. *Fofana et al.*, *supra* note 576, at para. 348.   [612] *Ibid.*, para. 351.

against lawful targets (fighters and military objectives), even though a side effect of such attacks is that civilians are terrorized by the carnage.[613]

(b) Starvation of civilians

466. Article 14 proscribes the '[s]tarvation of civilians as a method of combat', and the following actions are disallowed:

> to attack, destroy, remove or render useless, for that purpose, objects indispensable to the survival of the civilian population, such as food-stuffs, agricultural areas for the production of foodstuffs, crops, livestock, drinking water installations and supplies and irrigation works.[614]

467. The illegality of the starvation of civilians is linked to its use 'as a method of combat'. Of course, a breakdown in the supply system caused by the ravages of a NIAC may lead to famine even when there is no deliberate policy to starve civilians. In such circumstances, the solution lies in relief consignments, either local or foreign in origin: the topic is taken up in Paragraph (2) of Article 18 (*infra* 476–7).

468. As for the protection of objects indispensable to the survival of the civilian population – such as crops – the key words are 'for that purpose' (i.e. starvation of civilians). Thus, attacks against crops used for concealment by fighters are not detrimentally affected[615] (but see *supra* 429 on 'scorched earth' policy).

(c) Works or installations containing dangerous forces

469. Article 15 proclaims:

> Works or installations containing dangerous forces, namely dams, dykes and nuclear electrical generating stations, shall not be made the object of attack, even where these objects are military objectives, if such attack may cause the release of dangerous forces and consequent severe losses among the civilian population.[616]

The adverb 'namely' limits the category of works and installations containing dangerous forces to dams, dykes and nuclear electrical generating stations: no other civilian objects (not even petroleum storage facilities, the destruction of which may entail commensurate risks) come within the circumference of Article 15.[617] Still, this is a controversial provision.

---

[613] See Sivakumaran, *supra* note 144, at 341.   [614] AP/II, *supra* note 6, at 781.
[615] See *Commentary on the Additional Protocols, supra* note 95, at 1459.
[616] AP/II, *supra* note 6, at 781–2.
[617] See *Commentary on the Additional Protocols, supra* note 95, at 1462.

(d) Cultural property

470. Article 16[618] promulgates that, 'without prejudice' to the provisions of the 1954 CPCP, 'it is prohibited to commit any acts of hostility directed against historic monuments, works of art or places of worship which constitute the cultural or spiritual heritage of peoples, and to use them in support of the military effort'. The 'without prejudice' parlance denotes that the legal regime established in the CPCP is not modified. We shall come back to this subject *infra* 670.

(e) Forced movement of civilians

471. Article 17[619] sets forth, in Paragraph (1), that '[t]he displacement of the civilian population shall not be ordered for reasons related to the conflict' (thus excluding other reasons related, e.g., to epidemics or to natural disasters like earthquakes[620]), 'unless the security of the civilians involved or imperative military reasons so demand'. It ensues from this clause that 'ethnic cleansing' is banned in a NIAC, 'even when it is not carried out with mass murders and other atrocities'.[621]

472. The phraseology of Article 17 appears to single out the act of *ordering* the displacement of the civilian population. Article 8(2)(e)(viii) of the Rome Statute (*infra* 572) also uses the verb '[o]rdering', and the Elements of Crimes – designed to assist the ICC in the interpretation of Article 8 (in accordance with Article 9 of the Statute[622]) – consider the issuance of an order to be a crucial component of the war crime.[623] It has nevertheless been suggested (on the basis of State practice) that – irrespective of the correct interpretation of the Rome Statute – 'forced displacement does not need to have been ordered for a violation of Article 17 AP II to materialize'.[624]

473. When displacement of civilians has to be carried out, Paragraph (1) of Article 17 requires that all possible measures must be taken to ensure 'satisfactory conditions of shelter, hygiene, health, safety and nutrition'. Displacement is restricted to the territory of the State swept by the NIAC. Pursuant to Paragraph (2) of Article 17, '[c]ivilians shall not be

---

[618] AP/II, *supra* note 6, at 782. [619] *Ibid.*

[620] See *Commentary on the Additional Protocols, supra* note 95, at 1473; confirmed in *Prosecutor* v. *Blagojević* (ICTY, Trial Chamber, 2005), para. 600.

[621] N. Ronzitti, 'Civilian Population in Armed Conflict', II *MPEPIL* 197, 207.

[622] Rome Statute of the ICC, *supra* note 7, at 1321.

[623] *Elements of War Crimes under the Rome Statute, supra* note 590, at 472.

[624] See J. Willms, 'Without Order, Anything Goes? The Prohibition of Forced Displacement in Non-International Armed Conflict', 875 *IRRC* 547, 554 (2009).

compelled to leave their own territory for reasons connected with the conflict'.

(f) Relief action

474. Article 18[625] deals, in Paragraph (1), with relief societies located within the territory of the State (e.g., national Red Cross societies), allowing them to offer their services for the performance of their traditional functions in relation to the victims of a NIAC. The ICRC – usually at the vanguard of such activities – is not named, but it retains the right to offer similar services by virtue of Paragraph (2) of Common Article 3 (*supra* 409). 'Paradoxically, it can thus be said that in this respect it is common article 3 which "develops and supplements" the Protocol rather than vice versa'.[626]

475. Paragraph (1) of Article 18 also allows the civilian population – even on its own initiative – to offer to collect and care for the wounded, sick and shipwrecked. As with relief societies, the only entitlement of the civilian population is to offer services. In both instances, the authorities may actually decline the offer (although their refusal cannot be without rhyme or reason).[627]

476. Paragraph (2) of Article 18 provides that, '[i]f the civilian population is suffering undue hardship owing to a lack of the supplies essential for its survival, such as foodstuffs and medical supplies', relief action from the outside 'shall be undertaken'. But there are three conditions: the relief action must be (i) 'of an exclusively humanitarian and impartial nature'; (ii) 'conducted without any adverse distinction'; and, most importantly, (iii) 'subject to the consent of the High Contracting Party concerned'.

477. What is 'undue hardship'? Presumably, it can only be assessed on the basis of 'the usual living standard of the affected population and the needs provoked by the hostilities'.[628] The lack of supplies essential for the survival of the civilian population may be caused by the NIAC only in part. Natural disasters (such as earthquakes, volcanic eruptions or floods) may destroy harvests and disrupt communications, thus adding to civilian suffering (cf. *supra* 467): the fact that the Government cannot

---

[625] AP/II, *supra* note 6, at 782.   [626] See Abi-Saab, *supra* note 547, at 232.

[627] See *Commentary on the Additional Protocols, supra* note 95, at 1478.

[628] J. Pejic, 'The Right to Food in Situations of Armed Conflict: The Legal Framework', 844 *IRRC* 1097, 1108 (2001).

be rebuked for the plight of those affected does not lessen its duty to allow relief action from the outside.[629]

478. A blatant shortcoming of Paragraph (2) of Article 18 is that it ignores the issue of protection of relief personnel. Surely (as urged by the ICRC), if humanitarian assistance from the outside is to succeed, it is indispensable to vouchsafe such protection.[630] This is indeed done in Article 8(2)(e)(iii) of the Rome Statute of the ICC (*infra* 572).

479. The insistence in Paragraph (2) of Article 18 on obtaining the consent of the incumbent Government deprives the provision of much of its verve. All the same – arguably – consent can be withheld 'only for valid reasons, not for arbitrary and capricious ones'.[631] An arbitrary denial of consent may expose the Government to charges of resorting to starvation of civilians as an illicit method of conducting hostilities (see *supra* 466).[632] Consent may, however, be subject to conditions (such as insisting on inspection of convoys; imposing timetables, routes or air corridors; and closely monitoring the entire relief operation).[633] The Government is certainly within its right when it seeks to ensure that humanitarian relief will be strictly earmarked for the alleviation of the suffering of civilians, and that no supplies are siphoned off for consumption by fighters.

480. Paragraph (2) of Article 18 mentions only the need for consent by the incumbent Government ('the High Contracting Party concerned'). But, in reality, an area racked with 'undue hardship' for the civilian population may be under the effective control of the insurgents. If that is the case, any relief action from the outside will also require the *de facto* consent of the organized armed group in charge.[634]

481. Governmental reluctance to grant consent to humanitarian assistance from the outside will probably be at its zenith when the relief consignments are destined to insurgent-controlled tracts of land. It has been contended that – if assistance to the civilian population can be delivered without transiting through territory controlled by the Government –

---

[629] See D. Gavshon, 'The Applicability of IHL in Mixed Situations of Disaster and Conflict', 14 *JCSL* 243, 250–1 (2009).

[630] I *Customary International Humanitarian Law, supra* note 267, at 106.

[631] M. Bothe, 'Article 18', *New Rules for Victims of Armed Conflicts, supra* note 138, at 693, 696.

[632] See *Commentary on the Additional Protocols, supra* note 95, at 1479.

[633] See *Ibid.*, 1480.

[634] See H. Spieker, 'Humanitarian Assistance, Access in Armed Conflict and Occupation', V *MPEPIL* 31, 36.

consent by the latter is not needed.[635] But this does not comport with the language of Paragraph (2) of Article 18.

482. If relief missions from the outside are undertaken, undeterred by the absence of governmental consent, they are not protected by Article 18. Still, civilians engaging in such 'clandestine' relief missions do not thereby become participants in hostilities.[636]

483. The need for humanitarian assistance may be most acute where internally displaced persons are concerned.[637] These are civilians who – fleeing zones infested with hostilities – relocate from one part of the country to another, without crossing an international frontier. They may be living in dilapidated and sometimes unsanitary camps, lacking employment, deprived of minimum standards of living, etc. Their basic subsistence needs may be strained to the point that total refusal to grant consent to procuring for them humanitarian assistance from the outside may become incomprehensible.

---

[635] M.E. O'Connell, 'Humanitarian Assistance in Non-International Armed Conflict: The Fourth Wave of Rights, Duties and Remedies', 31 *Is.YHR* 183, 195 (2001).

[636] See R.A. Stoffels, 'Legal Regulation of Humanitarian Assistance in Armed Conflict: Achievements and Gaps', 855 *IRRC* 515, 535–6 (2004).

[637] See M. Jacques, *Armed Conflict and Displacement: The Protection of Refugees and Displaced Persons under International Humanitarian Law* 197–8 (2012).

9

Additional treaty texts

484. There are quite a few treaties relating to LONIAC in addition to Common Article 3 and AP/II. In Chapter 10, we shall address the war crimes texts. In the present chapter, we shall take stock of other treaty provisions. We shall deal separately with those treaties that expressly appertain to NIACs and those that are applicable only inferentially. Additionally, we shall take a look at treaties – not governing NIACs – that may convey the meaning of undefined terms-of-art with which LONIAC is interspersed.

I. Treaties explicitly apposite to NIACs

A. Cultural property

485. As indicated (*supra* 25), Paragraph (1) of Article 19 of the CPCP enunciates that the main provisions of the instrument will apply in NIACs, and the threshold is the same as that existing under Common Article 3 (see *supra* 115). Paragraph (1) of Article 22 of the 1999 Second Protocol to the CPCP applies the entire Protocol to NIACs (see *supra* 25).

486. The central provision regarding the protection of cultural property (defined *infra* 667) appears in Article 4 of the CPCP.[638] Paragraph (1) imposes – above all – the obligation of 'refraining from any act of hostility directed against' cultural property. This obligation is seriously weakened by Paragraph (2), which allows protection to be waived 'in cases where military necessity imperatively requires such a waiver'. A special protection for cultural property of 'very great importance', subject to an International Register, is heralded in Article 8 of the Convention.[639] Yet, the special protection (which, in any event, has not stood the test of time) is authoritatively viewed as inapplicable in NIACs.[640]

---

[638] CPCP, *supra* note 26, at 1002.   [639] *Ibid.*, 1003.

[640] See J. Toman, *Cultural Property in War: Improvement in Protection – Commentary on the 1999 Second Protocol to the Hague Convention of 1954 for the Protection of Cultural Property in the Event of Armed Conflict* 413 (UNESCO, 2009).

487. The Second Protocol to the CPCP, in Article 6(a), allows a waiver on the basis of imperative military necessity – pursuant to Paragraph 2 of Article 4 of the CPCP – to be invoked only if two conditions are met:

(i) that cultural property has, by its function, been made into a military objective; and

(ii) there is no feasible alternative available to obtain a similar military advantage to that offered by directing an act of hostility against that objective.[641]

488. The Second Protocol also fills certain gaps in AP/II, in the context of cultural property, through the importation of IAC law into NIACs. Article 7 of the Second Protocol accordingly stresses the need to take precautions in attack,[642] a theme missing altogether from AP/II (see *supra* 423).

489. The Second Protocol creates, in Article 10, a new rubric of 'enhanced protection' for cultural property ranking as 'cultural heritage of the greatest importance for humanity'[643] (subject to the supervision of a Special Committee, as per Article 11[644]). Unlike the special protection under the Convention, enhanced protection pursuant to the Second Protocol is applicable in NIACs.[645] But it is impossible to set great store by this new tool in the circumstances of a NIAC.

B. Weapons

490. In the *Tadić* Decision on appeal, the ICTY said:

> Indeed, elementary considerations of humanity and common sense make it preposterous that the use by States of weapons prohibited in armed conflicts between themselves be allowed when States try to put down rebellion by their own nationals on their own territory. What is inhumane and consequently proscribed in international wars, cannot but be inhumane and inadmissible in civil wars.[646]

These are firm words, but they do not fit in with the cautioning rider in the same Decision about there being no 'mechanical transplant' of IAC rules into NIACs (see *infra* 675). Furthermore, to quote M. Bothe (commenting on reliance on 'common sense' in the ICRC study of customary IHL), the trouble is that – judging by the track record – 'the relevant law makers'

---

[641] Second Protocol to the CPCP, *supra* note 27, at 1040.   [642] *Ibid.*   [643] *Ibid.*, 1041.

[644] *Ibid.*   [645] See Toman, *supra* note 640, at 413.

[646] *Prosecutor* v. *Tadić*, *supra* note 33, at 68.

often 'intentionally disregarded and discarded' what is considered by some as common sense.[647]

491. Assuredly, there has recently been a gradual harmonization of IAC and NIAC weapons law (culminating in Kampala in 2010; see *infra* 611). But that has not been brought about by deductions based on common sense. It came to fruition only through the conclusion of concrete amendments of earlier treaty texts.

492. The process of harmonization commenced in 1996, when Article 1(3) of Amended Protocol II to the 1980 CCCW applied the instrument to situations embodied in Common Article 3 (see *supra* 65). In this fashion, the requirement of taking feasible precautions to protect civilians from the pernicious effects of mines, booby-traps and other devices – laid down in Article 3(10)[648] – became applicable to NIACs (a matter of some importance, given the gap in AP/II; *supra* 423).

493. At the time, the innovation did not sit well with the other Protocols annexed to the CCCW. However, in 2001, in a revised version of Article 1(2) of the CCCW itself, a new provision was adopted to the effect that the original instrument and all its annexed Protocols shall apply to situations referred to in Common Article 3.[649] In consequence, the provisions of the CCCW *cum* Protocols apply to all NIACs without exception.

494. Altogether, there are five annexed Protocols to the CCCW (three appended at the outset and two added later). They cover the topics of non-detectable fragments;[650] mines and booby-traps;[651] incendiary weapons;[652] blinding laser weapons;[653] and explosive remnants of war.[654] The scope of the CCCW and its five Protocols is limited. The CCCW has rightly been seen from the start as 'a very modest achievement'.[655] All the texts relate to a finite set of weapons, the definitions of which are far from impermeable.

---

[647] M. Bothe, 'Customary International Humanitarian Law: Some Reflections on the ICRC Study', 8 *YIHL* 143, 153 (2005).

[648] Amended Protocol II to the CCCW, *supra* note 67, at 199.

[649] 2001 Amendment to CCCW, *supra* note 66, at 185 n. 4.

[650] CCCW Protocol on Non-Detectable Fragments (Protocol I), 1980, *supra* note 67, at 190.

[651] CCCW Protocol on Prohibitions or Restrictions on the Use of Mines, Booby-Traps and Other Devices (Protocol II), 1980, *ibid.*, 191.

[652] CCCW Protocol on Prohibitions or Restrictions on the Use of Incendiary Weapons (Protocol III), 1980, *ibid.*, 210.

[653] CCCW Protocol on Blinding Laser Weapons (Protocol IV), 1995, *ibid.*, 212.

[654] CCCW Protocol on Explosive Remnants of War (Protocol V), 2003, 45 *ILM* 1348 (2006).

[655] R.J. Mathews, 'The 1980 Convention on Certain Conventional Weapons: A Useful Framework Despite Earlier Disappointments', 844 *IRRC* 991, 996 (2001).

495. Thus, Amended Protocol II of 1996 – which began the process of equating NIAC and IAC law in the field of weapons – permits the use of some anti-personnel landmines (totally banned only in the 1997 Ottawa Convention on Anti-Personnel Mines[656]) and certainly of anti-vehicle landmines (which were not addressed in Ottawa).[657] As well, the use of diverse booby-traps is still allowed under Protocol II even as amended.[658] A number of the Protocols' prohibitions amount only to restrictions on use of weapons in prescribed circumstances. Along these lines, incendiaries (such as napalm) are forbidden – in Article 2 of Protocol III – against 'any military objectives located within a concentration of civilians', but not against other military objectives.[659]

C. Child-soldiers

496. Paragraph (3)(c) of Article 4 of AP/II (*supra* 443) interdicts the recruitment and participation in hostilities of children under the age of fifteen years. The provision applies both to the incumbent Government and to insurgent armed groups, and it drastically curtails the power of parties to a NIAC to turn children into fighters (thereby denying them the protection due to civilians).

497. The same age bar of fifteen years is fixed in Article 38(2)–(3) of the 1989 Convention on the Rights of the Child (CRC), which however is applicable only to States Parties and not to armed groups (see *infra* 762). On both points changes were introduced in 2000, in an Optional Protocol to the CRC.[660] While ratcheting up the age bar from fifteen to eighteen years, this instrument corrects the error of omission as regards armed groups.

498. With respect to Government forces, there are two discrete clauses in the Optional Protocol. Article 1 lays down that 'States Parties shall take all feasible measures to ensure that members of their armed forces who have not attained the age of 18 years do not take a direct part in

---

[656] Ottawa Convention on the Prohibition of the Use, Stockpiling, Production and Transfer of Anti-Personnel Mines and on Their Destruction, 1997, *Laws of Armed Conflicts* 285, 287.

[657] On anti-vehicle landmines, see D. Kaye and S.A. Solomon, 'The Second Review Conference of the 1980 Convention on Certain Conventional Weapons', 96 *AJIL* 922, 931–3 (2002).

[658] See A.P.V. Rogers, 'A Commentary on the Protocol on Prohibitions or Restrictions on the Use of Mines, Booby-Traps and Other Devices', 26 *Mil.LLWR* 185, 199 (1987).

[659] Protocol III to the CCCW, *supra* note 652, at 210–11.

[660] Optional Protocol to the Convention on the Rights of the Child on the Involvement of Children in Armed Conflict, 2000, *Laws of Armed Conflicts* 957, 959.

hostilities'.[661] Article 2 ordains that 'States Parties shall ensure that persons who have not attained the age of 18 years are not compulsorily recruited into their armed forces'.[662] There is consequently a discrepancy between a more lenient duty to 'take all feasible measures' to foil participation of child-soldiers in hostilities (Article 1) and an unvarnished obligation to preclude their compulsory recruitment (Article 2).

499. The malleable language of Article 1 of the Optional Protocol to the CRC is unfortunate, particularly when compared to the absolute duty – crafted in Paragraph (3) of Article 4 of AP/II (*supra* 443) – regarding both recruitment of child-soldiers and their participation in hostilities. Even the absolute duty in Article 2 of the Optional Protocol is weakened by the adverb 'compulsorily'. Granted, Article 3 of the Optional Protocol insists on safeguards ensuring that recruitment of child-soldiers under the age of eighteen years is genuinely voluntary (sealed by the informed consent of the parents or legal guardians).[663] But detractors have challenged the entire conception of children joining the armed forces on a voluntary basis, recalling the vulnerability of youth to all sorts of inducements and pressures.[664]

500. Article 4 of the Optional Protocol to the CRC[665] stipulates in Paragraph (1) that '[a]rmed groups that are distinct from the armed forces of a State should not, under any circumstances, recruit or use in hostilities persons under the age of 18 years'. No differentiation is made here between recruitment (compulsory or voluntary) and use in hostilities. A jarring note is the insertion of the permissive words 'should not' immediately preceding the stern phrase 'under any circumstances'.[666] The 'armed groups' under discussion are not limited to insurgents, but they are explicitly set apart from 'the armed forces of a State'.

501. Paragraph (2) of Article 4 of the Optional Protocol to the CRC adds that 'States Parties shall take all feasible measures to prevent such recruitment and use'. The repetition of the pliable formula of 'all feasible measures' makes more sense here than in Article 1 (*supra* 498–9). At the end of the day, where insurgent armed groups are concerned, Governments are largely powerless to block the recruitment and use of

---

[661] *Ibid.*   [662] *Ibid.*   [663] *Ibid.*

[664] See V. Popovski, 'Protection of Children in International Humanitarian Law and Human Rights Law', *International Humanitarian Law and Human Rights Law: Towards a New Merger in International Law* 383, 400 (R. Arnold and N. Quénivet eds., 2008).

[665] Optional Protocol to the CRC, *supra* note 660, at 958.

[666] See D. Helle, 'Optional Protocol on the Involvement of Children in Armed Conflict to the Convention on the Rights of the Child', 839 *IRRC* 797, 806 (2000).

child-soldiers against themselves (other than prosecuting offenders if they are apprehended).[667]

II. Treaties implicitly apposite to NIACs

A. Enforced disappearances

502. Some treaties do not mention NIACs *expressis verbis*, but they use such sweeping language that NIACs must be seen as coming within their fold. In this manner, Article 2(2) of the 2006 International Convention for the Protection of All Persons from Enforced Disappearance states: 'No exceptional circumstances whatsoever, whether a state of war or a threat of war, internal political instability or any other public emergency, may be invoked as a justification for enforced disappearance'.[668] Although NIACs are not named, they are captured by the amorphous phrase 'internal political instability or any other public emergency'.[669]

B. Weapons treaties

(a) Biological weapons

503. An all-inclusive language that covers all eventualities is symptomatic of weapons treaties. In Article I of the BWC of 1972, Contracting Parties undertake 'never in any circumstances to develop, produce, stockpile or otherwise acquire or retain' such weapons designed 'for hostile purposes or in armed conflict'.[670] The crucial verb 'use' does not feature in the litany of prohibited acts as quoted. However, the non-inclusion is partly compensated for by the Preambular paragraph:

> Determined, for the sake of all mankind, to exclude completely the possibility of bacteriological (biological) agents and toxins being used as weapons.[671]

Besides, logically, 'what is not possessed cannot be used'.[672]

---

[667] See M. Happold, *Child Soldiers in International Law* 79–80 (2005).

[668] International Convention for the Protection of All Persons from Enforced Disappearance, [2006] *UNJY* 309, *id.*

[669] Enforced disappearance is categorized as a crime against humanity in Article 7(1)(i) of the Rome Statute of the ICC, *supra* note 7, at 1316.

[670] BWC, *supra* note 310, at 136.   [671] *Ibid.*

[672] A.V. Lowe, '1972 Convention on the Prohibition of the Development, Production and Stockpiling of Bacteriological (Biological) and Toxin Weapons and Their Destruction', *The Law of Naval Warfare*, *supra* note 80, at 623, 643.

504. Although the BWC does not refer to NIACs, the admonition 'never in any circumstances' is broad enough to encompass them.[673] It is also noteworthy that, under Article IV, Contracting Parties are bound to take any necessary measures to prohibit and prevent development, production, stockpiling, acquisition or retention of biological weapons anywhere within their territories.[674]

505. The dialectics of disarmament has obvious repercussions for NIACs. Even had NIACs not come within the purview of the BWC, once possession of weapons of mass destruction is abjured by all armed forces – if only for purposes of IACs – they are no longer kept in the arsenals, and then the issue of using non-existing weapons in a NIAC may become moot.[675]

(b) Chemical weapons

506. In Article I(1) of the 1993 CWC, Contracting Parties are obligated 'never under any circumstances' to 'develop, produce, otherwise acquire, stockpile or retain chemical weapons', to transfer them 'to anyone', or to 'use' them.[676] 'Use' is thus added overtly to the list of illicit activities. If any doubt as to the intention of the framers of the CWC remains, it ought to be dissipated by the following Preambular paragraph:

> *Determined* for the sake of all mankind, to exclude completely the possibility of the use of chemical weapons.[677]

Unquestionably, the open-ended exclusion of the use of chemical weapons covers NIACs.[678]

507. Chemical weapons were used repetitively by the Assad Government in the Syrian NIAC. When a large-scale indiscriminate chemical attack took place in August 2013, it gave rise to international outrage and threats of US retaliatory air strikes. Following weeks of negotiations, the Security Council determined in a binding manner – in Resolution 2118 (2013) – that 'the use of chemical weapons anywhere constitutes a threat to international peace and security'; without assigning blame to the Assad Government, the Council condemned such use in the Syrian NIAC 'in violation of international law'.[679] Shortly before the adoption of the resolution, Syria was pressured to accede to the CWC. The resolution

---

[673] See W. Boothby, *Weapons and the Law of Armed Conflict* 324 (2009).
[674] BWC, *supra* note 310, at 137.   [675] See Hellestveit, *supra* note 179, at 96.
[676] CWC, *supra* note 71, at 241–2.   [677] *Ibid.*
[678] See Boothby, *supra* note 673, at 321.
[679] Security Council Resolution 2118 (2013), paras. 1–2.

established a special inspection regime to supervise the elimination of the Syrian chemical weapons programme and the destruction of existing stockpiles (coupled with a decision to impose measures under Chapter VII of the Charter in the event of non-compliance[680]).

(c) Other weapons

508. The modified formula of the BWC/CWC – 'never under any circumstances' plus a concrete mention of 'use' – is repeated in Article 1 of the 1997 Ottawa Convention on Anti-Personnel Mines.[681] The inference may therefore be drawn that the Ottawa Convention applies to NIACs.[682] The modified formula is also inserted in Article 2 of the 2008 Dublin Cluster Munitions Convention,[683] with the same consequences concerning NIACs.[684]

509. Despite the modern trend, it would be wrong to jump to the conclusion that every weapons treaty today is automatically pertinent to NIACs. Thus, the ENMOD Convention of 1976[685] – relating to the employment of environmental modification techniques as a weapon (by producing earthquakes, tsunamis, etc.) – is definitely inapposite to a NIAC.[686]

III. Search for definitions

510. Both Common Article 3 and AP/II use terms-of-art that are at times enigmatic, leaving intriguing questions as to their precise scope. Authentic definitions of these terms are missing from the texts, and any attempt to enforce the relevant norms may be stymied by sharp disagreements about their tenor. The predicament may be alleviated by relying on judicial pronouncements. But this is not a panacea: judges, too, are often confounded by the lack of reliable guideposts. The riddle is whether, and to what extent, the trajectory of existing IAC definitions can traverse the orbit of LONIAC.

---

[680] *Ibid.*, para. 21.   [681] Ottawa Convention, *supra* note 656, at 287.

[682] See Boothby, *supra* note 673, at 322.

[683] Dublin Convention on Cluster Munitions, *supra* note 226, at 358.

[684] See K. Hulme, 'The 2008 Cluster Munitions Convention: Stepping outside the CCW Framework (Again)', 58 *ICLQ* 219, 221 (2009).

[685] Convention on the Prohibition of Military or Any Other Hostile Use of Environmental Modification Techniques (ENMOD Convention), 1976, *Laws of Armed Conflicts* 163.

[686] See Y. Dinstein, *The Conduct of Hostilities under the Law of International Armed Conflict* 201 (2nd edn, 2010).

A. IAC definitions

511. IAC treaty law, especially AP/I, offers a veritable cornucopia of working definitions of key phrases relating to the *jus in bello*. When some of the same phrases reappear unalloyed in Common Article 3 and/or AP/II, there is no reason militating against the use of analogy in their interpretation. For sure, any transposition from IAC *jus in bello* to corresponding LONIAC norms must be done *mutatis mutandis*, bearing in mind contextual disparities. Still, *ceteris paribus*, the importation of definitions of the exact same terms from IAC to NIAC law need not create insuperable complications. We shall sketch out five examples that stand out.

(a) Attacks

512. AP/II uses the word 'attack' several times (principally, in Paragraph (2) of Article 13, *supra* 462). Although no definition appears in AP/II, the ICRC Commentary records that '[f]rom the beginning of the work of the Conference [which produced AP/I and AP/II] it was agreed that the same meaning should be given this term in both Protocols'.[687]

513. Article 49(1) of AP/I defines 'attacks' as 'acts of violence against the adversary, whether in offence or in defence'.[688] The definition, which hinges on violence, is counter-intuitive: it strays from the vernacular by categorizing defence as a mode of attack. All the more reason to appreciate its significance, and to commend its transplant from IAC to NIAC law.

514. Attacks are a subset of military operations. A host of military operations (related, for instance, to intelligence gathering or to psychological warfare) do not entail violence, and therefore do not amount to attacks. All military operations, whether or not deemed attacks, come under the awning of hostilities (see *supra* 35).

(b) Wounded, sick and shipwrecked

515. Paragraph (1) of Article 7 of AP/II focuses on 'wounded, sick and shipwrecked' (*supra* 452) without defining the phrase. Again, the ICRC Commentary argues for application of definitions incorporated in AP/I.[689] It is generally admitted that these definitions 'can be used as a guide even though they have no binding force' in NIACs.[690] Article 8 of AP/I says in Paragraphs (a)–(b):

---

[687] *Commentary on the Additional Protocols, supra* note 95, at 1452 n. 19.

[688] AP/I, *supra* note 21, at 735.

[689] *Commentary on the Additional Protocols, supra* note 95, at 1409–10.

[690] *UK Manual of the Law of Armed Conflict, supra* note 64, at 404.

(a) 'wounded' and 'sick' mean persons, whether military or civilian, who, because of trauma, disease or other physical or mental disorder or disability, are in need of medical assistance or care and who refrain from any act of hostility. These terms also cover maternity cases, newborn babies and other persons who may be in need of immediate medical assistance or care, such as the infirm or expectant mothers, and who refrain from any act of hostility;

(b) 'shipwrecked' means persons, whether military or civilian, who are in peril at sea or in other waters as a result of misfortune affecting them or the vessel or aircraft carrying them and who refrain from any act of hostility.[691]

516. There are two countervailing dimensions related to the wounded and sick:

(i) One dimension narrows the field. It is not enough for a person to be either wounded or sick, in order to come within the bounds of the definition. Entitlement to protection is conditioned on refraining from any act of hostility.

(ii) The other dimension broadens the span of the definition – and the protection it offers – to cover maternity cases and newborn babies. Once more, this is counter-intuitive: a person is considered wounded or sick without suffering from any wounds or sickness. Nevertheless, the need to lend protection to maternity cases and newborn babies – under whatever label – overcomes lexical semantics.

517. Two additional comments about shipwrecked:

(i) Just as 'wounded and sick' need not be quite wounded or sick, the term 'shipwrecked' as defined by AP/I goes beyond persons who are literally shipwrecked. The wreck may be that of an aircraft, and there may be other reasons for misfortune at sea like falling into the water.[692]

(ii) Since naval operations at sea are neither as common nor as extensive in NIACs as in IACs, it is worthwhile stressing the words 'or in other waters'. They indicate that shipwrecked include those who are in peril in lakes, rivers and canals (although not in perilous land areas, such as deserts).[693]

---

[691] AP/I, *supra* note 21, at 718.
[692] See *Commentary on the Additional Protocols*, *supra* note 95, at 119.
[693] See *ibid.*

(c) *Hors de combat*

518. Common Article 3 employs a well-known French locution: *hors de combat* (*supra* 409). Paragraph (1) of Article 4 of AP/II avoids it, resorting instead to the English translation of persons who 'have ceased to take part in hostilities' (*supra* 431). Either way, what is the definition of the protected category? The answer is given in Article 41(2) of AP/I:

> A person is *hors de combat* if:
> (a) he is in the power of an adverse Party;
> (b) he clearly expresses an intention to surrender; or
> (c) he has been rendered unconscious or is otherwise incapacitated by wounds or sickness, and therefore is incapable of defending himself, provided that in any of these cases he abstains from any hostile act and does not attempt to escape.[694]

There can be no possible objection to regarding this definition as applicable in the settings of both Common Article 3 and Paragraph (1) of Article 4 of AP/II.[695] Curiously, shipwrecked are not mentioned here expressly, although they cannot be excluded from the construct of *hors de combat*.[696]

519. The reference to those who have laid down their arms – as well as those who are wounded, sick or detained – already appears in Common Article 3. The most prominent new feature is the proviso at the end of the paragraph, which requires that persons who are *hors de combat* must not only abstain from any further hostile act but must also not attempt to escape. That is true of all contingencies of *hors de combat*.

(d) Medical and religious personnel

520. The expression 'medical and religious personnel' appears in Article 9 of AP/II (*supra* 456), but is left undefined. The ICRC Commentary reminds us that, like related provisions in the same part of AP/II, 'Article 9 was negotiated and drafted on the basis of definitions developed for the two Protocols together'.[697]

521. Article 8(c) of AP/I[698] states:

> 'medical personnel' means those persons assigned, by a Party to the conflict, exclusively to the medical purposes enumerated under sub-paragraph (e) [*infra* 523] or to the administration of medical units or to the operation

---

[694] AP/I, *supra* note 21, at 731.   [695] See Partsch, *supra* note 593, at 640.
[696] See *Commentary on the Additional Protocols*, *supra* note 95, at 487.
[697] *Ibid.*, 1418.   [698] AP/I, *supra* note 21, at 718.

or administration of medical transports. Such assignments may be either permanent or temporary.

Medical personnel are not only doctors and nurses but also ambulance drivers, paramedics and all those involved in running a hospital or any other medical installation (for the duration of their employment).

522. Article 8(d) of AP/I[699] clarifies that 'religious personnel' means 'military or civilian persons, such as chaplains, who are exclusively engaged in the work of their ministry' and are attached (even temporarily) to the armed forces or to medical units or transports. In NIAC circumstances, it must be perceived that they may also serve their mission when embedded in insurgent organized armed groups.

(e) Medical units and transports

523. Article 11 of AP/II bestows protection on 'medical units and transports' (*supra* 459). The phrase is not explained in AP/II, but a very comprehensive definition appears in Article 8(e) and (g) of AP/I:

> (e) 'medical units' means establishments and other units, whether military or civilian, organized for medical purposes, namely the search for, collection, transportation, diagnosis or treatment – including first-aid treatment – of the wounded, sick and shipwrecked, or for the prevention of disease. The term includes for example, hospitals and other similar units, blood transfusion centres, preventive medicine centres and institutes, medical depots and the medical and pharmaceutical stores of such units. Medical units may be fixed or mobile, permanent or temporary;

> . . .

> (g) 'medical transports' means any means of transportation, whether military or civilian, permanent or temporary, assigned exclusively to medical transportation and under the control of a competent authority of a Party to the conflict.[700]

Paragraph (f) elucidates that medical transportation can be by land, water or air.[701] As with the definition of medical and religious personnel, no valid reason can be adduced for regarding the ambit of medical units and transports as different in AP/II compared to AP/I.

B. General treaty definitions

524. When IAC texts fail to fill in a definitional lacuna in NIAC instruments, the next best thing is to consult general treaties that may

---

[699] *Ibid.*, 718–19. [700] *Ibid.*, 719. [701] *Ibid.*

shed light on the meaning of any abstract terms used. This needs to be done prudently, verifying that the general treaty definition can be adapted to the special ambience of a NIAC. Four premier examples will be presented.

(a) Slavery and the slave trade

525. The prohibition of 'slavery and the slave trade' is conveyed in Paragraph (2)(f) of Article 4 of AP/II (*supra* 431). The dual epithet 'slavery and the slave trade' is enshrined in the 1926 Slavery Convention.[702] Article 1 of the Convention comes up with a detailed definition of these terms:

> (1) Slavery is the status or condition of a person over whom any or all of the powers attaching to the right of ownership are exercised.
> (2) The slave trade includes all acts involved in the capture, acquisition or disposal of a person with intent to reduce him to slavery; all acts involved in the acquisition of a slave with a view to selling or exchanging him; all acts of disposal by sale or exchange of a slave acquired with a view to being sold or exchanged, and, in general, every act of trade or transport in slaves.[703]

526. The scourge of slavery still plagues several countries, and the text penned in 1926 is far from outmoded. A 1956 Supplementary Slavery Convention augments the original language with certain additional institutions and practices comparable to slavery, such as serfdom or debt bondage.[704] But, in Article 7, the new instrument retains verbatim the 1926 definition of slavery and only slightly recasts that of the slave trade.[705]

527. The 1926 definitions of slavery and the slave trade can now be considered a reflection of customary international law. This is confirmed by the ICTY Judgments in both instances in the *Kunarac et al.* case: more categorically in the Trial stage in 2001[706] and more circumspectly in the Appeals phase in 2002.[707] Although there are some practical issues that cannot be sidelined concerning the application of the two definitions in

---

[702] *Commentary on the Additional Protocols, supra* note 95, at 1335.

[703] Slavery Convention, 1926, 60 *LNTS* 254, 263.

[704] Supplementary Convention on the Abolition of Slavery, the Slave Trade, and Institutions and Practices Similar to Slavery, 1956, 266 *UNTS* 40, 41 (Article 1).

[705] *Ibid.*, 43.   [706] *Prosecutor* v. *Kunarac et al.* (ICTY, Trial Chamber, 2001), para. 520.

[707] *Prosecutor* v. *Kunarac et al., supra* note 50, at paras. 117–18.

concrete circumstances,[708] Paragraph (2)(f) of Article 4 of AP/II must be construed in harmony with the earlier texts.

528. Article 5 of the 1926 Slavery Convention expressly recognizes that forced or compulsory labour may be exacted for public purposes.[709] That is a general rider, but it has exceptional value in an armed conflict (either an IAC or a NIAC). Parties to the conflict are more than likely to summon civilians to compulsory labour connected with the hostilities (e.g., construction of fortifications).[710]

(b) Torture

529. The position is less simple regarding the interpretation of the term 'torture' appearing both in Common Article 3 and in Paragraph (2)(a) of Article 4 of AP/II (*supra* 409, 431). Here comes into the picture Article 1(1) of the 1984 Convention against Torture (CAT):

> For the purposes of this Convention, the term 'torture' means any act by which severe pain or suffering, whether physical or mental, is intentionally inflicted on a person for such purposes as obtaining from him or a third person information or a confession, punishing him for an act he or a third person has committed or is suspected of having committed, or intimidating or coercing him or a third person, or for any reason based on discrimination of any kind, when such pain or suffering is inflicted by or at the instigation of or with the consent or acquiescence of a public official or other person acting in an official capacity. It does not include pain or suffering arising only from, inherent in or incidental to lawful sanctions.[711]

530. Incontestably, the CAT is applicable to armed conflicts. In Article 2(2), the message is put across that '[n]o exceptional circumstances whatsoever, whether a state of war or a threat of war, internal political instability or any other public emergency, may be invoked as a justification of torture'.[712] The purpose of Article 2(2) was to underscore the absolute, non-derogable character of the prohibition of torture.[713] Yet,

---

[708] See J. Allain, *The Slavery Conventions: The Travaux Préparatoires of the 1926 League of Nations Convention and the 1956 United Nations Convention* 4–5 (2008).

[709] Slavery Convention, *supra* note 703, at 265.

[710] See M. Greenspan, 'The Protection of Human Rights in Time of Warfare', 1 *Is. YHR* 228, 237 (1971).

[711] Convention against Torture and Other Cruel, Inhuman or Degrading Treatment or Punishment (CAT), [1984] *UNJY* 135, *id.*

[712] *Ibid.*, 136.

[713] See J.H. Burgers and H. Danelius, *The United Nations Convention against Torture: A Handbook on the Convention against Torture and Other Cruel, Inhuman or Degrading Treatment or Punishment* 124 (1988).

there is a thorny question pertaining to the application in NIACs of Article 1(1), which puts weight on the involvement of 'a public official or other person acting in an official capacity'. This prerequisite gives short shrift to charges of torture committed by non-State actors, going off at a tangent from Paragraph (2)(a) of Article 4 of AP/II (which covers torture committed by both sides in a NIAC).[714]

531. The CAT definition of torture was taken for granted by the Trial Chamber of the ICTR in its *Akayesu* Judgment of 1998.[715] Torture was discussed at length in the *Furundžija* Judgment, delivered in the same year, where an ICTY Trial Chamber queried whether the CAT depiction of torture – limited, as it is, '[f]or the purposes of this Convention' – has 'extra-conventional effect'.[716] The crisp answer given was affirmative on the ground that the text reflects customary international law.[717] The Judgment also pronounced that the prohibition of torture 'has evolved into a peremptory norm or *jus cogens*, that is, a norm that enjoys a higher rank in the international hierarchy than treaty law and even "ordinary" customary rules'.[718] In 2012, the ICJ confirmed – in the *Questions Relating to the Obligation to Prosecute or Extradite (Belgium* v. *Senegal)* case – that 'the prohibition of torture is part of customary international law and it has become a peremptory norm (*jus cogens*)'.[719]

532. The awkward issue of torture committed in a non-official capacity was taken up in the ICTY 1998 *Delalić et al.* Judgment:

> Traditionally, an act of torture must be committed by, or at the instigation of, or with the consent or acquiescence of, a public official or person acting in an official capacity. In the context of international humanitarian law, this requirement must be interpreted to include officials of non-State parties to a conflict, in order for the prohibition to retain significance in situations of internal armed conflicts or international conflicts involving some non-State entities.[720]

533. The CAT linkage to official capacity was dropped from the Elements of Crimes accompanying Article 8(2)(c)(i) of the Rome Statute

---

[714] See C. Droege, '"In Truth the Leitmotiv": The Prohibition of Torture and Other Forms of Ill-Treatment in International Humanitarian Law', 867 *IRRC* 515, 518 (2007).

[715] *Prosecutor* v. *Akayesu, supra* note 103, at para. 593.

[716] *Prosecutor* v. *Furundžija* (ICTY, Trial Chamber, 1998), para. 160.

[717] *Ibid.*   [718] *Ibid.*, para. 153.

[719] *Questions Relating to the Obligation to Prosecute or Extradite (Belgium* v. *Senegal)* case, 51 *ILM* 709, 732 (2012).

[720] *Prosecutor* v. *Delalić et al., supra* note 37, at para. 473.

of the ICC (*infra* 559).[721] The topic was reexamined in the *Kunarac et al.* Judgment of 2001, where the Trial Chamber observed that – in turning to human rights law for guidance – one must be mindful of the fact that (i) a definition is largely a function of the environment in which it develops, and (ii) in contrast to human rights law, LONIAC applies equally to all parties to the conflict.[722] The Trial Chamber, duly noting that the CAT version of torture was meant to apply only '[f]or the purposes of this Convention',[723] arrived at the conclusion that it 'cannot be regarded as the definition of torture under customary international law which is binding regardless of the context in which it is applied'.[724] Although some aspects of the definition have become part of customary international law, the Trial Chamber characterized as 'contentious' the requirement that torture can only be inflicted by (or at the instigation of or with the consent or acquiescence of) a public official or other person acting in an official capacity.[725] The *Kunarac et al.* approach has been reaffirmed in subsequent proceedings.[726]

(c) Taking of hostages

534. Both Common Article 3 and Paragraph (2) of Article 4 of AP/II speak about the 'taking of hostages' (*supra* 409, 431). When can persons be regarded as 'hostages'? In particular, if civilians are coercively put in a position of 'human shields' in or near a military objective – with a view to inducing a calculus of potential excessive collateral damage to civilians (see *infra* 694), thus screening the target from attack by the opposing side – will they be considered 'hostages' for the purposes of Paragraph (2) of Article 4 of AP/II?[727] Despite some support for the idea in the legal literature,[728] it appears to be ill-conceived. In the end, captive 'human shields' – although put in harm's way – are not threatened directly by their captors: any death or injury will result from action by the opponents (which the captors are seeking to deter).

---

[721] *Elements of War Crimes under the Rome Statute*, *supra* note 590, at 402–3.

[722] *Prosecutor v. Kunarac et al.*, *supra* note 706, at paras. 469–70.

[723] *Ibid.*, para. 473.   [724] *Ibid.*, para. 482.   [725] *Ibid.*, paras. 483–4.

[726] See J. Marshall, 'Torture Committed by Non-State Actors: The Developing Jurisprudence from the *Ad Hoc* Tribunals', 5 *NSAIL* 171, 181 (2005).

[727] See M.N. Schmitt, 'Distinction and Loss of Civilian Protection in International Armed Conflicts', 38 *Is.YHR* 1, 30 (2008).

[728] See V. Rusinova, 'Human Shields', V *MPEPIL* 19, 21.

535. Other issues affecting the compass of the taking of hostages arise as well. Hence the temptation to rely on Article 1(1) of the 1979 Taking of Hostages Convention:

> Any person who seizes or detains and threatens to kill, to injure or to continue to detain another person (hereinafter referred to as the 'hostage') in order to compel a third party, namely, a State, an international intergovernmental organization, a natural or juridical person, or a group of persons, to do or abstain from doing any act as an explicit or implicit condition for the release of the hostage commits the offence of taking of hostages ('hostage-taking') within the meaning of this Convention.[729]

Article 1(1) appears to be germane to the taking of hostages in NIACs, inasmuch as it covers both States and groups of persons as targets. However, that is not all that the Convention has to say on the subject.

536. Article 12 of the Hostages Convention narrows its scope of application:

> In so far as the Geneva Conventions of 1949 for the protection of war victims or the Protocols Additional to those Conventions are applicable to a particular act of hostage-taking, and in so far as States Parties to this Convention are bound under those conventions to prosecute or hand over the hostage-taker, the present Convention shall not apply to an act of hostage-taking committed in the course of armed conflicts as defined in the Geneva Conventions of 1949 and the Protocols thereto.[730]

Standing by itself, Article 12 does not obstruct the operation of the Hostages Convention (including its definition) in NIACs. There is a disconnect between the general limitation of Article 12 and NIACs, since no obligation to prosecute or hand over the hostage-taker is contained in the relevant provisions of the Geneva Conventions and Protocols (i.e. Common Article 3 or AP/II).[731]

537. Article 13 of the Hostages Convention is more apposite to NIACs:

> This Convention shall not apply where the offence is committed within a single State, the hostage and the alleged offender are nationals of that State and the alleged offender is found in the territory of that State.[732]

---

[729] International Convention against the Taking of Hostages, [1979] *UNJY* 124, *id.*
[730] *Ibid.*, 127.
[731] See J.J. Lambert, *Terrorism and Hostages in International Law – A Commentary on the Hostages Convention 1979* 273–82 (1990).
[732] International Convention against the Taking of Hostages, *supra* note 729, at 127.

Without mentioning the Geneva Conventions or Protocols, Article 13 seems to vitiate the application of any part of the Hostages Convention to civil strife. After all, only a single State is involved and the hostages as well as hostage-takers would generally be its nationals.

538. Nonetheless, the merits of the definition embroidered in Article 1(1) of the Hostages Convention are such that they sometimes overcome the barriers created by Article 13. The Rome Statute's Elements of Crimes cite the definition when construing the phrase 'taking of hostages' in the setting of both NIAC and IAC war crimes.[733] In the *Sesay et al.* Judgment of 2009, the Appeals Chamber of the SCSL also remarked that an analysis of the Hostages Convention's definition can 'prove useful' in a NIAC setting.[734] The remark cannot be gainsaid. Still, proving 'useful' does not mean that the Hostages Convention's definition is conclusive in every NIAC setting.

(d) Acts of terrorism

539. 'Acts of terrorism' are forbidden in Paragraph (2)(d) of Article 4 of AP/II (*supra* 431), but no attempt has been made to elaborate. The term 'terrorism' (although common to the point of banality) unmistakably invites a definition. Thus far, no comprehensive definition of terrorism has been adopted in a general treaty in force. Yet, a most useful and relevant definition[735] – certainly, the clearest[736] – appears in Article 2(1)(b) of the 1999 International Convention for the Suppression of the Financing of Terrorism.[737]

540. After acknowledging a series of treaties relating to specific acts of terrorism, this clause refers residually to:

> Any other act intended to cause death or serious bodily injury to a civilian, or to any other person not taking an active part in the hostilities in a situation of armed conflict, when the purpose of such act, by its nature or context, is to intimidate a population, or to compel a government or an international organization to do or to abstain from doing any act.

---

[733] *Elements of War Crimes under the Rome Statute, supra* note 590, at 126–7, 406.

[734] *Prosecutor* v. *Sesay et al.* (SCSL, Appeals Chamber, 2009), para. 579.

[735] See L. Martinez, 'Prosecuting Terrorists at the International Criminal Court: Possibilities and Problems', 34 *Rut.LJ* 1, 6 (2002–3).

[736] See Special Tribunal for Lebanon, Interlocutory Decision on the Applicable Law: Terrorism, Conspiracy, Homicide, Perpetration, Cumulative Charging (2011), para. 88.

[737] International Convention for the Suppression of the Financing of Terrorism, 1999, 39 *ILM* 270, 271 (2000).

Here is the first binding definition of acts of terrorism appearing in a 'treaty in force at the world level'.[738] Since the Convention's definition – albeit residual – is all about acts lethal or injurious to 'a civilian, or to any other person not taking an active part in the hostilities in a situation of armed conflict', it can be very handy in a NIAC context.

541. To quote G. Guillaume, the Convention's definition implies that:

> a distinction should be made between the victim that the terrorist seeks to harm, the target that he wishes to attain and the results he is looking to secure. Terrorism is a method of combat in which the victims are not chosen on an individual basis but are struck either at random or for symbolic effect. The ultimate goal pursued in attacking them is not the killing or injuring of the victims themselves but to spread terror among the group to which they belong. By doing so, terrorists generally seek to compel governments or public opinion to make some concession towards them, if only to consider their position more favourably.[739]

The triple distinction (by victim, target and results) is praiseworthy in that it manages to partition 'acts of terrorism' from any other acts of violence, either in a NIAC or otherwise.

542. We have mentioned (*supra* 540) the series of treaties relevant to specific terrorist activities. A treaty of that type may exclude its application in any armed conflict (IAC or NIAC). Article 19(2) of the 1997 International Convention for the Suppression of Terrorist Bombings makes no bones about it: 'The activities of armed forces during an armed conflict, as those terms are understood under international humanitarian law, which are governed by that law, are not governed by this Convention'.[740] A similar provision appears in Article 4(2) of the 2005 International Convention for the Suppression of Acts of Nuclear Terrorism.[741]

---

[738] A. Gioia, 'The UN Conventions on the Prevention and Suppression of International Terrorism', *International Cooperation in Counter-Terrorism: The United Nations and Regional Organizations in the Fight against Terrorism* 3, 13 (G. Nesi ed., 2005).

[739] G. Guillaume, 'Terrorism and International Law', 53 *ICLQ* 537, 540–1 (2004).

[740] International Convention for the Suppression of Terrorist Bombings, [1997] *UNJY* 277, 285.

[741] International Convention for the Suppression of Acts of Nuclear Terrorism, 2005, 44 *ILM* 815, 818 (2005).

10

NIAC war crimes

I. Individual criminal responsibility

A. *The nexus to a NIAC*

(a) Crimes against humanity and genocide

543. In the present chapter, we shall concentrate on NIAC war crimes. This is shorthand for serious violations of LONIAC for which individuals are personally accountable (see *supra* 42). We shall not canvass other international crimes that are possibly relevant to NIACs. In particular, we shall not enquire into crimes against humanity or genocide, although these international crimes can be – and have been – committed while a country is consumed by a NIAC. The elision is due to the fact that there is no built-in direct linkage between crimes against humanity or genocide and a NIAC.

544. Since its treaty origins in 1948, it has consistently been made clear that the crime of genocide (as defined in Article 1 of the Genocide Convention[742]) can be 'committed in time of peace or in time of war'. A NIAC is not posited. In the *Kayishema et al.* Judgment of 1999, the ICTR Trial Chamber held that a NIAC under AP/II was in progress in Rwanda, yet massacres of Tutsis (emanating from an elaborate policy of genocide) were perpetrated in certain areas without any direct link to the hostilities.[743]

545. As for crimes against humanity, at the outset there was a requirement of a nexus to IACs.[744] Over the years, the linkage was incrementally corroded. Article 5 of the ICTY Statute already relates to crimes against humanity 'when committed in armed conflict, whether international or

---

[742] Genocide Convention, *supra* note 239, at 840.

[743] *Prosecutor* v. *Kayishema et al.*, *supra* note 47, at para. 603.

[744] See Y. Dinstein, 'Crimes against Humanity after Tadić', 13 *LJIL* 373, 383–4 (2000).

internal in character'.[745] In the *Tadić* Decision on appeal, the ICTY went a step further:

> customary international law may not require a connection between crimes against humanity and any conflict at all. Thus, by requiring that crimes against humanity be committed in either internal or international armed conflict, the Security Council may have defined the crime in Article 3 more narrowly than necessary under customary international law.[746]

The Rome Statute, in Article 7, does not retain any nexus between crimes against humanity and either IACs or NIACs.[747]

(b) The growth of NIAC war crimes

546. When LONIAC first surfaced in Common Article 3, the framers of the Geneva Conventions did not think that its violation should carry individual criminal accountability. In the *Tadić* Decision on appeal, the ICTY held that such a violation does not come within the spectrum of 'grave breaches' (a coinage equivalent to war crimes) as inventoried in the Conventions,[748] since grave breaches are restricted to acts committed in IACs.[749] The criminalization of serious violations of LONIAC occurred much later (well past the adoption of AP/II), and it goes hand in hand with the emergence of international courts and tribunals vested with jurisdiction over perpetrators.

547. Article 10 of the Rome Statute prescribes that nothing in the part containing Article 8 (defining IAC and NIAC war crimes) 'shall be interpreted as limiting or prejudicing in any way existing or developing rules of international law for purposes other than this Statute'.[750] The chief purpose of Article 10 was to reassure Contracting Parties to the Statute that the list of war crimes in Article 8 is not an 'exhaustive codification' of the existing law relating to serious violations of IAC and NIAC law.[751] As a matter of fact, both treaty and customary LONIAC can and do go beyond the span of Article 8.

---

[745] Statute of the ICTY, 1993, *Laws of Armed Conflicts* 1288, 1289.

[746] *Prosecutor* v. *Tadić, supra* note 33, at 72.

[747] Rome Statute of the ICC, *supra* note 7, at 1316–17.

[748] The list of 'grave breaches' appears in Geneva Convention (I), *supra* note 536, at 477 (Article 50); Geneva Convention (II), *ibid.*, 501 (Article 51); Geneva Convention (III), *ibid.*, 557 (Article 130); Geneva Convention (IV), *ibid.*, 624–5 (Article 147).

[749] *Prosecutor* v. *Tadić, supra* note 33, at 59.

[750] Rome Statute of the ICC, *supra* note 7, at 1321.

[751] W.A. Schabas, *The International Criminal Court: A Commentary on the Rome Statute* 270 (2010).

548. Article 10 does not 'foreclose arguments that customary international law now includes the Statute's definitions' of serious violations of LONIAC.[752] This is confirmed by the ICTY Trial Chamber 1998 Judgment in the *Furundžija* case.[753] Indeed, the incorporation of a NIAC war crime in the Rome Statute provides strong evidence that the kernel of the crime amounts to a breach of customary LONIAC.

549. Like all other international crimes, NIAC war crimes have two constituent elements: (i) the criminal act (*actus reus*), and (ii) a criminal intent or at least a criminal consciousness (*mens rea*). The vital function of *mens rea* as an indispensable component of international crimes is attested in Article 30 of the Rome Statute.[754] Unlike international criminal law, LONIAC focuses on the *actus reus*. Still, even LONIAC usually presupposes that its breaches are intentional, and do not stem from accidental action or a technical malfunction.[755]

B. The Statutes of the ad hoc international tribunals

550. The first time that serious violations of Common Article 3, as well as certain breaches of AP/II, were authoritatively identified *per se* as war crimes – to which individual criminal responsibility is attached – was in 1994, when the Security Council adopted the Statute of the ICTR Tribunal.[756] At that juncture, it was felt necessary to debate whether the Statute did or did not represent *ex post facto* legislation.[757] The case law even showed some hesitation about prosecuting NIAC war crimes for acts happening before 1994.[758] But soon the flow of State practice and *opinio juris* dispelled any lingering doubt about how well embedded are NIAC war crimes in current law.

551. Article 4 of the ICTR Statute reads:

> The International Tribunal for Rwanda shall have the power to prosecute persons committing or ordering to be committed serious violations of

---

[752] L. Sadat, 'Custom, Codification and Some Thoughts about the Relationship between the Two: Article 10 of the ICC Statute', 49 *DPLR* 909, 920 (1999–2000).

[753] *Prosecutor* v. *Furundžija, supra* note 716, at para. 227.

[754] Rome Statute of the ICC, *supra* note 7, at 1328.

[755] See Klabbers, *supra* note 57, at 225.

[756] See T. Graditzky, 'Individual Criminal Responsibility for Violations of International Humanitarian Law Committed in Non-International Armed Conflicts', 322 *IRRC* 29, 49–50 (1998).

[757] See T. Meron, 'International Criminalization of Internal Atrocities', 89 *AJIL* 554, 565–8 (1995).

[758] See E.M. Salgado, 'The Judgment of the International Criminal Tribunal for the Former Yugoslavia in the *Vasiljević* Case', 16 *LJIL* 321, 325 (2003).

Article 3 common to the Geneva Conventions of 12 August 1949 for the Protection of War Victims, and of Additional Protocol II thereto of 8 June 1977. These violations shall include, but shall not be limited to:

(a) Violence to life, health and physical or mental well-being of persons, in particular murder as well as cruel treatment such as torture, mutilation or any form of corporal punishment;

(b) Collective punishments;

(c) Taking of hostages;

(d) Acts of terrorism;

(e) Outrages upon personal dignity, in particular humiliating and degrading treatment, rape, enforced prostitution and any form of indecent assault;

(f) Pillage;

(g) The passing of sentences and the carrying out of executions without previous judgement pronounced by a regularly constituted court, affording all the judicial guarantees which are recognized as indispensable by civilized peoples;

(h) Threats to commit any of the foregoing acts.[759]

552. When the Statute of the ICTY was approved by the Security Council in 1993, no specific provision was inserted relating to violations of Common Article 3 and AP/II. Article 2 of the Statute encompasses grave breaches of the Geneva Conventions.[760] Article 3 adds violations of the laws or customs of war:

The International Tribunal shall have the power to prosecute persons violating the laws or customs of war. Such violations shall include, but not be limited to:

(a) employment of poisonous weapons or other weapons calculated to cause unnecessary suffering;

(b) wanton destruction of cities, towns or villages, or devastation not justified by military necessity;

(c) attack, or bombardment, by whatever means, of undefended towns, villages, dwellings, or buildings;

(d) seizure of, destruction or wilful damage done to institutions dedicated to religion, charity and education, the arts and sciences, historic monuments and works of art and science;

(e) plunder of public or private property.[761]

553. There is no hint in the text of Article 3 of the ICTY Statute that it appertains to NIACs. Moreover, when one examines the official commentary (submitted by the UN Secretary-General) attached to this

---

[759] Statute of the ICTR, *supra* note 89, at 1300–1.
[760] Statute of the ICTY, *supra* note 745, at 1288.   [761] *Ibid.*

clause,[762] it is quite evident that the authors had solely IACs in mind. However, a wider interpretation of Article 3 gained traction in light of Security Council debates when the ICTY Statute was approved.[763] In the 1995 *Tadić* Decision on appeal, the ICTY entertained no doubt that (unlike Article 2 of the Statute) Article 3 extends also to 'violations of common Article 3 and other customary rules on internal conflicts'.[764]

554. It is noteworthy that not all NIAC war crimes listed in the Statutes of the *ad hoc* international tribunals are reiterated in Article 8 of the Rome Statute of the ICC (see, e.g., the ICTR Statute's references to collective punishments and acts of terrorism, *supra* 551). Such deletions exclude certain acts from the jurisdiction of the ICC. They do not necessarily erode the standing of the acts in question as violations of customary LONIAC.

II. The Rome Statute of the ICC

555. Within a few short years of the adoption of the Statutes of the *ad hoc* international tribunals, all remaining misgivings about the existence of NIAC war crimes have vanished. The 1998 Rome Statute of the ICC gave a final seal of approval to the postulate of individual criminal responsibility for serious violations of LONIAC. In Article 8 of the Rome Statute, the framers selected those serious infractions that they deemed fit for the stigma of NIAC war crimes (which are subject to the jurisdiction of the ICC).

556. One can cavil about omissions from the Statute of some serious violations of LONIAC (see *infra* 600), as well as about the specific definition of this or that NIAC war crime. But the message conveyed in the Statute is loud and clear: the international community is nowadays responsive to the idea that perpetrators of serious violations of LONIAC may be personally prosecuted and punished for their misdeeds by the ICC. NIAC war criminals – congruently with Article 8 – are both insurgents and persons in the employ of the Government, and all tiers of command

---

[762] Secretary-General's Report on Aspects of Establishing an International Tribunal for the Prosecution of Persons Responsible for Serious Violations of International Humanitarian Law Committed in the Territory of the Former Yugoslavia (1993), 32 *ILM* 1159, 1171–2 (1993).

[763] See D. Robinson and H. von Hebel, 'War Crimes in Internal Conflicts: Article 8 of the ICC Statute', 2 *YIHL* 193, 196 (1999).

[764] *Prosecutor* v. *Tadić, supra* note 33, at 61.

are affected. It is important to allude here to the irrelevance of action in an official capacity (Article 27 of the Rome Statute).[765]

557. Under Article 29 of the Statute, '[t]he crimes within the jurisdiction of the Court shall not be subject to any statute of limitations'.[766] NIAC war crimes, as enumerated in the Statute, are among these crimes.

558. Article 8 of the Statute streamlines IAC and NIAC war crimes in different layers. The latter are subdivided into two segments: (i) war crimes based on Common Article 3, and (ii) additional NIAC war crimes.

A. NIAC war crimes based on Common Article 3

(a) The crimes

559. Article 8(2)(c) of the Rome Statute reads:

> In the case of an armed conflict not of an international character, serious violations of article 3 common to the four Geneva Conventions of 12 August 1949, namely, any of the following acts committed against persons taking no active part in the hostilities, including members of armed forces who have laid down their arms and those placed *hors de combat* by sickness, wounds, detention or any other cause:
>
> (i) Violence to life and person, in particular murder of all kinds, mutilation, cruel treatment and torture;
> (ii) Committing outrages upon personal dignity, in particular humiliating and degrading treatment;
> (iii) Taking of hostages;
> (iv) The passing of sentences and the carrying out of executions without previous judgement pronounced by a regularly constituted court, affording all judicial guarantees which are generally recognized as indispensable.[767]

560. This text retains verbatim the bulk of Paragraph (1) of Common Article 3 (*supra* 409). However:

(i) Only 'serious' violations of Common Article 3 are penalized.[768]
(ii) Because of the use of the adverb 'namely', the crimes listed by the framers of Article 8(2)(c) are circumscribed to the four categories itemized therein, so that the generic requirement of humane treatment without any adverse distinction – featuring prominently in

---

[765] Rome Statute of the ICC, *supra* note 7, at 1327.   [766] *Ibid.*, 1328.   [767] *Ibid.*, 1319.
[768] See S. Estreicher, 'Privileging Asymmetric Warfare (Part III)? The Intentional Killing of Civilians under International Humanitarian Law', 12 *Chi.JIL* 589, 599 (2011–12).

Paragraph (1) of Common Article 3 – does not entail criminal accountability.[769]

(iii) One minor change also came about: the words 'by civilized people' – ending sub-paragraph (iv) in Common Article 3 – were dropped, owing to a sense of 'political correctness'. The omission does not impact on the substance.

561. The Elements of Crimes illuminate the identity of victims of the war crimes catalogued in Article 8(2)(c): persons who 'were either *hors de combat*, or were civilians, medical personnel or religious personnel taking no active part in the hostilities' ('religious personnel' being defined as including non-confessional, non-combatant military personnel carrying out a similar function).[770] The attention paid to medical or religious personnel fills a transparent lacuna in the original text of Common Article 3 (see *supra* 414).

562. In *sub-paragraph (i)*, the Elements of Crimes throw light on the expression 'mutilation, cruel treatment and torture', which is left undefined in Paragraph (1) of Common Article 3 and, for that matter, in Paragraph (2) of Article 4 of AP/II (*supra* 409, 431). Mutilation is perpetrated 'in particular by permanently disfiguring' a protected person, 'permanently disabling' him, 'or removing an organ or appendage' without medical justification.[771] Acts of mutilation must consist of physical violence.[772] But the words 'in particular' indicate that the war crime is not limited to the acts specified.[773]

563. Cruel treatment, according to the Elements of Crimes, denotes the infliction of 'severe physical or mental pain or suffering'.[774] By bringing in mental pain or suffering, this definition is broader than mutilation. It is also wider than torture. In the words of the ICTY Trial Chamber, in the 1998 *Delalić et al.* Judgment, 'all torture is encapsulated in the offence of cruel treatment': cruel treatment is a more extensive construct, not as 'purposive' as torture.[775]

---

[769] See H. Spieker, 'The International Criminal Court and Non-International Armed Conflicts', 13 *LJIL* 395, 414 (2000).

[770] *Elements of War Crimes under the Rome Statute, supra* note 590, at 383.

[771] *Ibid.*, 395.   [772] *Ibid.*, 397.

[773] See L. Moir, 'Conduct of Hostilities – War Crimes', *The Legal Regime of the International Criminal Court: Essays in Honour of Professor Igor Blischenko* 487, 511 (J. Dorta, H.-P. Gasser and M.C. Bassiouni eds., 2009).

[774] *Elements of War Crimes under the Rome Statute, supra* note 590, at 397.

[775] *Prosecutor v. Delalić et al., supra* note 37, at para. 443.

564. As for torture, the Elements of Crimes enunciate that the 'severe physical or mental pain or suffering' has to be 'for such purposes as: obtaining information or a confession, intimidation or coercion or for any reason based on discrimination of any kind'.[776] We have here the essence of the definition espoused by the CAT, minus the reference to official capacity (see *supra* 529 *et seq.*).

565. *Sub-paragraph (ii)* identifies humiliation and degradation as the staple of 'outrages upon personal dignity'. In the *Aleksovski* case of 1999, an ICTY Trial Chamber held that what counts is not the purely subjective sensitivity of the victim but an objective evaluation as to whether a reasonable person would be outraged.[777] There are still numerous issues that have not been entirely settled. For instance, can the coercive shaving off of beards grown for religious reasons be warranted by medical reasons (such as the need to purge lice)?[778]

566. The Elements of Crimes add (in a footnote) a new factor in the appraisal of 'outrages upon personal dignity': the victims include dead persons, and – if alive – they need not be aware of the humiliation or degradation.[779] The text consequently covers outrages against those who are mentally impaired or unconscious, and it takes into account what is looked upon as a degradation only in the eyes of others.[780]

567. The taking of hostages, listed in *sub-paragraph (iii)*, has already been addressed *supra* 534 *et seq*. *Sub-paragraph (iv)* adverts to indispensable 'judicial guarantees'. The framers of the provision made no attempt to expatiate on those guarantees, which had been sketched out in much greater detail in Paragraph (2) of Article 6 of AP/II (see *supra* 448).

568. The Elements of Crimes tack on the caveat that 'the Court should consider whether, in the light of all relevant circumstances, the cumulative effect of factors with respect to guarantees deprived the person or persons of a fair trial'.[781] The observation is astute, inasmuch as the central issue in criminal adjudication is not mechanical compliance with this or that

---

[776] *Elements of War Crimes under the Rome Statute, supra* note 590, at 401.

[777] *Prosecutor* v. *Aleksovski* (ICTY, Trial Chamber, 1999), para. 56.

[778] See S. Erikkson, 'Humiliating and Degrading Treatment under International Humanitarian Law: Criminal Accountability, State Responsibility, and Cultural Considerations', 55 *AFLR* 269, 299–300 (2004).

[779] *Elements of War Crimes under the Rome Statute, supra* note 590, at 404.

[780] See L. Moir, 'Violations of Common Article 3 of the Geneva Conventions', *The Legal Regime of the International Criminal Court, supra* note 773, at 619, 630.

[781] *Elements of War Crimes under the Rome Statute, supra* note 590, at 408.

individual guarantee. The decisive factor is the overall fairness of the trial vouching for due process of law.

569. As for the problematic phrase 'regularly constituted court' in sub-paragraph (iv), the Elements of Crimes define it as a court affording the 'essential guarantees of independence and impartiality'.[782] The language follows in the footsteps of Paragraph (2) of Article 6 of AP/II and the human rights instruments (see *supra* 446).

(b) Scope of application

570. Paragraph (d) of Article 8(2) demarcates the scope of application of the preceding clause:

> Paragraph 2 (c) applies to armed conflicts not of an international character and thus does not apply to situations of internal disturbances and tensions, such as riots, isolated and sporadic acts of violence or other acts of a similar nature.[783]

571. The text reiterates the language of Paragraph (2) of Article 1 of AP/II (*supra* 65), the sole difference being the use of the conjunction 'or' instead of 'and' antecedent to 'other acts'. The nature of below-the-threshold internal disturbances was examined *supra* 111 *et seq.*

B. *Additional NIAC war crimes*

(a) The crimes

572. If Paragraph (c) of Article 8(2) is tethered to Common Article 3, Paragraph (e) is largely self-reliant:

> Other serious violations of the laws and customs applicable in armed con-flicts not of an international character, within the established framework of international law, namely, any of the following acts:
>   (i) Intentionally directing attacks against the civilian population as such or against individual civilians not taking direct part in hostilities;
>   (ii) Intentionally directing attacks against buildings, material, medical units and transport, and personnel using the distinctive emblems of the Geneva Conventions in conformity with international law;
>   (iii) Intentionally directing attacks against personnel, installations, mate-rial, units or vehicles involved in a humanitarian assistance or peacekeeping mission in accordance with the Charter of the United Nations, as long as they are entitled to the protection given to civil-ians or civilian objects under the international law of armed conflict;

---

[782] *Ibid.*   [783] Rome Statute of the ICC, *supra* note 7, at 1319–20.

   (iv) Intentionally directing attacks against buildings dedicated to reli-
        gion, education, art, science or charitable purposes, historic mon-
        uments, hospitals and places where the sick and wounded are col-
        lected, provided they are not military objectives;
    (v) Pillaging a town or place, even when taken by assault;
   (vi) Committing rape, sexual slavery, enforced prostitution, forced preg-
        nancy, as defined in article 7, paragraph 2(f), enforced sterilization,
        and any other form of sexual violence also constituting a serious
        violation of article 3 common to the four Geneva Conventions;
  (vii) Conscripting or enlisting children under the age of fifteen years
        into armed forces or groups or using them to participate actively in
        hostilities;
 (viii) Ordering the displacement of the civilian population for reasons
        related to the conflict, unless the security of the civilians involved or
        imperative military reasons so demand;
   (ix) Killing or wounding treacherously a combatant adversary;
    (x) Declaring that no quarter will be given;
   (xi) Subjecting persons who are in the power of another party to the
        conflict to physical mutilation or to medical or scientific experiments
        of any kind which are neither justified by the medical, dental or
        hospital treatment of the person concerned nor carried out in his
        or her interest, and which cause death to or seriously endanger the
        health of such person or persons;
  (xii) Destroying or seizing the property of an adversary unless such
        destruction or seizure be imperatively demanded by the necessi-
        ties of the conflict.[784]

(b) Analysis

573. *Sub-paragraph (i)* of Article 8(2)(e) is derived from Paragraph (2) of Article 13 of AP/II (*supra* 462) concerning the protection of the civilian population from attacks, except that it correctly appends the qualifying limitation of 'not taking direct part in hostilities' (see *supra* 183).

574. *Sub-paragraph (ii)* is linked to Articles 9 and 11 of AP/II regarding the protection of medical personnel, units and transports (see *supra* 456, 459), as well as Article 12 about the distinctive emblem (see *supra* 460). The straightforward expansion of the protection to buildings and material fills a glaring gap (hospitals as such are adverted to only in sub-paragraph (iv)).

575. *Sub-paragraph (iii)* is a criminal corollary devised to ensure protection from attack to two categories of personnel (as long as they retain their civilian character), as well as their installations, material, units or vehicles:

---

[784] Rome Statute of the ICC, *supra* note 7, at 1320.

(i) Personnel engaged in humanitarian assistance. The basic activity is the subject of Paragraph (2) of Article 18 of AP/II, but – as mentioned (*supra* 478) – there is no allusion in that provision to protection of relief personnel as such.

(ii) Personnel involved in peacekeeping missions. The progenitor of this provision is the 1994 Convention on the Safety of UN and Associated Personnel (see *supra* 292).

576. Sub-paragraph (iii) relates in a roundabout manner – as part of the proviso ('as long as', etc.) – to the protection given to 'civilian objects' under LONIAC. Sub-paragraphs (ii) and (iv) cover particular civilian objects (e.g., buildings): those using the distinctive emblem and those dedicated to medical, religious, cultural and other charitable purposes. Yet, surprisingly, Article 8(2)(e) does not reckon an attack against other civilian objects as a war crime.[785]

577. *Sub-paragraph (iv)* has to do with cultural property, places of worship, hospitals, and so on. The wording is identical to the corresponding provision on the same subject in the context of IACs: Article 8(2)(b)(ix),[786] which is primarily derived from Hague Regulations 27 and 56 of 1899/1907.[787] Article 16 of AP/II (*supra* 470) is also devoted to cultural property and places of worship, but the Rome phraseology is studiously different. Whereas AP/II talks about 'historic monuments, works of art or places of worship which constitute the cultural or spiritual heritage of peoples', the Rome Statute concentrates on historic monuments and buildings dedicated to religion, education, art (works of art are kept out) or science, removing altogether the requirement that they constitute 'the cultural or spiritual heritage of peoples'.

578. *Sub-paragraph (v)* on pillage of towns or places again repeats the language of the counterpart IAC war crime provision (Article 8(2)(b)(xvi)),[788] spawned by Hague Regulation 28 (*supra* 436). Paragraph (2)(g) of Article 4 of AP/II is different, forbidding only pillage of protected persons (see *supra* 431).[789]

579. *Sub-paragraph (vi)* on sexual offences is in part an extrapolation of AP/II (rape and enforced prostitution are mentioned specifically in Paragraph (2)(e) of Article 4 and sexual slavery is a segment of slavery

---

[785] See La Haye, *supra* note 2, at 144.   [786] Rome Statute of the ICC, *supra* note 7, at 1318.

[787] Hague Regulations Respecting the Laws and Customs of War on Land, *supra* note 572, at 74, 81.

[788] Rome Statute of the ICC, *supra* note 7, at 1318.

[789] See *Elements of War Crimes under the Rome Statute, supra* note 590, at 464.

forbidden in Paragraph (2)(f) of the same Article; *supra ibid.*). By comparison, forced pregnancy and enforced sterilization are definitely novel.
The fount of sub-paragraph (vi) is the parallel IAC provision (Article
8(2)(b)(xxii)).[790]

580. The most important crime listed in sub-paragraph (vi) is, of
course, rape. There is no consensus in the case law as regards the reach
of this crime.[791] But the Elements of Crimes provide a comprehensive
definition of rape, which is gender-neutral and is based on any sexual
invasion of the body.[792] Forced pregnancy is linked in sub-paragraph (vi)
to the definition of the phrase in Article 7(2)(f) of the Statute – in connection with crimes against humanity – where a number of characteristics
are introduced, mainly the intent to affect the ethnic composition of the
population.[793] As for sterilization, the Elements of Crimes clarify that
here – in contrast to medical experimentation (see *infra* 594) – genuine
consent of the victim may be a justification for the act.[794]

581. The reference to Common Article 3 (*supra* 409) in the residual limb
of sub-paragraph (vi) – pointing to 'any other form of sexual violence' –
comes in lieu of the original IAC mention of grave breaches of the Geneva
Conventions, thus adapting the terminology to the NIAC setting. What
this leads to is that acts of sexual violence – other than those (like rape)
that are explicitly mentioned in sub-paragraph (vi) – would be deemed
NIAC war crimes only 'if, and to the extent, that they also constitute by
the same token a serious violation of common Article 3'.[795]

582. *Sub-paragraph (vii)* on child-soldiers is founded on Paragraph
(3)(c) of Article 4 of AP/II (*supra* 443). In both the Rome Statute and AP/II
there is a bifurcation in the banned activity. One prong is 'using them to
participate actively in hostilities' (a more proactive phrase than the AP/II
version of 'allowed to take part in hostilities'). The other relates to children
being only 'recruited' to armed forces or groups (the AP/II language). The
Rome Statute employs two verbs ('[c]onscripting' or 'enlisting') instead
of one (recruiting). Patently, both conscription and enlistment are forms
of recruitment.

---

[790] Rome Statute of the ICC, *supra* note 7, at 1319.
[791] See, e.g., *Prosecutor* v. *Furundžija, supra* note 716, at paras. 174–86.
[792] *Elements of War Crimes under the Rome Statute, supra* note 590, at 466.
[793] Rome Statute of the ICC, *supra* note 7, at 1316.
[794] *Elements of War Crimes under the Rome Statute, supra* note 590, at 327, 331.
[795] A. Zimmermann, 'Article 8(2)(c)–(f)', *Commentary on the Rome Statute of the ICC, supra* note 8, at 475, 495–6.

583. In the *Brima et al.* Judgment of 2007, a Trial Chamber of the SCSL propounded that the distinction between conscription and enlistment is 'somewhat contrived', and that there is both voluntary and forced enlistment.[796] However, if that is the case, the distinction between conscription and enlistment loses its punch. The better view, confirmed by the Trial Chamber of the ICC, in the *Lubanga* Judgment of 2012, is that conscription is coercive whereas enlistment is voluntary.[797]

584. Whether in the form conscription or enlistment, recruitment is not interchangeable with the use of child-soldiers in hostilities. The *Lubanga* Judgment admitted that sub-paragraph (vii) – taken on its own – may be potentially ambiguous on this point, but (bolstered by the Elements of Crimes) pronounced that the two alternative modes of proscribed recruitment are independent of the use of child-soldiers in hostilities.[798] In consequence, the offence of using child-soldiers in hostilities can be committed separately from the earlier delict of conscription or enlistment of those children into the relevant armed force or group.[799]

585. As for children's participation in hostilities, the *Brima et al.* Judgment stated:

> the use of children to participate actively in hostilities is not limited to participation in combat. An armed force requires logistical support to maintain its operations. Any labour or support that gives effect to, or helps maintain, operations in a conflict constitutes active participation. Hence carrying loads for the fighting faction, finding and/or acquiring food, ammunition or equipment, acting as decoys, carrying messages, making trails or finding routes, manning checkpoints or acting as human shields are some examples of active participation as much as actual fighting and combat.[800]

586. The main drift of this articulation of the law is incontrovertible: active (or direct) participation in hostilities is not confined to combat and covers a spate of auxiliary activities (see *supra* 191). But the list of such activities, as outlined in the passage quoted (e.g., carrying loads or procuring food), appears to exceed the usual definition of direct participation in hostilities.

---

[796] *Prosecutor* v. *Brima et al.* (SCSL, Trial Chamber, 2007), para. 192.
[797] *Prosecutor* v. *Lubanga, supra* note 202, at 1065.   [798] *Ibid.*   [799] See *ibid.*, 1066–7.
[800] *Prosecutor* v. *Brima et al., supra* note 796, at para. 737.

587. Justifiable concern has been expressed about the wide range of auxiliary activities carried out by children as charted in *Brima et al*.[801] It would be myopic not to notice that the desire to expand the boundaries of the war crime of using children to participate actively in hostilities is apt to boomerang. The scales have to balance individual accountability (by those who manipulate child-soldiers) with protection for the victims (the children themselves). When they directly participate in hostilities, child-soldiers are excluded from the protective rubric of civilians and are exposed to attack as fighters.[802] If more activities count as direct participation in hostilities, a greater number of manipulators of child-soldiers are caught in the net as war criminals. Yet, fewer children are entitled to protection from attack.

588. The war crime in sub-paragraph (vii) sustains AP/II's age limit of fifteen years for child-soldiers. This cut-off point is lower than the more recent cap of eighteen years, set in the Optional Protocol to the CRC (see *infra* 758). But it is the Rome–AP/II bar that reflects existing customary international law.[803]

589. *Sub-paragraph (viii)* on displacement of the civilian population is impelled by Paragraph (1) of Article 17 of AP/II (*supra* 471). This is a particularly important war crime when a party to the NIAC is scrambling to bring about 'ethnic cleansing' in a given area.[804] We have already touched upon the difficulty with which the use of the word '[o]rdering' is fraught (*supra* 472).

590. *Sub-paragraph (ix)* on treacherous killing or wounding is an echo of the IAC war crime provision (Article 8(2)(b)(ix)),[805] animated by Hague Regulation 23(b).[806] AP/I (Article 37(1) cited *supra* 423) prefers the modern terminology of perfidy over that of treachery, but the retagging is purely semantic. A substantive dissonance relates to another matter. Unlike Article 37(1) of AP/I, the war crime pursuant to sub-paragraph (ix) relates only to killing or injuring the victim. Perfidious

---

[801] See V. Oosterveld, 'The Special Court for Sierra Leone, Child Soldiers, and Forced Marriage, Providing Clarity or Confusion?', 45 *Can.YIL* 131, 148 (2007).

[802] See N. Guibert and T. Blumenstock, 'The First Judgement of the Special Court for Sierra Leone: A Missed Opportunity?', 6 *LPICT* 367, 381 (2007).

[803] See I *Customary International Humanitarian Law, supra* note 267, at 488.

[804] See Zimmermann, *supra* note 795, at 497.

[805] Rome Statute of the ICC, *supra* note 7, at 1318.

[806] Hague Regulations Respecting the Laws and Customs of War on Land, *supra* note 572, at 73.

capture, embodied in Article 37(1), is glossed over as a crime in the Rome Statute.

591. Considering that the notion of 'combatants' is not consonant with NIAC phraseology (see *infra* 705), the use of the phrase 'combatant adversary' in sub-paragraph (ix) – in a NIAC context – grates on the ears. This is aggravated by the fact that, although the expression 'combatant' would have been normal in an IAC setting, Article 37(1) of AP/I speaks only about 'adversary'. The framers of sub-paragraph (ix) probably did not have in their sights combatants (as a term of art) but only adversaries who are taking part in NIAC combat (or hostilities).[807] The idiom 'combatant adversary' would thus exclude a 'civilian adversary'.[808] However, the exclusion is redundant: a true civilian cannot be an adversary.

592. The Elements of Crimes transmit the essence of perfidy from Article 37(1) of AP/I into sub-paragraph (ix):

1. The perpetrator invited the confidence or belief of one or more combatant adversaries that they were entitled to, or were obliged to accord, protection under rules of international law applicable in armed conflict.
2. The perpetrator intended to betray that confidence or belief.
3. The perpetrator killed or injured such person or persons.[809]

Falsely inviting the adversary's confidence or belief that international legal protection is in play goes to the core of perfidy.

593. *Sub-paragraph (x)* pertaining to a declaration that no quarter will be given is the equivalent of the AP/II prohibition of ordering that there shall be no survivors (Paragraph (1) of Article 4; *supra* 431). The emphasis in sub-paragraph (x) is on the very declaration that quarter will be denied. 'There is no requirement of a result'.[810] In other words, sub-paragraph (x) disallows a no-quarter declaration not only when it is converted into a concrete order to execute persons who are *hors de combat*. An abstract threat that there shall be no survivors is a war crime.

594. *Sub-paragraph (xi)* with respect to mutilation or unjustified medical/scientific experiments is also related to AP/II (Paragraph (2)(a) of Article 4 and Paragraph (2)(e) of Article 5; *supra* 431, 445). Mutilation

---

[807] See Zimmermann, *supra* note 795, at 498–9.
[808] See K. Kittichaisaree, *International Criminal Law* 204 (2001).
[809] *Elements of War Crimes under the Rome Statute*, *supra* note 590, at 476.
[810] Schabas, *supra* note 751, at 239.

is already covered in Article 8(2)(c)(i) of the Statute (*supra* 559). As for medical/scientific experiments, what strikes the eye is that there is no diminution in the crime in the event of consent by the victim.[811]

595. *Sub-paragraph (xii)* on destruction or seizure of property – unless imperatively demanded by the necessities of the conflict – is a projection from an IAC war crime provision (Article 8(2)(b)(xiii)),[812] originating in Hague Regulation 23(g)).[813] The Elements of Crimes relating to sub-paragraph (xii) make plain that the property involved must, in the first place, be protected from destruction or seizure by LONIAC.[814] This is a *renvoi* to the relevant rules of AP/II and customary international law.[815]

596. It is asseverated by the ICRC study of customary IHL that attacks against civilian objects in general constitute a war crime under sub-paragraph (xii), inasmuch as – *ex hypothesi* – their destruction cannot be 'imperatively demanded by the necessities of the conflict'.[816] But the hypothesis wrenches the realities of hostilities to fit a legal preconception. In actuality, the destruction of civilian objects is often inevitable in the course of hostilities. The essence of the war crime, as per sub-paragraph (xii), is not the civilian nature of the object destroyed. It is the wanton character of the destruction, namely, the fact that such a measure is not vindicated by military necessity.

597. Article 8(2)(e) is highly evocative of the trend of osmosis from IAC to NIAC law (cf. *infra* 671 *et seq.*). The roster of twelve NIAC war crimes is much shorter than the comparable roll of twenty-six IAC war crimes mustered in Article 8(2)(b) of the Rome Statute.[817] Nevertheless, when one considers the evolution of LONIAC, the Rome Statute may be seen as a quantum leap forward.

(c) Interaction with AP/II

598. When the twelve sub-paragraphs of Article 8(2)(e) are evaluated, various features of interaction with AP/II become prominent. The first is that a number of paragraphs are closely knit with corresponding AP/II norms (see *supra* 573–4, 579, 582, 589, 593–4). The odium of war crimes

---

[811] See *Elements of War Crimes under the Rome Statute*, *supra* note 590, at 482.

[812] Rome Statute of the ICC, *supra* note 7, at 1318.

[813] Hague Regulations Respecting the Laws and Customs of War on Land, *supra* note 572, at 73.

[814] *Elements of War Crimes under the Rome Statute*, *supra* note 590, at 491.

[815] See *ibid.*, 250, 486.

[816] I *Customary International Humanitarian Law*, *supra* note 267, at 27.

[817] See Rome Statute of the ICC, *supra* note 7, at 1317–19.

reinforces the argument that the interdiction of certain acts by AP/II has become an integral part of customary international law (cf. *supra* 548).

599. The second point is that some of the paragraphs of Article 8(2)(e) fill loopholes in AP/II: the protection of relief personnel (see *supra* 575) and the prohibition of perfidy (see *supra* 590–2) are good examples. These instances have to be viewed as customary developments of LONIAC, bringing it into greater harmony with IAC *jus in bello*. Still, numerous gaps in AP/II are not redressed in Article 8(2)(e). The lacunae are particularly deplorable as regards attacks against civilian objects in general; indiscriminate attacks; the principle of proportionality; and precautions in attack (see *supra* 423–4).

600. The third point is even more striking. Some provisions of AP/II are conspicuous by the absence of matching war crimes in Article 8(2)(e). This is understandable in the case of controversial stipulations (e.g., Article 15 of AP/II concerning the special protection of works or installations containing dangerous forces; *supra* 469). But the omissions are more surprising as regards other matters: (i) slavery in other than a sexual connotation (Paragraph (2)(f) of Article 4 of AP/II; *supra* 431); (ii) collective punishments (Paragraph (2)(b) Article 4 of AP/II; *supra ibid.*); (iii) acts of terrorism (Paragraph (2)(d) of Article 4 of AP/II; *supra ibid.*); (iv) improper use of the Red Cross emblem and its counterparts (Article 12 of AP/II; *supra* 460); and (v) the starvation of civilians as a method of conducting hostilities (Article 14 of AP/II; *supra* 466).

601. Slavery may appear to some to be an arcane issue, yet recent NIACs demonstrate that several of its manifestations are as relevant as ever. Certain aspects of slavery have even attracted the attention of the ICTY (see *infra* 657).

602. The non-inclusion in Article 8(2)(e) of collective punishments and acts of terrorism is disconcerting, since both are recognized as NIAC war crimes in Article 4 of the 1994 ICTR Statute (*supra* 551), and in Article 20(f) of the ILC's 1996 Draft Code of Crimes against Peace and Security of Mankind.[818] The omission of acts of terrorism from the list of NIAC war crimes in the Rome Statute was hashed out in a vigorous discussion.[819] The hiatus concerning collective

---

[818] Draft Code of Crimes against the Peace and Security of Mankind, Report of the ILC, 48th Session, [1996] II (2) *ILC Ybk* 17, 53–4.

[819] See G. Venturini, 'War Crimes', I *Essays on the Rome Statute of the International Criminal Court* 171, 180–1 (F. Lattanzi and W.A. Schabas eds., 1999).

punishments has elicited scholarly calls for an amendment of the Rome Statute.[820]

603. Not branding as a NIAC war crime the improper use of the Red Cross and related distinctive emblems of protection is hard to explain, recollecting that such conduct is defined as an IAC war crime in Article 8(2)(b)(vii) of the Rome Statute.[821]

604. The framers' decision to overlook starvation of civilians as a war crime in Article 8(2)(e) has been widely reprimanded by commentators.[822] It makes inroads into the position taken by the ICRC that Article 14 of AP/II has a customary standing.[823]

(d) Scope of application

605. Paragraph (f) of Article 8(2) sets a different scope of application for the crimes catalogued in Paragraph (d), compared to those slated in Paragraph (c):

> Paragraph 2 (e) applies to armed conflicts not of an international character and thus does not apply to situations of internal disturbances and tensions, such as riots, isolated and sporadic acts of violence or other acts of a similar nature. It applies to armed conflicts that take place in the territory of a State when there is protracted armed conflict between governmental authorities and organized armed groups or between such groups.[824]

606. The striking element in Paragraph (f) is that it goes beyond insurgencies and applies also to NIACs between organized armed groups *inter se* (see *supra* 89). In doing that, the Rome Statute breaks away from AP/II and acknowledges the realities of modern NIACs (especially within 'failing States'; see *supra* 261).

607. Paragraph (f) also employs the adjective 'protracted', derived from the *Tadić* Decision on appeal (see *supra* 96). What is baffling is that the same adjective does not appear in Paragraph (d) as well, for 'protracted armed violence' – in line with *Tadić* – is a precondition to all NIACs, even those waged under Common Article 3.[825] The inclusion of 'protracted' in Paragraph (f), when juxtaposed next to its exclusion from Paragraph (d),

---

[820] See S. Darcy, 'Prosecuting the War Crime of Collective Punishment: Is It Time to Amend the Rome Statute?', 8 *JICJ* 29, 49 (2010).

[821] Rome Statute of the ICC, *supra* note 7, at 1318.

[822] See, e.g., C. Kress, 'War Crimes Committed in Non-International Armed Conflict and the Emerging System of International Criminal Justice', 30 *Is.YHR* 103, 134 (2000).

[823] See I *Customary International Humanitarian Law*, *supra* note 267, at 187–8.

[824] Rome Statute of the ICC, *supra* note 7, at 1320–1.

[825] See Kress, *supra* note 822, at 118.

is apt to create the false impression that only NIAC war crimes specified in Paragraph (e) – as distinct from those spelt out in Paragraph (c) – must occur during protracted hostilities.[826] The wrong impression is exacerbated, perhaps, by the figure of speech 'protracted armed conflict' – in lieu of 'protracted armed violence' – as a constituent element of a NIAC.[827] It is unnecessarily repetitive to say that a (non-international) armed conflict is protracted, since no NIAC is possible unless violence is protracted.[828]

608. Although several of the war crimes defined in Paragraph (e) are stamped with the footprints of AP/II, it is interesting that Paragraph (f) does not reproduce the prerequisites of Paragraph (1) of Article 1 of AP/II (*supra* 118) that organized armed groups: (i) be 'under responsible command'; (ii) exercise control over part of the territory; (iii) carry out 'sustained and concerted military operations'; and (iv) have the ability to implement obligations under AP/II. As a result, certain conduct – for instance, by an organized armed group not exercising control over territory – may amount to a war crime defined in Paragraph (e) without constituting a breach of AP/II. This may look paradoxical when the *actus reus* is lifted from AP/II.

609. A central AP/II requirement retained in Paragraph (f) is the existence of organized armed groups. In doing so, Paragraph (f) denotes that its tier of application is higher than the first threshold of NIACs established in Common Article 3. In the *Lubanga* case of 2012, the ICC Trial Chamber pronounced that organized armed groups must 'have a sufficient degree of organisation, in order to enable them to carry out protracted armed violence', picking out telltale signs of organization (such as the ability to plan military operations and put them in effect).[829] This is certainly more than the minimum required by Common Article 3 (see *supra* 90 *et seq.*).

610. However, since the deletion of other AP/II prerequisites shows that the second threshold of NIACs need not be crossed in full under Paragraph (f), the inevitable conclusion is that – notwithstanding a disinclination to admit this[830] – a new, 'intermediary' threshold (in between the first and

---

[826] Cf. L. Condorelli, 'War Crimes and Internal Conflicts in the Statute of the International Criminal Court', *The Rome Statute of the International Criminal Court: A Challenge to Impunity* 107, 112–13 (M. Politi and G. Nesi eds., 2001).

[827] See Kress, *supra* note 822, at 118.

[828] See *Elements of War Crimes under the Rome Statute, supra* note 590, at 441.

[829] *Prosecutor* v. *Lubanga, supra* note 202, at 1055.

[830] See Cullen, *supra* note 432, at 179.

the second) is set up for the specific purpose of trials by the ICC of war crimes defined in Paragraph (e) of Article 8(2).[831]

(e) The Kampala amendment

611. An important milestone in the evolution of NIAC war crimes was reached in a Review Conference of the ICC Statute, held in Kampala in 2010. Three new sub-paragraphs relating to weapons were inserted as an amendment to Article 8(2)(e) of the Rome Statute (*supra* 572):

> (xiii) Employing poison or poisoned weapons;
> (xiv) Employing asphyxiating, poisonous or other gases, and all analogous liquids, materials or devices;
> (xv) Employing bullets which expand or flatten easily in the human body, such as bullets with a hard envelope which does not entirely cover the core or is pierced with incisions.[832]

The new sub-paragraphs correspond to the IAC provisions incorporated from the very beginning in Article 8(2)(b)(xvii)–(xix) of the Rome Statute.[833]

612. The Kampala amendment dissolved any plausible doubts concerning the customary standing of the prohibitions of poison and gas warfare. The Review Conference's resolution, to which the Kampala text is annexed, ascribed the drawing up of new sub-paragraphs (xiii) and (xiv) to the fact that they reflect customary international law.[834] Failure to mention such weapons in the forerunner text of Article 8(2)(e) of the Rome Statute was indeed hard to explain, in light not only of the lucid IAC rules contained in Article 8(2)(b) but also of the provision of Article 3(a) of the ICTY Statute (*supra* 552), which considers the 'employment of poisonous weapons' to be a crime.

613. As for sub-paragraph (xv), the resolution evinces an 'understanding that the crime is committed only if the perpetrator employs the bullets to uselessly aggravate suffering or the wounding effect upon the target of such bullets, as reflected in customary international law'.[835] The pith is in the words 'to uselessly aggravate', denoting that no crime

---

[831] I *How Does Law Protect in War?, supra* note 44, at 123.

[832] First ICC Review Conference (Kampala): Resolutions and Declarations, 2010, 49 *ILM* 1328, 1332 (2010).

[833] Rome Statute of the ICC, *supra* note 7, at 1318–19.

[834] First ICC Review Conference, *supra* note 832, at 1332.   [835] *Ibid.*

is committed if military utility justifies resorting to expanding bullets.[836] The aim of the understanding was to inculcate the idea that the use of hollow-point expanding ('dum-dum') bullets in a NIAC (albeit not in an IAC[837]) may be for a justifiable and lawful purpose, especially in a hostage-taking situation.[838]

614. Although the Kampala interpolation into the Rome text of three new NIAC war crimes has been a major breakthrough where means of hostilities are concerned, it is necessary to register that the opportunity was not availed of to expand NIAC war crimes into the arena of methods of hostilities (such as starvation of civilians; see *supra* 466, 600, 604). From a more holistic perspective, it is of singular significance that no attempt was made in Kampala to follow some outré academic proposals to do away with the allegedly artificial distinction between IAC and NIAC war crimes (cf. *supra* 73).[839]

III. The Second Protocol to the CPCP

615. The 1954 CPCP already requires (in Article 28) that all necessary steps be taken 'to prosecute and impose penal or disciplinary sanctions' against those who breach the CPCP.[840] Yet, this provision 'largely remained a dead letter, mainly because it does not list the violations which require a criminal sanction'.[841]

616. A development in the law of cultural property took place in 1999, when the Second Protocol to the CPCP – in Article 15[842] – indicated which violations of the prohibitions of the CPCP and the Protocol are to be regarded as criminal. Paragraph (1) lists the following five offences:

(a) making cultural property under enhanced protection the object of attack;

---

[836] See W.H. Boothby, 'Differences in the Law of Weaponry When Applied to Non-International Armed Conflicts', 88 *ILS*, *supra* note 55, at 197, 201.

[837] There is no similar understanding with respect to Article 8(2)(b)(xix) of the Rome Statute, cited *supra* note 833.

[838] See W.A. Schabas, *An Introduction to the International Criminal Court* 146 (4th edn, 2011).

[839] For such a proposal, see D. Willmot, 'Removing the Distinction between International and Non-International Armed Conflict in the *Rome Statute of the International Criminal Court*', 5 *Mel.JIL* 196–219 (2004).

[840] CPCP, *supra* note 26, at 1009.

[841] See J.-M. Henckaerts, 'New Rules for the Protection of Cultural Property in Armed Conflict', 835 *IRRC* 593, 613 (1999).

[842] Second Protocol to the CPCP, *supra* note 27, at 1043.

(b) using cultural property under enhanced protection or its immediate surroundings in support of military action;

(c) extensive destruction or appropriation of cultural property protected under the Convention and this Protocol;

(d) making cultural property protected under the Convention and this Protocol the object of attack;

(e) theft, pillage or misappropriation of, or acts of vandalism directed against cultural property protected under the Convention.

Paragraph (2) provides that each Contracting Party to the Protocol shall adopt the necessary measures to establish these acts as punishable criminal offences under its domestic law.

617. Several observations are called for:

(i) Of the five offences mentioned in Article 15, the first two relate to enhanced protection (see *supra* 489) and the others to general protection of cultural property.

(ii) All five offences can be committed in NIACs as well as in IACs.[843]

(iii) The five offences are to be penalized under the domestic law of Contracting Parties. Since the Second Protocol is not linked to the Rome Statute, no criminal accountability exists insofar as the ICC is concerned (unless the acts also constitute NIAC war crimes under Article 8; see *infra* 572).

IV. Prosecution in a foreign State and extradition

618. NIAC war crimes committed in Ruritania may be tried by Ruritanian domestic courts or by insurgents' tribunals. Such penal proceedings must be conducted subject to the judicial guarantees of fair trial itemized in Article 6 of AP/II (*supra* 448) and mirrored in customary international law (see *infra* 654). The pitfall in these proceedings is that – although in theory the court must be independent and impartial – in practice, there is always an apprehension of an innate bias on the part of the judges: either in favour of defendants who belong to the same side or against those who are adversaries.[844] The desire to have judges who are above the fray is the *point d'appui* of the creation of international courts and tribunals.

619. NIAC war crimes charges may also be lodged before the domestic courts of a foreign State (Arcadia) when Ruritanian perpetrators

---

[843] See Toman, *supra* note 640, at 413–14.

[844] See L. Perna, *The Formation of the Treaty Law of Non-International Armed Conflicts* 142–3 (2006).

flee there (or just enter Arcadian borders, during or after the conclusion of the NIAC, even as tourists). There are two issues that emerge in this context: (i) the right of Arcadia to prosecute persons accused of having committed NIAC war crimes within Ruritanian territory, and (ii) potential extradition of the accused to Ruritania, if and when their rendition for trial in that State is requested.

A. Universal jurisdiction

620. Universal jurisdiction over certain NIAC war crimes may be engendered by treaty. Thus, Article 16(1)(c) of the Second Protocol to the CPCP prescribes that jurisdiction over offenders will be established by each Contracting Party not only on the grounds of territoriality and nationality, but, 'in the case of offences set forth in Article 15 sub-paragraphs (a) to (c), when the alleged offender is present in its territory'.[845] This relates to only three of the five offences encapsulated in Article 15(1)(a)–(c) (*supra* 616), and – since (a)–(b) pertain to enhanced protection – to a single albeit major offence against the general protection of cultural property, i.e. extensive destruction.

621. The establishment of universal jurisdiction in Article 16(1)(c) is subject to the provision of Paragraph (4) of Article 22 of the Second Protocol (cited *supra* 25), which sets forth:

> Nothing in this Protocol shall prejudice the primary jurisdiction of a Party in whose territory an armed conflict not of an international character occurs over the violations set forth in Article 15.

The effect of the clause is that, when there are concurrent jurisdictions over the NIAC crimes listed in Article 15(1)(a)–(c), universality must defer to territoriality.[846]

622. More generally, in the Krakow session of 2005, the *Institut de Droit International* forcefully declared that universal jurisdiction may be exercised by any State over (*inter alia*) 'serious violations of international humanitarian law committed in international or non-international armed conflict'.[847] Three important conditions were set out by the *Institut*:

---

[845] Second Protocol to the CPCP, *supra* note 27, at 1043.

[846] See R. O'Keefe, *The Protection of Cultural Property in Armed Conflict* 275–6 (2006).

[847] *Institut de Droit International*, Resolution on 'Universal Jurisdiction with Respect to the Crime of Genocide, Crimes against Humanity and War Crimes', 71 (II) *AIDI* 297, 299 (Krakow, 2005) (Article 3(a)).

(i) The competence to exercise universal jurisdiction – not counting acts of investigation and requests for extradition – is contingent on the State concerned having custody over the accused. Consequently, *in absentia* proceedings are excluded.

(ii) Priority has to be given to the exercise of jurisdiction by a State having a 'significant link' – primarily, territoriality or nationality – to the crime, the offender or the victim, provided that the significantly linked State is able and willing to prosecute the offender.

(iii) Account has to be taken of the jurisdiction of international criminal courts.[848]

Unlike the Second Protocol, the *Institut* equates territoriality with nationality for purposes of priority in the exercise of jurisdiction. But the primacy of territoriality over universality is shared by both texts.

623. Recent State practice shows that dozens of countries have enacted domestic legislation enabling prosecution and punishment of NIAC war crimes committed in foreign lands, although only in a handful of States have such trials actually been held.[849] There is also a problem sparked by the application of statutes of limitations. Whereas there are treaty provisions excluding IAC war crimes from the purview of domestic statutes of limitations,[850] no similar treaty stipulations exist with respect to the prosecution of NIAC war crimes. The only relevant treaty provision appears in the Rome Statute, in connection with the jurisdiction of the ICC itself (see *supra* 557).

B. Extradition

(a) Political offences

624. Mere participation in hostilities by an insurgent in the course of a NIAC in Ruritania is not deemed a crime under international law, as distinct from the domestic law of Ruritania (see *supra* 34). If a rebel crosses the border into Arcadia, and Ruritania requests his extradition – in order to prosecute him for engaging in hostilities – does Arcadia have to oblige? Even if there is a bilateral or regional extradition treaty in force between Ruritania and Arcadia, a stumbling block is encountered due to the political nature of the offence. Numerous extradition treaties explicitly

---

[848] *Ibid.* (Article 3(b)–(d)).   [849] See La Haye, *supra* note 2, at 254.

[850] See Convention on the Non-Applicability of Statutory Limitations to War Crimes and Crimes against Humanity, 1968, *Laws of Armed Conflicts* 1267, 1268 (Article 1).

state that political offences are not extraditable.[851] When they do not, the exception may be read into the treaty, as resolved by the *Institut de Droit International* in its Cambridge session of 1983:

> Where the extradition treaty does not expressly contain the right to refuse extradition for political offences, a State may nevertheless invoke this defence in support of its refusal.[852]

625. The political offences dispensation from extradition emerged in the nineteenth century. From the starting point, it was designed for the benefit of 'those who committed crimes while attempting to overthrow a government'.[853] Currently, the rule is subject to many exceptions,[854] but these do not cover mere participation in NIAC hostilities.

(b) NIAC war crimes

626. Extradition of NIAC war criminals is the crux of the issue. First and foremost, the ICC may request the surrender of any person – from any State in the territory of which he is found – with a view to international prosecution for NIAC war crimes. Contracting Parties to the Rome Statute must comply with such request, subject to the principle *ne bis in idem*, in accordance with Article 89 of the Statute.[855]

627. Extradition of a person accused of NIAC war crimes may be requested not only by international courts and tribunals. Arcadia – where the alleged offender is present – may be requested to extradite him to Ruritania (where the NIAC takes or took place) and/or by Utopia (especially if it is linked to the offence, e.g., by the nationality of the accused or the victim). A preliminary issue is whether Arcadia is required to hand over the accused in the absence of a specific treaty decreeing extradition.

628. The obligation of *aut dedere aut judicare* does not form part of either Common Article 3 or AP/II (which is no wonder, considering that they anteceded the recognition of the construct of NIAC war crimes; see *supra* 546, 550). However, the obligation to extradite or prosecute certain NIAC war crimes does appear in Article 17(1) of the Second Protocol to

---

[851] See, e.g., Article 3(1) of the European Convention on Extradition, 1957, I *ECA* 173, 175 (1971).

[852] *Institut de Droit International*, Resolution on 'New Problems of Extradition', 60 (II) *AIDI* 304, 306 (Cambridge, 1983) (Article II(1)).

[853] G. Gilbert, *Transnational Fugitive Offenders in International Law: Extradition and Other Mechanisms* 387 (1998).

[854] See, e.g., European Convention on the Suppression of Terrorism, 1977, IV *ECA* 41, 42 (1983).

[855] Rome Statute of the ICC, *supra* note 7, at 1359–60.

the CPCP.[856] In more general terms, the obligation appears in Article 9 of the non-binding Draft Code of Crimes against the Peace and Security of Mankind (penned by the ILC).[857] While some scholars assert that there is now a customary law obligation of *aut dedere aut judicare* as regards core international crimes,[858] it is very doubtful that general State practice concurs.

629. The extradition option in *aut dedere aut judicare* is covered from every possible angle by Article 18 of the Second Protocol to the CPCP:

1. The offences set forth in Article 15 sub-paragraphs 1 (a) to (c) shall be deemed to be included as extraditable offences in any extradition treaty existing between any of the Parties before the entry into force of this Protocol. Parties undertake to include such offences in every extradition treaty to be subsequently concluded between them.
2. When a Party which makes extradition conditional on the existence of a treaty receives a request for extradition from another Party with which it has no extradition treaty, the requested Party may, at its option, consider the present Protocol as the legal basis for extradition in respect of offences as set forth in Article 15 sub-paragraphs 1 (a) to (c).
3. Parties which do not make extradition conditional on the existence of a treaty shall recognise the offences set forth in Article 15 sub-paragraphs 1 (a) to (c) as extraditable offences between them, subject to the conditions provided by the law of the requested Party.
4. If necessary, offences set forth in Article 15 sub-paragraphs 1 (a) to (c) shall be treated, for the purposes of extradition between Parties, as if they had been committed not only in the place in which they occurred but also in the territory of the Parties that have established jurisdiction in accordance with Article 16 paragraph 1.[859]

Paragraph (4) should be seen as a 'safety valve', enlarging as it does the application of the notion of territoriality.[860] But it is necessary to recall the primary status of real territoriality in the prosecution of NIAC war crimes (see *supra* 622).

---

[856] Second Protocol to the CPCP, *supra* note 27, at 1043–4.
[857] Draft Code of Crimes against the Peace and Security of Mankind, *supra* note 818, at 30.
[858] See R. van Steenberghe, 'The Obligation to Extradite or Prosecute: Clarifying Its Nature', 9 *JICJ* 1089–116 (2011).
[859] Second Protocol to the CPCP, *supra* note 27, at 1044.
[860] Toman, *supra* note 640, at 358.

630. Assuming that NIAC war crimes are extraditable offences under a bilateral or multilateral treaty in force between Ruritania (or Utopia) and Arcadia, the key question is whether the obstacle of the classification of the crimes as political offences (see *supra* 625) can be overcome. The answer is twofold:

(i) There may be a treaty provision removing the obstacle where war crimes are concerned. Thus, the Second Protocol to the CPCP expressly prescribes, in Paragraph (1) of Article 20,[861] that – for the purpose of extradition – offences set forth in sub-paragraphs 1 (a) to (c) of Article 15 'shall not be regarded as political offences'.

(ii) Recent trends in extradition law suggest that perhaps no war crimes (or other international crimes) should be regarded as political offences for the purposes of extradition.[862] But the matter is not free from doubt.

631. Even if a NIAC war crime is not labelled as political, there may be another hurdle. It is stressed by Paragraph (2) of Article 20 of the Second Protocol that there is no obligation to extradite when the requested State has substantial grounds for believing that an extradition of a person – accused of an Article 15 offence – is designed for prosecuting or punishing him on account of his 'race, religion, nationality, ethnic origin or political opinion'. This blends well with the human right of refugees to 'non-refoulement' (see *infra* 781).

632. The Second Protocol is supposed to apply to all parties to a NIAC: insurgent armed groups as much as the incumbent Government.[863] Still, when it comes to measures such as extradition, their application to the insurgents may be hampered by barriers that are both legal and factual.[864] The obligations undertaken by Governments in these matters are not easily translated to non-State actors.

V. Post-NIAC amnesties

633. An intransigent post-conflict demand by the winning side is liable to be the instigation of wholesale prosecutions and punishment of those

---

[861] Second Protocol to the CPCP, *supra* note 27, at 1044.
[862] See Gilbert, *supra* note 853, at 395.   [863] See Henckaerts, *supra* note 841, at 618.
[864] See T. Desch, 'The Second Protocol to the 1954 Hague Convention for the Protection of Cultural Property in the Event of Armed Conflict', 2 *YIHL* 63, 83–4 (1999).

who fought for the lost cause.[865] Such trials can give rise to much friction and derail efforts of healing the NIAC wounds. To keep at bay a resumption of the tensions of the past, there is often a no less ardent counter-pressure to close the books on the NIAC and start a process of national accommodation. In many instances, a NIAC 'can be ended only at the cost of agreeing not to prosecute' offenders.[866]

634. Post-NIAC trials can be waived *a priori* by legislation, or convictions may be set aside *a posteriori* by amnesties and pardons (of which there are multifarious patterns[867]). We shall concentrate here on amnesty in the sense of waiver by legislation of post-NIAC trials related to crimes committed in connection with the NIAC.

A. AP/II on amnesty

635. Paragraph (5) of Article 6 of AP/II (cited *supra* 446) proclaims:

> At the end of hostilities, the authorities in power shall endeavour to grant the broadest possible amnesty to persons who have participated in the armed conflict, or those deprived of their liberty for reasons related to the armed conflict, whether they are interned or detained.

636. The grant of a general amnesty, in conformity with Paragraph (5) of Article 6 of AP/II, has been described as 'a surrogate for the missing status of combatancy in internal armed conflicts'.[868] But it is necessary to be alert to the hortatory nature of Paragraph (5). No outright amnesty obligation is imposed by AP/II: all that Contracting Parties undertake to do is endeavour to impart – by law – a broad amnesty, in a manner that 'stops prosecutions and quashes convictions', with a view to the reconciliation of a divided nation.[869]

637. Paragraph (5) of Article 6 – which was framed well before the nascence of NIAC war crimes – seems to encourage a general amnesty embracing all offences, even if they amount to breaches of Common

---

[865] See A. Plattner, 'The Penal Repression of Violations of International Humanitarian Law Applicable in Non-International Armed Conflicts', 278 *IRRC* 409, 417 (1990).

[866] Werle, *supra* note 244, at 77.

[867] For a typology of amnesties and pardons, see L.M. Olson, 'Provoking the Dragon on the Patio – Matters of Transitional Justice: Penal Repression vs. Amnesties', 862 *IRRC* 275, 283–4 (2004).

[868] S. Oeter, 'Civil War, Humanitarian Law and the United Nations', 1 *MPYUNL* 195, 209 (1997).

[869] *Commentary on the Additional Protocols, supra* note 95, at 1402.

Article 3 and AP/II itself.[870] If so, that 'would now be out of step' with more modern developments.[871] Some scholars maintain that the correct interpretation of Paragraph (5) is that amnesty should be confined to those who have merely taken up arms against the incumbent Government, as distinct from the perpetrators of war crimes.[872] The ICRC shares this interpretation.[873]

638. Whatever the accurate purport of Paragraph (5), a choice has to be made between justice and reconciliation. When emerging from a ruinous NIAC, can a State focus exclusively on the past (looking through the prism of penal justice) or should it also set its sights on the future (cultivating prospects of national reconciliation)? Despite arguments to the contrary, it is impossible to discount the view that the need to end the internecine conflict may sometimes trump any duty to prosecute.[874]

B. Amnesty and impunity

(a) The validity of an amnesty for NIAC war crimes

639. In the *Furundžija* Judgment, the Trial Chamber of the ICTY pronounced that 'national measures authorising or condoning torture or absolving its perpetrators through an amnesty law' would not be 'accorded international legal recognition'.[875] In connecting the dots, it is not clear (i) whether the Chamber had in mind only the prohibition of torture or the wider tapestry of NIAC war crimes, and (ii) whether this statement – averse to the idea of 'condoning torture' – relates solely to individual amnesties or also to general amnesties designed to bring to bear national reconciliation at the close of a NIAC. The dimensions of non-accordance of 'international legal recognition' are also somewhat opaque.

640. The validity of a domestic general amnesty law granting impunity for NIAC war crimes is disputed. There are those who think that any amnesty for war crimes is incompatible with international

---

[870] See F. Domb, 'Treatment of War Crimes in Peace Settlements: Prosecution or Amnesty?', *War Crimes in International Law, supra* note 260, at 305, 319.

[871] See J. Gavron, 'Amnesties in the Light of Developments in International Law and the Establishment of the International Criminal Court', 51 *ICLQ* 91, 103 (2002).

[872] See R. Müllerson, *Ordering Anarchy: International Law in International Society* 351 (2000).

[873] See I *Customary International Humanitarian Law, supra* note 267, at 611–12.

[874] See C. Villa-Vicencio, 'Why Perpetrators Should Not Always Be Prosecuted: Where the International Criminal Court and Truth Commissions Meet', 49 *Em.LJ* 205, 220 (2000).

[875] *Prosecutor* v. *Furundžija, supra* note 716, at para. 155.

law,[876] but that is not of a piece with the Decision of the Appeals Chamber of the SCSL in the *Kallon et al.* case.[877] State practice divulges that a large number of countries have offered general amnesties for NIAC war crimes, and others are prepared to broker deals making such amnesties possible in foreign lands. In all, practice 'suggests that many states believe the exchange of justice for peace is an acceptable tradeoff.'[878] A dispassionate analysis of the *lex lata* does not confirm the existence of any norm of international law, at the present time, precluding a domestic general amnesty for NIAC war crimes aimed at national reconciliation.[879]

641. A post-NIAC domestic amnesty, although meaning impunity, need not be unconditional. The most famous process of conditional amnesty took place in South Africa following the demise of the apartheid regime. In the Promotion of National Unity and Reconciliation Act of 1995,[880] a 'Truth and Reconciliation Commission' was established for the investigation of gross violations of human rights 'emanating from the conflicts of the past' (as from 1960), with amnesty granted to offenders on condition that they make full disclosure of their wrongdoing.[881] There was a *quid pro quo*: impunity from prosecution in return for full disclosure. It was hoped that the disclosure would lead to 'closure' of a traumatic experience for the victims (or their families) and perhaps for the entire nation. This dividend has been gauged by many, although not by everybody, as counterbalancing the competing need for penal justice.[882]

642. Whatever their form, domestic general amnesties for NIAC war crimes 'cannot "travel" with efficacy to other jurisdictions, and, in particular, are without force before international courts and tribunals'.[883]

---

[876] See C. Stahn, 'Complementarity, Amnesties and Alternative Forms of Justice: Some Interpretative Guidelines for the International Criminal Court', 3 *JICJ* 695, 701–3 (2005).

[877] *Prosecutor* v. *Kallon et al.*, *supra* note 230, at para. 71.

[878] C.P. Trumbull, 'Giving Amnesties a Second Chance', 25 *Berk.JIL* 283, 298 (2007).

[879] See S.M. Meisenberg, 'Legality of Amnesties in International Humanitarian Law: The Lomé Amnesty Decision of the Special Court for Sierra Leone', 856 *IRRC* 837, 847–8 (2004).

[880] South Africa, Promotion of National Unity and Reconciliation Act, No. 34, 1995, H.J. Steiner, P. Alston and R. Goodman, *International Human Rights in Context: Law, Politics, Morals – Text and Materials* 1353 (3rd edn, 2008).

[881] The Report of the Commission was submitted in 1998 and published (in five volumes) in 1999.

[882] For an overall assessment, see B.N. Schiff, 'Do Truth Commissions Promote Accountability or Impunity? The Case of the South African Truth and Reconciliation Commission', *Post-Conflict Justice* 325–42 (M.C. Bassiouni ed., 2002).

[883] L.N. Sadat, 'Exile, Amnesty and International Law', 81 *NDLR* 955, 1034 (2005–6).

Thus, Article 10 of the Statute of the SCSL (established by an Agreement concluded between Sierra Leone and the UN in 2002)[884] expressly promulgates that an amnesty granted to any person falling within the jurisdiction of the SCSL 'shall not be a bar to prosecution'.[885]

(b) The Rome Statute of the ICC

643. The Preamble of the Rome Statute of the ICC declares a determination 'to put an end to impunity' for the crimes spelt out in its text.[886] However, the operative clauses of the Statute are silent on the issue of domestic amnesties. What the Statute does say, in Article 17, is that a case is admissible by the ICC when a State vested with jurisdiction 'is unwilling or unable' to investigate or prosecute it genuinely (shielding a person from criminal responsibility under the Statute).[887] A penetrating question is whether the establishment of a mechanism such as the South African Truth and Reconciliation Commission may be construed as unwillingness on the part of the State to investigate or prosecute NIAC war crimes.[888]

644. When a challenge to admissibility is made, Article 19(1) of the Rome Statute decrees that the ICC shall 'satisfy itself' that it has jurisdiction.[889] As the 'final arbiter', the Court 'may use its own autonomous criteria and standards to assess whether an amnesty or other alternative forms of justice are compatible with the Statute', and it may proceed to trial despite the functioning of a truth and reconciliation commission.[890]

645. There is a measure of flexibility immanent in the discretion granted to the Prosecutor of the ICC (subject to review by a Pre-Trial Chamber) not to proceed with a trial when this 'is not in the interests of justice, taking into account all the circumstances' (Article 53(2)(c)).[891] The Prosecutor (and the Pre-Trial Chamber) may not be inclined to jeopardize a national reconciliation process predicated on a general amnesty clause.[892] Much may depend on the nature of the general amnesty and whether it provides

---

[884] Agreement between the UN and Sierra Leone on the Establishment of the SCSL, 2000, Appendix to *Post-Conflict Justice*, *supra* note 882, at 601.

[885] Statute of the SCSL, 2000, *ibid.*, 605, 608.

[886] Rome Statute of the ICC, *supra* note 7, at 1314.   [887] *Ibid.*, 1323.

[888] See R. Cryer, 'Post-Conflict Accountability: A Matter of Judgement, Practice or Principle?', *The UN, Human Rights and Post-Conflict Situations* 267, 277–8 (N.D. White and D. Klassen eds., 2005).

[889] Rome Statute of the ICC, *supra* note 7, at 1324.   [890] Stahn, *supra* note 876, at 702.

[891] Rome Statute of the ICC, *supra* note 7, at 1339.

[892] See M. Freeman, *Necessary Evils: Amnesties and the Search for Justice* 83 (2009).

for modes of 'accountability and redress' or merely constitutes an attempt to bury past crimes.[893]

(c) The exercise of universal jurisdiction

646. Even if the ICC steps away from the trial of NIAC war crimes in light of a domestic general amnesty in Ruritania for NIAC war crimes, that is not the end of the story. The Ruritanian general amnesty cannot vitiate the right of Arcadia, Utopia, etc., to prosecute and punish Ruritanian NIAC war criminals in the exercise of universal jurisdiction (see *supra* 620 *et seq.*). The Appeals Chamber of the SCSL pronounced in the *Kallon et al.* case: 'Where jurisdiction is universal, a State cannot deprive another State of its jurisdiction to prosecute the offender by the grant of amnesty'.[894]

647. The universal jurisdiction right of Arcadia, Utopia, etc., to prosecute and punish war crimes committed in a NIAC in Ruritania is not affected by a decision by the ICC to shelve a case owing to a truth and reconciliation process: each State is free to decide whether it wishes to lodge criminal charges before its own courts.[895] All the same, it has been argued persuasively by A. Cassese that 'if the amnesty results from a specific individual decision of a court or a Truth and Reconciliation Commission, the exigencies of justice could be held to be fulfilled and foreign courts should refrain from adjudicating these crimes'.[896]

---

[893]　M.P. Scharf, 'The Amnesty Exception to the Jurisdiction of the International Criminal Court', 32 *Cor.ILJ* 507, 526 (1999).

[894]　*Prosecutor* v. *Kallon et al.*, *supra* note 230, at para. 67.

[895]　See A. Seibert-Fohr, 'The Relevance of the Rome Statute of the International Criminal Court for Amnesties and Truth Commissions', 7 *MPYUNL* 553, 576 (2003).

[896]　A. Cassese, *International Criminal Law* 316 (1st edn, 2003).

11

LONIAC customary international law

I. The evolution of LONIAC customary law

A. The pace of the evolution

648. Customary LONIAC has begun to develop only in the aftermath of the adoption of the Geneva Conventions in 1949, but since the *Nicaragua* Judgment of 1986 (see *supra* 30) Common Article 3 has been universally recognized as a true reflection of customary international law. That being the case, there is no need to dwell in the present chapter on the standing of the various norms enshrined in Common Article 3 (*supra* 409). It must be taken for granted that each and every one of them is imbued with customary nature. We shall therefore commence our examination of LONIAC norms that have acquired customary status by looking at the supplementary provisions of AP/II (see *infra* 654 *et seq.*).

649. Customary LONIAC norms may develop not only alongside and in connection with treaty law as framed in Common Article 3 and AP/II.[897] Nowadays the zeitgeist is palpably different, compared to the eras when Common Article 3 and even AP/II were negotiated (the late 1940s and 1970s respectively). Since the 1990s we have witnessed the inexorable emergence of a new customary LONIAC, going well beyond existing treaty law and in fact filling some of its gaps.[898] L. Condorelli calls this 'high speed custom' (as in high speed trains),[899] and the dynamic development has been veritably phenomenal.

B. Lex lata *and* lex ferenda

650. General State practice is the umbilical cord connecting LONIAC norms to customary international law (see *supra* 26–7). When there is a dearth of raw material indicating what general State practice is on a specific

---

[897] See T. Meron, *Human Rights and Humanitarian Norms as Customary Law* 56 (1989).
[898] See Akande, *supra* note 178, at 36.   [899] Condorelli, *supra* note 826, at 109.

issue, it is pointless to pretend that custom exists. Some commentators – goaded by humanitarian considerations – are keen on giving customary LONIAC a push forward. Such efforts are impeccable as long as the dividing line between *lex lata* and *lex ferenda* is duly noted and plumbed in depth. Problems arise when that line remains hazy, as happens in the ICRC study of customary IHL which requires parties to a NIAC – for example – to act with 'due regard for the protection and preservation of the natural environment'.[900] There is hardly any 'ringing endorsement' in general State practice for that rule.[901] The natural environment is simply 'not yet the subject at customary law of special protection in the course of NIAC'.[902] Portions of the natural environment – like forests – can perhaps be considered civilian objects, but even this may change if (e.g., through concealment of adversary fighters) they become military objectives.[903]

651. In the last two decades, the delicate process of determining the existence of customary LONIAC has gained tremendously from the input of a plethora of judicial decisions rendered by international criminal courts and tribunals. These decisions may lump together IACs and NIACs. In the present chapter, we shall spotlight rulings that relate *sub specie* to NIACs, confirming authoritatively the existence of customary LONIAC beyond the boundaries of Common Article 3.

II. The temporal and spatial scope of application

652. As pointed out by the ICTY in the *Tadić* Decision on appeal, the 'geographical and temporal frame of reference' of customary LONIAC is broad.[904] Temporally, customary LONIAC applies from the moment that a NIAC begins (i.e. the moment that it is past the first threshold) to the moment that it ends, and beyond (certain norms are applicable even after the termination of the NIAC; *supra* 160, 635).

653. Spatially, once customary LONIAC is in play, it is potentially applicable throughout the entire territory of the State in which the NIAC is seething. Although there may be oases of calm untouched by the violence whirling around them, one cannot identify a set frontline in a NIAC, and

---

[900]   I *Customary International Humanitarian Law, supra* note 267, at 143–58.
[901]   See K. Hulme, 'Natural Environment', *Perspectives on the ICRC Study on Customary International Humanitarian Law, supra* note 88, at 204, 220–2.
[902]   W. Boothby, *The Law of Targeting* 450 (2012).
[903]   Cf. Article 2(4) of Protocol III to the CCCW, *supra* note 652, at 211.
[904]   *Prosecutor* v. *Tadić, supra* note 33, at 69.

the 'contact zone' between the parties to the conflict is fluid. In the words of the Appeals Chamber of the ICTY, in the 2002 case of *Kunarac et al.*, a violation of LONIAC may 'occur at a time when and in a place where no fighting is actually taking place'.[905]

III. The customary standing of LONIAC treaty provisions (beyond Common Article 3)

A. AP/II

654. We have already seen (*supra* 434) that some provisions of AP/II simply repeat obligations initiated by Common Article 3: they may therefore be deemed customary in character from the outset. The same can be said about clauses based on well-entrenched human rights law, preeminently the concretization of judicial guarantees of fair trial (see *supra* 446 *et seq.*). Other stipulations – originally innovative in nature – have generated custom subsequent to the conclusion of AP/II (on treaties generating custom, see *supra* 29). Largely speaking, as pronounced by the ICTY in the *Tadić* Decision on appeal (*supra* 30), much of the core of AP/II has gradually become part of customary international law over the years. We shall now turn to specific international judicial holdings with respect to concrete provisions of AP/II.

655. In the *Brima et al.* Judgment of 2007, the Trial Chamber of the SCSL held that collective punishments – forbidden in Paragraph (2)(b) of Article 4 of AP/II (*supra* 431) – are a violation of customary international law.[906]

656. In the *Furundžija* case of 1998, the Trial Chamber of the ICTY reached the conclusion that the prohibition of rape – incorporated in Paragraph (2)(e) of Article 4 of AP/II (*supra ibid.*) – constitutes a part of customary international law.[907]

657. In the *Krnojelac* case of 2002, a Trial Chamber of the ICTY, citing the prohibition of slavery in NIACs – engraved in Paragraph (2)(f) of Article 4 of AP/II (*supra ibid.*) – confirmed that this 'is an inalienable, non-derogable and fundamental right, one of the core rules of general customary and conventional international law'.[908]

---

[905] *Prosecutor* v. *Kunarac et al., supra* note 50, at para. 57.
[906] *Prosecutor* v. *Brima et al., supra* note 796, at paras. 673, 675.
[907] *Prosecutor* v. *Furundžija, supra* note 716, at paras. 165–6, 168.
[908] *Prosecutor* v. *Krnojelac* (ICTY, Trial Chamber, 2002), para. 353.

658. In the 2004 *Norman* case, the Appeals Chamber of the SCSL – relying on Paragraph (3)(c) of Article 4 of AP/II (*supra* 443) – enunciated that by 1996 (the critical date for the proceedings) the injunction against the recruitment and use of child-soldiers had 'crystallized as customary international law'.[909] Although the reasoning of the Court has been questioned, the finding about the customary status of the prohibition is not in dispute.[910]

659. Citing Paragraph (2) of Article 13 of AP/II (*supra* 462), the ICTY Appeals Chamber – in its 2004 *Blaškić* Judgment – stated: 'The protection of civilians reflects a principle of customary international law that is applicable in internal and international armed conflicts'.[911] As for the second sentence of Paragraph (2), prohibiting the spread of terror among the civilian population, the ICTY Appeals Chamber in the *Galić* case of 2006 found that it (like the first sentence) 'constituted an affirmation of existing customary international law' already at the time of the adoption of AP/II (namely, 1977).[912] In *Brima et al.*, the SCSL Trial Chamber extended the customary imposition of individual criminal liability to the prohibition of 'acts of terrorism' under Paragraph (2)(d) of Article 4 of AP/II (*supra* 431).[913] But the extension is quite dubious. See on this issue the criticism expressed *supra* 464 as regards the SCSL Appeals Judgment of 2008 in the *Fofana et al.* case.

660. In the *Krnojelac* case of 2003, the Appeals Chamber of the ICTY took the position that Article 17 of AP/II – relating to the forced displacement of civilians (see *supra* 471) – is declaratory of customary international law.[914]

661. Manifestly, not every single stipulation of AP/II passes muster in this fashion. Thus, as conceded even in the ICRC study of customary IHL, the provision of Article 15 of AP/II concerning the special protection of works or installations containing dangerous forces is transformed in customary LONIAC from a flat prohibition to a mere duty of particular care in attack.[915]

---

[909] *Prosecutor* v. *Norman*, *supra* note 223, at 1135–7.
[910] See M. Happold, 'International Humanitarian Law, War Criminality and Child Recruitment: The Special Court for Sierra Leone's Decision in *Prosecutor* v. *Samuel Hinga Norman*', 18 *LJIL* 284, 288–9 (2005).
[911] *Prosecutor* v. *Blaškić*, *supra* note 211, at para. 157.
[912] *Prosecutor* v. *Galić* (ICTY, Appeals Chamber, 2006), para. 87.
[913] *Prosecutor* v. *Brima et al.*, *supra* note 796, at para. 664, 666.
[914] *Prosecutor* v. *Krnojelac* (ICTY, Appeals Chamber, 2003), para. 220.
[915] I *Customary International Humanitarian Law*, *supra* note 267, at 139.

B. Other treaties

(a) Weapons

662. Contemporary developments in treaty prohibitions of the use of certain weapons display a seemingly intractable trend of expansion of their applicability to NIACs (see especially *supra* 611). Yet, are LONIAC treaty obligations matched by customary international law? The question has to be pored over in light of general State practice pertaining to each weapon separately.

663. Where chemical weapons are concerned, the ICTY *Tadić* Decision on appeal pointed out that 'there indisputably emerged a general consensus in the international community on the principle that the use of those weapons is also prohibited in internal armed conflicts' as a matter of customary international law.[916] This is corroborated by the Kampala amendment to the Rome Statute (see *supra* 612), and confirmed by the Security Council response to use of chemical weapons in the Syrian NIAC (see *supra* 507).

664. There is every reason to believe that the prohibition of the use of biological weapons is equally a part of NIAC customary law.[917] In Resolution 1540 (2004), the Security Council – acting under Chapter VII – determined that proliferation of nuclear, chemical and biological weapons constitutes a threat to international peace and security, and decided to take action preventing non-State actors from acquiring, possessing or using such weapons.[918] Resolution 2118 (2013) expressly mentioned biological weapons in reiterating the ban in the context of the Syrian NIAC.[919]

665. As far as conventional weapons prohibited in the CCCW and its Protocols are concerned, opinions are divided on whether the general practice of States has crested at a level justifying an avowal that the treaty regime already mirrors customary international law applicable to NIACs.[920] The flat prohibitions of anti-personnel landmines and cluster munitions – as per the Ottawa and Dublin Conventions (see *supra* 508) – are certainly not customary in nature in NIACs (nor, for that matter, in IACs), inasmuch as (i) they were innovative at the point of entering into

---

[916] *Prosecutor* v. *Tadić, supra* note 33, at 69.   [917] See Boothby, *supra* note 673, at 324.
[918] Security Council Resolution 1540 (2004), Preamble, paras. 1–2.
[919] Security Council Resolution 2118 (2013), *supra* note 679, at paras. 18–19.
[920] See Boothby, *supra* note 673, at 326–30.

force, and (ii) State practice is not abundant enough to venture to suggest that they have generated custom thereafter.[921]

(b) Cultural property

666. It will be recalled (see *supra* 30) that the *Tadić* Decision on appeal resolved that Article 19 of the CPCP – which expressly applies most of the instrument to NIACs – had become part of customary law. But it must also be taken into account that the protection of cultural property in NIACs is covered separately in Article 16 of AP/II (*supra* 470). Article 16 safeguards 'places of worship', which are not mentioned as such in the CPCP. On the other hand, Article 16 speaks only about two categories of cultural property: 'historic monuments' and 'works of art'.

667. The limited scope of the AP/II provision stands out when compared with the compendious definition appearing in Article 1 of the CPCP:

> For the purposes of the present Convention, the term 'cultural property' shall cover, irrespective of origin or ownership:
> (a) movable or immovable property of great importance to the cultural heritage of every people, such as monuments of architecture, art or history, whether religious or secular; archaeological sites; groups of buildings which, as a whole, are of historical or artistic interest; works of art; manuscripts, books and other objects of artistic, historical or archaeological interest; as well as scientific collections and important collections of books or archives or of reproductions of the property defined above;
> (b) buildings whose main and effective purpose is to preserve or exhibit the movable cultural property defined in sub-paragraph (a) such as museums, large libraries and depositories of archives, and refuges intended to shelter, in the event of armed conflict, the movable cultural property defined in sub-paragraph (a);
> (c) centres containing a large amount of cultural property as defined in sub-paragraphs (a) and (b), to be known as 'centres containing monuments'.[922]

The definition encloses not only historic monuments and works of art, but also archaeological sites, museums, libraries, scientific collections, archives, etc.

---

[921] See *HPCR Manual on International Law Applicable to Air and Missile Warfare* 72, 75–7 (2013).
[922] CPCP, *supra* note 26, at 1001.

668. While the CPCP is applicable to 'property of great importance to the cultural heritage of every people',[923] Article 16 of AP/II resorts to the formula: 'which constitute the cultural or spiritual heritage of peoples'. The adjective 'spiritual' is thus added (presumably because of places of worship), and the expression 'every people' (in the singular) becomes 'peoples' (in the plural). Is this a difference that amounts to a distinction?

669. In its study of customary IHL, the ICRC advocates the view that 'peoples' in Article 16 mean mankind as a whole, justifying a restrictive attitude on the dual ground that (i) Article 16 (unlike the CPCP[924]) does not posit a distinctive emblem marking out objects under protection, and (ii) AP/II (again unlike the CPCP: see *supra* 486) does not provide for a waiver of protection from attack in case of imperative military necessity.[925] Admittedly, not everybody agrees with that interpretation.[926]

670. The issue of a possible waiver of protection profoundly disconnects AP/II from the CPCP: each instrument pursues a painstakingly divergent approach to the subject.[927] The attempt to bridge over the discord, made in the 1999 Second Protocol to the CPCP (see *supra* 487), is a matter of treaty law. But which (if any) of the two disparate treaty regimes is endorsed by customary international law? There is no way to ignore the fact that Article 16 was formulated 'without prejudice' to the provisions of the CPCP (*supra* 470). In light of the 'without prejudice' rider, an ICTY Trial Chamber in the *Strugar* case of 2005 said that AP/II 'may not have affected the operation of the waiver provision of the Hague Convention of 1954 in cases where military necessity imperatively requires waiver'.[928]

IV. The process of osmosis from IAC *jus in bello*

A. Convergence of LONIAC and IAC jus in bello?

671. Since there is a relative paucity of treaty law concerning NIACs compared to IACs, there is a burgeoning penchant for administering to NIAC hostilities norms carved out by and for IAC *jus in bello* (on the ground that they reflect customary international law applicable to all types of armed conflict). Some commentators proceed to suggest – without any

---

[923] *Ibid.*   [924] *Ibid.*, 1005 (Article 16).
[925] I *Customary International Humanitarian Law, supra* note 267, at 130.
[926] See O'Keefe, *supra* note 846, at 210–12, 231.
[927] See R. Wolfrum, 'Protection of Cultural Property in Armed Conflict', 32 *Is.YHR* 305, 329 (2002).
[928] *Prosecutor* v. *Strugar* (ICTY, Trial Chamber, 2005), para. 309.

hard proof – that certain IAC cum NIAC norms have acquired the status of *jus cogens*, so that they cannot be modified by an ordinary treaty.[929]

672. The propensity to show convergence of IAC *jus in bello* and LONIAC is apt to go to great lengths. This is attested by the ICRC study of customary IHL (cited *infra* 228), where '136 (and arguably even 141) out of 161 rules' under review are found to apply both in IACs and in NIACs.[930] A rate of overlap of some 85 per cent is exaggerated even on the face of it.

673. Whatever the actual rate of overlap, the abundant evidence for an increasing harmonization between IAC and NIAC customary rules speaks for itself. Consequently, there have been scholarly calls for blending the law regulating the two types of armed conflicts into a single amorphous module.[931] There is even a vogue to conflate IAC and NIAC law by interlacing *lex lata* with *lex ferenda*[932] (cf. *supra* 650). More cautiously, in its Berlin session of 1999 the *Institut de Droit International* expressed its support for the *lex ferenda* idea of drafting and adopting a new 'convention designed to regulate all armed conflicts and protect all victims, regardless of whether such conflicts are international, non-international or of a mixed character'.[933]

674. *De lege lata*, it would be wrong to maintain that 'recent developments have sufficiently erased differences between the two traditionally separate and distinct parts of international humanitarian law to allow them to be considered as a single body of principles and rules applicable in armed conflicts'.[934] The distinction between IAC and NIAC law of armed conflict is far from being 'an outdated phenomenon'.[935] It most certainly 'remains in place' in the practice and perception of States[936] (cf. the observation about the Kampala amendment *supra* 614).

---

[929] See D. Fleck, 'The Protocols Additional to the Geneva Conventions and Customary International Law', 29 *Mil.LLWR* 497, 501 (1990).

[930] This is the ICRC's own tabulation: I *How Does Law Protect in War?*, *supra* note 44, at 324.

[931] See E. Crawford, 'Unequal before the Law: The Case for the Elimination of the Distinction between International and Non-International Armed Conflicts', 20 *LJIL* 441, 449–52 (2002).

[932] See D. Turns, 'At the "Vanishing Point" of International Humanitarian Law: Methods and Means of Warfare in Non-International Armed Conflicts', 45 *Ger.YIL* 115, 131 (2002).

[933] *Institut de Droit International*, *supra* note 224, 399 (Article XI).

[934] See Müllerson, *supra* note 872, at 343.

[935] An expression used by E. Kwakwa, *The International Law of Armed Conflict: Personal and Material Fields of Application* 23 (1992).

[936] R. Bartels, 'Timelines, Borderlines and Conflicts: the Historical Evolution of the Legal Divide between International and Non-International Armed Conflicts', 873 *IRRC* 35, 40–1 (2009).

675. There is little benefit in a discourse *in abstracto* on the complex coexistence of IAC *jus in bello* and LONIAC customary norms. Even when it is demonstrated that certain IAC and LONIAC customary rules correspond *grosso modo*, it does not follow that the LONIAC rights and obligations match their IAC counterparts in every detail. Here are some words of caution from the *Tadić* Decision on appeal (a decision that, in multiple ways, 'pushed the envelope' of NIAC customary international law):

> The emergence of the aforementioned general rules on internal armed conflicts does not imply that internal strife is regulated by general international law in all its aspects. Two particular limitations may be noted: (i) only a number of rules and principles governing international armed conflicts have gradually been extended to apply to internal conflicts; and (ii) this extension has not taken place in the form of a full and mechanical transplant of those rules to internal conflicts, rather, the general essence of those rules, and not the detailed regulation they may contain, has become applicable to internal conflicts.[937]

676. In the next two sections, we shall trace evidence in the case law for the convergence of IAC and LONIAC general principles and specific norms in present-day customary law. Then, we shall take a look at the opposite side of the coin, namely, the congenital divergence – which cannot be dismissed – between certain aspects of IAC and NIAC customary international law.

B. General principles

677. Two general principles radiate from IAC *jus in bello* onto customary LONIAC. These are the principles concerning distinction and unnecessary suffering. Many, if not most, of the concrete LONIAC prohibitions affecting either the means or the methods of hostilities are derived from these two principles. Both principles were declared by the ICJ, in its 1996 Advisory Opinion on the *Legality of Nuclear Weapons*, to be 'cardinal' in the realm of humanitarian law.[938]

(a) Distinction

678. In its Advisory Opinion, the ICJ described the principle of distinction as 'aimed at the protection of the civilian population and civilian

---

[937] *Prosecutor* v. *Tadić, supra* note 33, at 69.
[938] Advisory Opinion on the *Legality of the Threat or Use of Nuclear Weapons*, [1996] *ICJ Reports* 226, 257.

objects and establishes the distinction between combatants and non-combatants'.[939] The expression 'combatants' does not suit NIACs (see *infra* 705). But it is incontrovertible that, even in NIACs, it is essential to distinguish in attack fighters from civilians (provided that the latter do not take a direct part in hostilities). In the words of an ICTY Trial Chamber in the *Kupreškić* Judgment of 2000, '[t]he protection of civilians in time of armed conflict, whether international or internal, is the bedrock of modern humanitarian law'.[940] This general principle is 'inherent' in AP/II, 'which provides for the protection of civilians': after all, '[f]or them to be protected, they must be distinguished'.[941]

679. The general principle of civilian protection is translated concretely into Paragraph (1) of Article 13 of AP/II, whereby the civilian population and individual civilians are entitled to protection against the dangers arising from military operations (*supra* 462). The ICTY case law constantly refers to civilian protection under Article 13 as one of the main building blocks of LONIAC customary law (see *supra* 659). There is much doctrinal support for broadening this protection under customary law, for instance by banning the use of civilians as 'human shields'.[942]

680. The foremost practical problem with the application of the principle of distinction in NIACs is that, unlike Government troops, insurgents do not usually wear uniforms or use other external marks identifying them as fighters. There is no authoritative guidance as to what an insurgent fighter is supposed to do in order to enable an adversary to tell him apart from civilians.[943] This leads to congeries of confusing incidents in which Government armed forces (especially air forces) claim that civilians in a NIAC were struck by mistake since they looked from a distance or high altitude like fighters (especially if they were carrying arms for self-protection).

681. Distinction is not confined to persons. Article 52 of AP/I (cited *supra* 424) draws a carefully drafted dual structure of 'military objectives' (determined by nature, location, purpose or use) versus 'civilian objects': the latter, as a reverse of the former, are protected from attack. Inexplicably, no analogous general provision appears in AP/II (see *supra ibid.*). The

---

[939] *Ibid.*   [940] *Prosecutor* v. *Kupreškić et al.* (ICTY Trial Chamber 2000), para. 521.

[941] *Fight It Right: Model Manual on the Law of Armed Conflict for Armed Forces* 233 (ICRC, A.P.V. Rogers and P. Malherbe eds., 1999).

[942] See *San Remo Manual on the Law of Non-International Armed Conflict*, *supra* note 208, at 44.

[943] See A.W. Dahl, 'The Legal Status of the Opposition Fighter in International Armed Conflict', 43(3) *Mil.LLWR* 137, 144–5 (2004).

linchpin expression 'military objectives' appears in AP/II solely *en passant* in Article 15 (*supra* 469), apropos of works and installations containing dangerous forces. The application to NIACs of the CCCW and its Protocols brought in more mentions of military objectives (see *supra* 495). As far as cultural property is concerned, the concept of 'military objectives' is given its right place only in Article 6(a) of the Second Protocol to the CPCP, in connection with waiver of protection under the Convention (see *supra* 487).

682. Once the principle of distinction between civilians and fighters is recognized in NIACs, the idea of segregating in hostilities military objectives from civilian objects becomes almost irresistible. 'It would be absurd to claim that in a non-international armed conflict, an attack upon a weapons factory and upon a school are equivalent under IHL simply because in both cases civilians are killed'.[944] Article 3(7) of Amended Protocol II to the CCCW (cited *supra* 440), which applies to NIACs, does prohibit in all circumstances to direct relevant weapons (mines, boobytraps and similar devices) against civilian objects. So does Article 2 of Protocol III to the CCCW about incendiaries (see *supra* 495).

683. In the *Hadžihasanović et al.* Decision of 2005, the Appeals Chamber of the ICTY was confident that the prohibition on attacks on civilian objects in NIACs 'has attained the status of customary international law', and that this covers wanton destruction of civilian property.[945] Wanton destruction of property (civilian or otherwise) must, however, be dealt with separately from attacks on civilian objects (see *supra* 596).

684. The fact that objects (like bridges or railroads) have been verified to constitute military objectives does not mean that they will be automatically attacked. In a NIAC there is a constant policy dilemma whether a party to the conflict is well advised to destroy them. When victory in the NIAC seems within reach, reason dictates not to rush to bring about such destruction – even if it is permissible under LONIAC – inasmuch as the cost of post-conflict reconstruction may be daunting.

(b) Unnecessary suffering

685. The principle of unnecessary suffering is presented by the ICJ – in its Advisory Opinion on the *Legality of Nuclear Weapons* – as a prohibition

---

[944] M. Sassòli and L. Cameron, 'The Protection of Civilian Objects – Current State of the Law and Issues *de lege ferenda*', *The Law of Air Warfare: Contemporary Issues* 35, 45 (N. Ronzitti and G. Venturini eds., 2006).

[945] *Prosecutor* v. *Hadžihasanović et al.* (Decision) (ICTY, Appeals Chamber, 2005), para. 30.

of inflicting on combatants 'a harm greater than that unavoidable to achieve legitimate military objectives', covering the use of weapons 'uselessly aggravating' their suffering.[946] Although the ICJ talked expressly about combatants in IACs, the principle applies equally to fighters in NIACs.

686. Concrete references to 'unnecessary suffering' (or superfluous injury) appear in Article 3(3) of Amended Protocol II to the CCCW,[947] Article 3(a) of the ICTY Statute (*supra* 552), and the Preamble to the Ottawa Convention on Anti-Personnel Mines,[948] all of which are applicable in NIACs.

687. In practice, it is not always clear whether a particular weapon can be viewed as causing suffering that is unnecessary. Hence the need to conclude treaties spelling this out in a binding fashion, and it is then required to determine the applicability of each treaty to NIACs.

688. Weapons can cause unnecessary suffering not only when they are deliberately designed and manufactured to do so. Ordinary munitions – like standard-issue bullets – can be altered in the field by frontline fighters, in order to cause inflammation of wounds or otherwise intensify the agony of targeted adversaries. Such conduct comes squarely within the prohibition.[949]

C. Specific norms

689. A number of crucial IAC *jus in bello* norms have been imported into customary LONIAC, independently of treaty texts. Indeed, they have been ingested into LONIAC – by international courts or tribunals – in order to fill flagrant gaps in existing LONIAC instruments.

(a) Indiscriminate attacks

690. As pointed out (*supra* 423), there is no mention in AP/II of the prohibition of indiscriminate attacks. However, the *Tadić* Decision on appeal stated succinctly that the protection of civilians from indiscriminate attacks is a customary rule that has developed in NIACs.[950] The

---

[946] Advisory Opinion on the *Legality of the Threat or Use of Nuclear Weapons, supra* note 938, at 257.

[947] Amended Protocol II to the CCCW, *supra* note 67, at 198.

[948] Ottawa Convention, *supra* note 656, at 287.

[949] See *San Remo Manual on the Law of Non-International Armed Conflict, supra* note 208, at 31.

[950] *Prosecutor v. Tadić, supra* note 33, at 69.

ruling was reinvigorated by a Trial Chamber in the 2003 *Galić* Judgment, which held that the prohibition of indiscriminate attacks 'reflects a well-established rule of customary law applicable in all armed conflicts'.[951]

691. Indiscriminate attacks are defined in Article 51(4) of AP/I (cited *supra ibid.*) as attacks that are not directed specifically at military objectives (or personnel). Indiscriminate attacks cut across methods and means of hostilities. The blind use of indiscriminate weapons is forbidden in the 1996 Amended Protocol II to the CCCW[952] (which is applicable in NIACs).

692. Diametrically opposed to indiscriminate weapons are precision-guided munitions (PGM), capable of being delivered to targets 'on the nose'. Accurate targeting with PGM can be done even beyond visual range and in poor weather conditions, so that the indiscriminate character of an attack cannot be established merely on the basis of range or visibility.

(b) Proportionality

693. The *Galić* Judgment explained that '[o]ne type of indiscriminate attack violates the principle of proportionality'.[953] This is an understatement, in light of the vital importance of proportionality in practice. The customary nature of proportionality cannot be rebutted, despite its perplexing absence from AP/II (see *supra ibid.*).

694. The principle of proportionality is derived from IAC *jus in bello*. Whether in an IAC or in a NIAC, proportionality protects solely civilians and civilian objects.[954] That is to say, the principle of proportionality does not protect fighters. Its exclusive concern is to eliminate or minimize collateral damage (viz. incidental harm) to civilians or their property. The *Galić* Judgment correctly summarized the principle as follows: before an attack against a lawful target is launched, it is imperative to examine whether a reasonably well-apprised person in the concrete circumstances – making use of the information available at the time – could have expected that incidental civilian casualties resulting from the attack (or damage to civilian property) would be excessive in relation to the concrete and direct military advantage anticipated.[955] The anticipated military advantage has to be evaluated in a holistic manner.

---

[951] *Prosecutor* v. *Galić*, *supra* note 209, at para. 57.
[952] Amended Protocol II to the CCCW, *supra* note 67, at 198 (Article 3(8)(a)–(b)).
[953] *Prosecutor* v. *Galić*, *supra* note 209, at para. 58.
[954] See I. Henderson, *The Contemporary Law of Targeting: Military Objectives, Proportionality and Precautions in Attack under Additional Protocol I* 206 (2009).
[955] *Prosecutor* v. *Galić*, *supra* note 209, at para. 58.

695. The principle of proportionality is incorporated in Amended Protocol II to the CCCW,[956] and in Paragraph (c) of Article 7 of the Second Protocol to the CPCP (cited *supra* 488). Both provisions are applicable in NIACs.

(c) Precautions

696. Another significant conclusion, arrived at by the *Galić* Judgment, was that '[t]he practical application of the principle of distinction requires that those who plan or launch an attack take all feasible precautions to verify that the objectives attacked are neither civilians nor civilian objects, so as to spare civilians as much as possible'.[957] Feasible precautions in attack are also the subject of Article 7 of the Second Protocol to CPCP (see *supra ibid.*), which applies in NIACs.

697. The obligation to take feasible precautions devolves not only on high-ranking, long-term planners who benefit from the availability of time on their hands to figure out what is transpiring and what is to be expected. Even lower-echelon fighters confronted by targets of opportunity – which call for spur-of-the-moment decisions – are not absolved from the need to verify that those are lawful targets and that the principle of proportionality can be respected.

698. The ICRC contends that precautions in NIACs include the issuance of effective advance warnings of attacks affecting civilians, unless circumstances do not permit.[958] This is based, in essence, on the IAC norms, specifically Paragraph 2(c) of Article 57 of AP/I (cited *supra* 423). But advance warnings are not in evidence in NIAC general State practice.

(d) Perfidy

699. We have seen (*supra ibid.*) that AP/II does not incorporate the prohibition of perfidy, which appears in AP/I (Article 37(1)) and relates to acts of killing, injuring or capturing an adversary by inviting his confidence, leading him to believe that he is entitled to – or is obliged to accord – protection under the IAC *jus in bello*. Despite the gap in AP/II, the *Tadić* Decision on appeal pronounced that 'the general principles of customary international law have evolved with regard to internal armed conflicts' so

---

[956] Amended Protocol II to the CCCW, *supra* note 67, at 196, 198 (Article 3(8)(c)).
[957] *Prosecutor* v. *Galić*, *supra* note 209, at para. 58.
[958] See I *Customary International Humanitarian Law*, *supra* note 267, at 62–4.

as to bring forth a 'prohibition of perfidy'.[959] This ruling has been criticized in the legal literature,[960] but it can be buoyed up by the Rome Statute insofar as killing or injuring – although not capturing – an adversary is concerned (see *supra* 590).

700. The customary prohibition of perfidy does not impede the lawful use of ordinary ruses in hostilities (not inviting the adversary's confidence re protection under LONIAC), such as recourse to camouflage, decoys, mock operations or misinformation.[961]

V. Divergence from IAC *jus in bello*

701. The increasing resemblance between IAC *jus in bello* and LONIAC should not be taken as an indication that a full convergence between the two legal regimes is verging on completion. There are serious obstacles, some of which appear to be insurmountable, standing in the way of such a fusion being effected in the general practice of States.

A. POW status

702. In IACs, combatants – provided that they satisfy certain *jus in bello* conditions categorizing them as lawful combatants – are entitled to the privileged status of POW, meaning that if captured their life and health must be protected, and they cannot be prosecuted for ordinary acts of hostilities untainted as war crimes.[962] By contrast, in NIACs (absent 'recognition of belligerency'), captured insurgents do not benefit from an entitlement to the privileged status of POW.[963] In the words of M. Sassòli:

> no State accepts that its own citizens waging an armed conflict against the government or against each other have a right to commit acts of hostility and may not be punished for such acts – even if they conform to international humanitarian law – a privilege inherent to combatant status.[964]

---

[959] *Prosecutor* v. *Tadić*, *supra* note 33, at 69.
[960] See C. Greenwood, 'International Humanitarian Law and the *Tadić* Case', 7 *EJIL* 265, 278 (1996).
[961] See AP/I, *supra* note 21, at 730–1 (Article 37(2)).
[962] See Dinstein, *supra* note 686, at 33–55.
[963] See W.A. Solf, 'The Status of Combatants in Non-International Armed Conflicts under Domestic Law and Transnational Practice', 33 *AULR* 53, 54–5 (1983–4).
[964] M. Sassòli, 'Combatants', II *MPEPIL* 350, 357.

703. The rationale for this fundamental distinction between IAC *jus in bello* and LONIAC is that every domestic legal system looks upon an insurgency as pathogenic. Insurgents are regarded as criminals; perhaps even traitors (depending on the definition of treason in the domestic penal code). When captured by Government forces, they are liable to be prosecuted and severely punished by domestic courts (military or civilian) for their criminal conduct under the domestic law, even if they have complied with LONIAC (see *supra* 53). There is the additional possibility that the captives have committed violations of LONIAC. However, the quintessential point is that insurgents may be brought to trial – by domestic courts – not only for actions that run afoul of LONIAC but also for their very participation in hostilities (see *supra* 37). The disclaimer in Common Article 3 about not affecting the 'legal status' of the Parties to the conflict (*supra* 409) only strengthens an inference that the incumbent Government 'remains entitled to try captured rebels for treason and rebellion', denying them POW privileges.[965]

704. The LONIAC obligation to allow insurgents to surrender (see *supra* 433) does not attenuate the possibility of subsequent prosecution and punishment of the captives for treason or other crimes.[966] LONIAC norms steer clear of the issue, concentrating on a prohibition of summary executions of insurgents (see *supra* 92, 431). It follows that, if due process of law is guaranteed, the stakes can be mortal in those countries where criminal conviction may entail capital punishment (cf. *infra* 766).

705. This is the key reason why it is misleading to consider insurgents to be 'combatants'.[967] The 2006 San Remo Manual on Non-International Armed Conflict prefers the more suitable term 'fighters' instead.[968] The expression – used also in the present volume – is loose enough to cover both (i) members of the State's armed forces, and (ii) any civilians taking a direct part in the hostilities, either as insurgents or as members of organized armed groups opposing each other.

706. There is an interesting question relating to the treatment of captured personnel in a NIAC fought between organized armed groups in a 'failing State' (see *supra* 261). Since no Government is left, and all the organized armed groups in the field are equally shorn of any authority

---

965   M.S. McDougal and F.P. Feliciano, *The International Law of War: Transnational Coercion and World Public Order* 537–8 (1961).
966   See *San Remo Manual on the Law of Non-International Armed Conflict, supra* note 208, at 41.
967   See Kleffner, *supra* note 60, at 321.
968   *San Remo Manual on the Law of Non-International Armed Conflict, supra* note 208, at 4.

to cloak themselves with the mantle of the State – all of them operating on the same unconstitutional footing – the pejorative concept of treason cannot be factored into the equation. The diverse groups are estopped from claiming that opponents owe them any allegiance. That being the case, why should these groups not apply to captured adversaries the rules pertaining to POW status?

B. Neutrality

707. The law of neutrality is irrelevant to LONIAC.[969] This is a corollary of the separate line-up of Belligerent Parties and neutral States, which is a prominent feature of all IACs (even world wars) but is alien to NIACs. Since a NIAC occurs within the territory of a single country (see *supra* 74–6), the construct of a neutral as a 'third State' does not make sense. The position of an incumbent Government wrestling with an insurgency is not similar to that of an inter-State contest between peers (save in the extraordinary setting of 'recognition of belligerency', which warps the legal light beams; see *supra* 338 *et seq.*). It is precisely because the theorem of neutrality is non-existent in NIACs that Utopia is entitled to intervene militarily in a NIAC in Ruritania, at the request of its Government (see *supra* 244).

708. The inapplicability of neutrality law in the conduct of NIAC hostilities has far-reaching reverberations in LONIAC. There is no need to recap here all types of *jus in bello* norms, affected by the status of neutrality, which have no parallel in LONIAC. A few select examples – on land, at sea and in the air – will do.

709. On land, the movement of troops or munitions of war belonging to the incumbent Government of Ruritania through the territory of Utopia (with the latter's consent) is not forbidden. This is in contradiction to the IAC *jus in bello* rule of Hague Convention (V) of 1907 Respecting the Rights and Duties of Neutral Powers and Persons in Case of War on Land (Articles 2 and 5).[970]

710. On the high seas, the IAC *jus in bello* institution of blockade is inadmissible in a NIAC (see *supra* 350). Equally, there is no application in LONIAC[971] of the *jus in bello* rule relating to the right of visit and

---

[969] *HPCR Manual, supra* note 921, at 382.
[970] Hague Convention (V) Respecting the Rights and Duties of Neutral Powers and Persons in Case of War on Land, 1907, *Laws of Armed Conflicts* 1399, 1401.
[971] See C.J. Colombos, *The International Law of the Sea* 754 (6th edn, 1967).

search of neutral merchant vessels (monitoring contraband goods) or the corresponding entitlement to capture such vessels and cargoes as prize.[972]

711. In the air:

(i) An incursion of military aircraft of the incumbent Government of Ruritania into Utopian airspace during a NIAC does not result in the IAC *jus in bello* obligation for Utopia to intern the aircraft with their crews.[973]

(ii) An aerial blockade, like a maritime blockade, cannot be established over the high seas in a NIAC. The same rule would apply to any putative exclusion zone in international airspace. However, there is no legal hindrance preventing the incumbent Ruritanian Government from establishing no-fly zones within Ruritanian territory, including zones over insurgent-controlled territory.[974]

C. Additional hurdles

712. The whole complex body of law relating to belligerent occupation is out of tune with LONIAC. The legal architecture of belligerent occupation does not fit NIACs, since neither areas seized by insurgents nor those retained or recovered by the Government can be regarded as occupied territories in the sense of IAC *jus in bello*.[975]

713. There are other, far from trivial dissimilarities between IAC *jus in bello* and LONIAC. By way of illustration, as an ICTY Trial Chamber noted in the *Hadžihasanović et al.* Judgment of 2006, there are no NIAC rules pertaining to booty of war.[976] The customary *jus in bello* on booty of war is of vast practical importance, allowing capture on the battlefield of all types of enemy movable property.[977]

714. A great emphasis is put in IAC *jus in bello* on the strict definitions of warships and military aircraft, which must belong to – or be operated by – the armed forces of a State, and which alone are entitled to exercise belligerent rights.[978] Non-State actors cannot operate warships or

---

[972] On the IAC law, see *San Remo Manual on International Law Applicable to Armed Conflicts at Sea, supra* note 438, at 212–13.

[973] For the *jus in bello* norm, see *HPCR Manual, supra* note 921, at lx (Rule 170(c)).

[974] See *ibid.*, 289.

[975] See Y. Dinstein, *The International Law of Belligerent Occupation* 34 (2009).

[976] *Prosecutor v. Hadžihasanović et al.* (ICTY, Trial Chamber, 2006), para. 52.

[977] See Y. Dinstein, 'Booty of War', I *MPEPIL* 990, *id.*

[978] See *San Remo Manual on International Law Applicable to Armed Conflicts at Sea, supra* note 438, at 85, 90; *HPCR Manual, supra* note 921, at xxv, xxix (Rules 1(x), 17(a)).

military aircraft. As the Commentary on the HPCR Manual on Air and Missile Warfare says: 'By definition, aircraft operated by non-State organized armed groups (whatever the nature of the armed conflict) cannot qualify as military aircraft, although they may be military objectives'.[979] In addressing the *jus in bello* rule that belligerent rights can be exercised solely by military aircraft, the Commentary unambiguously declares that this does not apply to NIACs and that the incumbent Government may employ non-military aircraft to conduct operations against the insurgents.[980]

715. Unlike IAC *jus in bello*, LONIAC ignores the topic of espionage.[981] The reason is simple enough. The *jus in bello* sanction against members of the armed forces engaged in espionage – as stated in AP/I (Article 46(1))[982] – is that they lose their entitlement to POW status. Plainly, such a sanction is meaningless in the setting of NIACs (see *supra* 702).

[979] *HPCR Manual, ibid.*, at 39.   [980] *Ibid.*, 101.
[981] See C. Schaller, 'Spies', IX *MPEPIL* 435, 436.   [982] AP/I, *supra* note 21, at 734.

12

LONIAC and human rights law

I. The inter-relationship between LONIAC and human rights law

716. In the *Kunarac et al.* Judgment of 2001, the ICTY Trial Chamber pressed the right button when it said that there is often a resemblance (and, in some aspects, fusion) between LONIAC and human rights law 'in terms of goals, values and terminology'.[983] All the same, one should not be carried away by the extent of that resemblance. It is necessary to beware the wish that is father to the thought – expressed by some scholars – that the norms of human rights law and the law of armed conflict can or should be unified.[984] This idea, which is not seriously considered by States, ignores the need to fine-tune the law with a view to achieving its maximum performance in different sets of circumstances.

717. Even if human rights law is taken as the baseline, it is useful to consult Article 2(2)(c) of the European Convention on Human Rights:

> Deprivation of life shall not be regarded as inflicted in contravention of this article when it results from the use of force which is no more than absolutely necessary:
>
> ...
>
> c) in action lawfully taken for the purpose of quelling a riot or insurrection.[985]

Quelling a riot or an insurrection (two dissimilar events that are treated here jointly) is thus recognized as a justification for departure from the general human rights rules with respect to the deprivation of life. But the words 'no more than absolutely necessary' limit the range of the use of

---

[983] *Prosecutor* v. *Kunarac et al.*, *supra* note 706, at para. 467.

[984] For such a suggestion, see F.F. Martin, 'Using International Human Rights Law for Establishing a Unified Use of Force Rule in the Law of Armed Conflict', 64 *Sas.LR* 347–96 (2001).

[985] European Convention for the Protection of Human Rights and Fundamental Freedoms, 1950, *Human Rights Instruments* 81, 82.

force that is permissible. When a NIAC is in progress, more is needed, and LONIAC is summoned to meet the shortfall in the system. Article 2(2) was applied in the *McCann et al.* case (see *supra* 114), in which the ECHR – not treating the surrounding circumstances as a NIAC – was unpersuaded that automatic recourse to lethal force was absolutely required.[986] In a NIAC, a ruling of this nature would be incomprehensible. NIAC hostilities demand going beyond Article 2(2). Civilian victims would acquire supplementary rights (cf. *infra* 737),[987] but these would operate hand in hand with additional obligations (and hazards).

718. There are multiple ingrained differences between the two legal regimes of human rights law and the law of armed conflict (whether it is IAC *jus in bello* or LONIAC). As phrased in the *Kunarac et al.* Judgment:

> Firstly, the role and position of the state as an actor is completely different in both regimes. Human rights law is essentially born out of the abuses of the state over its citizens and out of the need to protect the latter from state-organised or state-sponsored violence. Humanitarian law aims at placing restraints on the conduct of warfare so as to diminish its effects on the victims of the hostilities.[988]

And then:

> Moreover, international humanitarian law purports to apply equally to and expressly bind all parties to the armed conflict whereas, in contrast, human rights law generally applies to only one party, namely the state involved, and its agents.[989]

719. Holding insurgent armed groups responsible for human rights violations can be quite problematic.[990] It is unclear what can be done, under human rights law, when the fundamental freedoms of an individual are trampled underfoot by insurrectionists placed in effective control over territory in a NIAC. Many scholars advance the view that 'human rights obligations are binding on Governments only'.[991] Even writers whose thinking is at odds with that outlook find it necessary to focus on context,

---

[986] *McCann et al.* v. *UK, supra* note 131, at para. 213.
[987] See A.H. Robertson and J.G. Merrills, *Human Rights in the World: An Introduction to the Study of the International Protection of Human Rights* 311 (4th edn, 1996).
[988] *Prosecutor* v. *Kunarac et al., supra* note 706, at para. 470.   [989] *Ibid.*
[990] See T. Hadden and C. Harvey, 'The Law of Internal Crisis and Conflict', 833 *IRRC* 119, 129 (1999).
[991] Moir, *supra* note 170, at 194.

inasmuch as insurgent armed groups are plainly unable to fulfil at least some human rights obligations.[992]

720. There are further compelling pragmatic reasons to avoid any mix-up between LONIAC and human rights law. In the words of T. Meron:

> We must, of course, look realistically at the relationship between human rights and humanitarian law. They are different and will remain different in many respects. It makes no sense to pretend that international humanitarian law and human rights are one and the same.
>
> Humanitarian law allows lawful killing, even on a large scale, of the enemy, in some circumstances even including civilians; it authorizes various measures of deprivation of freedom which are not recognized by human rights law.[993]

721. Meron's comment relates to humanitarian law in general, applying to both IACs and NIACs. Two elements concerning lawful killing in a NIAC are of particular import:

(i) LONIAC takes wilful killing of adversaries for granted (see *supra* 50). The killing is done in the course of hostilities, in a manner that is completely alien to the most basic assumptions and requirements of human rights law.

(ii) Even civilians can bear the brunt of NIAC hostilities, losing their lives as an incidental – fully expected – consequence of a permissible attack directed against lawful targets (see *supra* 694 on collateral damage and proportionality).

722. It would nevertheless be wrong to view LONIAC and human rights law as incompatible monolithic regimes, scanning them solely on the macro level.[994] When considered on the micro level (see *infra* 749 *et seq.*), it becomes apparent that a perception of LONIAC and human rights law as 'mutually exclusive' is a fallacy.[995] The interaction between the two legal regimes is nuanced, and it ought to be considered in terms of coexistence, *lex specialis*, derogation and limitation.

---

[992] See A. Clapham, *Human Rights Obligations of Non-State Actors* 284 (2006).

[993] T. Meron, 'Convergence of International Humanitarian Law and Human Rights Law', *Human Rights and Humanitarian Law, supra* note 551, at 97, 99–100.

[994] See R. Cryer, 'The Interplay of Human Rights and Humanitarian Law: The Approach of the ICTY', 14 *JCSL* 511, 525 (2009).

[995] Human Rights Committee, General Comment No. 31, Doc. CCPR/C/21/Rev.1/Add.13 (2004), para. 11.

A. Coexistence of LONIAC with human rights law

723. In principle, international human rights law does not cease to apply during an armed conflict (be it an IAC or a NIAC). The continued application of human rights law in an armed conflict has been certified by the ICJ – in its two Advisory Opinions on *Nuclear Weapons* (see quotation *infra* 727) and on the *Wall* (see quotations *infra* 724, 726) – and it can now be regarded as unassailable. Consequently, whenever possible, LONIAC and human rights law must find a way of coexisting in the course of a NIAC.

724. Coexistence of two separate legal regimes at the same time and space prompts an inescapable question as to how their concurrent application can be worked out. In the *Wall* Advisory Opinion, the Court stated:

> As regards the relationship between international humanitarian law and human rights law, there are thus three possible situations: some rights may be exclusively matters of international humanitarian law; others may be exclusively matters of human rights law; yet others may be matters of both these branches of international law.[996]

Standing by itself, this observation is virtually self-evident, almost to the point of being supererogatory.

725. The first two possibilities mentioned by the ICJ leave no reason for contest between the law of armed conflict and human rights law. It is only the third possibility that lays the ground for a potential clash. Should a fissure exist between the competing positions of the two arms of international law, one of the two will have to give way. What is required is a guiding principle allocating priority. That guiding principle is the construct of *lex specialis*.

B. LONIAC as lex specialis

726. In the *Wall* Advisory Opinion, after listing the three logical relationships between the law of armed conflict and human rights law, the ICJ went on to say:

> In order to answer the question put to it, the Court will have to take into consideration both these branches of international law, namely human rights law and, as *lex specialis*, international humanitarian law.[997]

---

[996] Advisory Opinion on *Legal Consequences of the Construction of a Wall in the Occupied Palestinian Territory*, 2004, 43 *ILM* 1009, 1038 (2004).

[997] *Ibid.*, 1038–9.

727. When adverting in 2004 to the status of the law of armed conflict as *lex specialis*, the ICJ reaffirmed the legal acumen articulated in the 1996 *Nuclear Weapons* Advisory Opinion (in connection with the arbitrary deprivation of life):

> In principle, the right not arbitrarily to be deprived of one's life applies also in hostilities. The test of what is an arbitrary deprivation of life, however, then falls to be determined by the applicable *lex specialis*, namely, the law applicable in armed conflict which is designed to regulate the conduct of hostilities. Thus whether a particular loss of life, through the use of a certain weapon in warfare, is to be considered an arbitrary deprivation of life contrary to Article 6 of the Covenant, can only be decided by reference to the law applicable in armed conflict and not deduced from the terms of the Covenant itself.[998]

728. The *lex specialis* precept was also endorsed in the *Kunarac et al.* Judgment, where the ICTY Trial Chamber cautioned that 'notions developed in the field of human rights can be transposed in international humanitarian law only if they take into consideration the specificities of the latter body of law'.[999]

729. Although the case law looks at humanitarian law generically, there can be little doubt that LONIAC is meant to be covered by the *lex specialis* principle.[1000] As in so many other spheres, a few academics chafe at the implications of the principle, suggesting that it should normally be abandoned or avoided.[1001] But the criticism is spurious.

730. The expression *lex specialis* is derived from the time-honoured adage *lex specialis derogat lex generali*. That is to say, the *lex specialis* (in this instance, the law of armed conflict) overrides the *lex generalis* (human rights law). In its Draft Articles on State Responsibility, the ILC devoted a special provision (Article 55) to *lex specialis*.[1002] In the Commentary, the ILC stated: 'For the *lex specialis* principle to apply it is not enough that the same subject matter is dealt with by two provisions; there must be some actual inconsistency between them'.[1003] The *lex specialis* solution to

---

[998] Advisory Opinion on the *Legality of the Threat or Use of Nuclear Weapons, supra* note 938, at 240.

[999] *Prosecutor* v. *Kunarac et al., supra* note 706, at para. 471.

[1000] See Pejic, *supra* note 331, at 113.

[1001] See M. Milanović, 'Norm Conflicts, International Humanitarian Law, and Human Rights Law', *International Humanitarian Law and International Human Rights Law* 95, 98, 116 (O. Ben-Naftali ed., 2011).

[1002] Draft Articles, *supra* note 249, at 30.   [1003] *Ibid.*, 140.

problems of disharmony between the law of armed conflict and human rights law may not be perfect,[1004] but it does resolve most practical issues.

731. What the *lex specialis* principle tells us is that, if a discord emerges between LONIAC and human rights law, LONIAC prevails. Differently phrased, the *lex generalis* (human rights law) ceases to be dispositive of the situation, and the *lex specialis* (LONIAC) takes over.[1005] There is no suggestion that, in consequence of the application of the *lex specialis* maxim in favour of LONIAC, human rights law is 'abolished' in an armed conflict.[1006] After all, an actual divergence between LONIAC and human rights law does not necessarily arise in every set of circumstances. If they are reconcilable, the two legal regimes continue to be applicable in synch.

732. When the LONIAC regime has gaps, it can only profit from their being filled by human rights law.[1007] The human rights law will then apply, so to speak, by default. Yet, the existence of a gap must be determined not only on the basis of treaty law (e.g., AP/II) but also in light of customary international law. Certain judgments of the ECHR (primarily, the *Isayeva* case of 2005[1008] relating to a NIAC in Chechnya) may be construed as suggesting that, since the principle of proportionality in attack is not entrenched in LONIAC treaty law, it has no *lex specialis* standing and can be 'bypassed' in favour of general human rights law.[1009] If this is the correct interpretation of what the ECHR had in mind (and the matter is not free of doubt[1010]), it is a mistaken approach.

733. The approach is mistaken because, as noted (*supra* 693–4), the principle of proportionality in attack constitutes an essential part of customary LONIAC. Once customary rules solidify, LONIAC no longer leaves the gate open for the application of inconsistent general norms of human rights law. By being absorbed into customary LONIAC, the principle of

---

[1004] See N. Prud'homme, '*Lex Specialis*: Oversimplifying More Complex and Multifaceted Relationship', 40 *Is.LR* 356–94 (2007).

[1005] See N. Balendra, 'Defining Armed Conflict', 29 *Car.LR* 2461, 2489 (2007–8).

[1006] See M. Koskenniemi, 'Fragmentation of International Law: Difficulties Arising from the Diversification and Expansion of International Law' (ILC, Report of Study Group, Doc. A/CN.4/L.682, 2006), para. 104.

[1007] See W. A. Schabas, '*Lex Specialis*? Belt and Suspenders? The Parallel Operation of Human Rights Law and the Law of Armed Conflict, and the Conundrum of *Jus ad Bellum*', 40 *Is.LR* 592, 598 (2007).

[1008] *Isayeva* v. *Russia* (ECHR, 2005), paras. 168–201.

[1009] W. Abresch, 'A Human Rights Law of Internal Armed Conflict: The European Court of Human Rights in Chechnya', 16 *EJIL* 741, 743–9 (2005).

[1010] See C. Byron, 'A Blurring of the Boundaries: The Application of International Humanitarian Law by Human Rights Bodies', 47 *Vir.JIL* 839, 853–6 (2006–7).

proportionality in attack has acquired a *lex specialis* status, trumping any incompatible norm of the human rights *lex generalis*.

734. Proportionality plays an important role in human rights law as well, but it has a profoundly divergent meaning – and consequences – in LONIAC.[1011] In contrast to general human rights law, the LONIAC principle of proportionality permits an attack against a lawful target – even though the attacker is cognizant of the fact that the action taken is liable to cause incidental death or injury to civilians – provided that the expected collateral damage is not excessive compared to the military advantage anticipated[1012] (see *supra* 694, 721). A choice between human rights law and LONIAC has to be made. Given the unique constraints of NIAC, LONIAC takes precedence.

C. Derogations from human rights

(a) The right to derogate

735. The application of human rights law is subject to derogations. Article 4(1) of the 1966 International Covenant on Civil and Political Rights sets forth:

> In time of public emergency which threatens the life of the nation and the existence of which is officially proclaimed, the States Parties to the present Covenant may take measures derogating from their obligations under the present Covenant to the extent strictly required by the exigencies of the situation, provided that such measures are not inconsistent with their other obligations under international law and do not involve discrimination solely on the ground of race, colour, sex, language, religion or social origin.[1013]

Similar provisions appear in the European and American Conventions of Human Rights.[1014]

736. 'Civil war and insurrection are the main categories' of situations in which a State may derogate from its human rights obligations by dint

---

[1011] See R. McLaughlin, 'The Law of Armed Conflict and International Human Rights Law: Some Paradigmatic Differences and Operational Implications', 13 *YIHL* 213, 231–8 (2010).

[1012] See D. Kretzmer, 'Rethinking the Application of IHL in Non-International Armed Conflicts', 42 *Is.LR* 8, 27–8 (2009).

[1013] International Covenant on Civil and Political Rights, *supra* note 233, at 180.

[1014] European Convention for the Protection of Human Rights and Fundamental Freedoms, *supra* note 985, at 85 (Article 15(1)); American Convention on Human Rights, 1969, *Human Rights Instruments* 155, 163 (Article 27(1)).

of a 'time of public emergency which threatens the life of the nation'.[1015]
Obviously, the very fact that derogation is required in order to suspend
the operation of certain provisions of the Covenant in a NIAC (subject to
conditions stipulated in the text of Article 4(1)) authenticates the insight
that as long as no permissible derogation is in effect, human rights law
continues to be in force (see *supra* 723). In the words of the ICJ in the
Nuclear Weapons Advisory Opinion:

> The Court observes that the protection of the International Covenant of
> [*sic*] Civil and Political Rights does not cease in times of war, except by
> operation of Article 4 of the Covenant whereby certain provisions may be
> derogated from in a time of national emergency.[1016]

737. The possibility of derogation from the protection of human rights –
in the exceptional circumstances of a NIAC – should nevertheless dampen
doctrinal enthusiasm about human rights law. There is a systemic disparity in this crucial respect between human rights law and LONIAC. By
its very nature, LONIAC is tailor-made for the unique demands of an
armed conflict. Coming into play upon the onset of a NIAC, rights and
duties established by LONIAC cannot be suspended on the ground that
this is a 'time of public emergency which threatens the life of the nation'.
Whereas the outbreak of a NIAC may bring about a derogation of human
rights, it cannot impair or weaken 'the unwavering legal force' of LONIAC
norms.[1017] Non-derogability of LONIAC is an extra bonus of immense
proportions. One must also keep in mind that LONIAC 'will apply not
because there is a limitation on the right to derogate within human
rights law but because an autonomous source of law prescribes its direct
application'.[1018]

(b) Non-use of the right to derogate

738. Even when the requisite conditions for derogation from human
rights during a NIAC are fulfilled, States do not always avail themselves
in practice of the theoretical right to derogate. Thus, in the *Isayeva*

[1015] D.J. Harris, M. O'Boyle and C. Warbrick, *Law of the European Convention on Human Rights* 492 (1995).

[1016] See Advisory Opinion on the *Legality of the Threat or Use of Nuclear Weapons*, *supra* note 938, at 240.

[1017] See H. Montealegre, 'The Compatibility of a State Party's Derogation under Human Rights Conventions with Its Obligations under Protocol II and Common Article 3', 33 *AULR* 41, 48 (1983–4).

[1018] R.E. Vinuesa, 'Interface, Correspondence and Convergence of Human Rights and International Humanitarian Law', 1 *YIHL* 69, 81 (1998).

Judgment, the ECHR noted that – in the case of the Chechnya insurgency – Russia had not made any derogation under the relevant provision of the European Convention on Human Rights.[1019] If no derogation has been made, human rights law is not suspended during the NIAC. Still, we are back to the guiding principle that, if human rights law is irreconcilable with LONIAC, the latter would prevail as *lex specialis* (see *supra* 732–3).

(c) Non-derogable human rights

739. Not all human rights are derogable. Article 4(2) of the Covenant[1020] prescribes that no derogation can be made from enumerated provisions. These relate to: the right to life; freedom from torture and cruel, inhuman or degrading treatment or punishment; freedom from slavery and the slave trade in all their forms or servitude; freedom from imprisonment merely on the ground of inability to fulfil a contractual obligation; freedom from being held guilty of any act or omission which did not constitute a criminal offence at the time of its commission, or being subject to a heavier penalty than the one applicable at that time; the right to recognition as a person before the law; and freedom of thought, conscience and religion. The European and American Conventions on Human Rights set out their own separate, and non-identical, recitals of non-derogable human rights.[1021]

740. The line-up of non-derogable human rights, as it appears in Article 4(2) of the Covenant, is marred by some tantalizing omissions. Thus, there is no reference in this provision to judicial guarantees of fair trial (which are protected in Article 14 of the Covenant; see *supra* 450). Admittedly, the Human Rights Committee expressed a non-binding opinion – in General Comment No. 29 of 2001 – that the catalogue of non-derogable rights in Article 4(2) is not exhaustive, and that there can be no derogation (in particular) from judicial guarantees.[1022] But, whatever the correct interpretation of Article 4(2), what stands out is that the protection of judicial guarantees during a NIAC is safer under LONIAC.[1023]

[1019] *Isayeva v. Russia, supra* note 1008, at para. 133.

[1020] International Covenant on Civil and Political Rights, *supra* note 233, at 180.

[1021] European Convention for the Protection of Human Rights and Fundamental Freedoms, *supra* note 985, at 86 (Article 15(2)); American Convention on Human Rights, *supra* note 1014, at 164 (Article 27(2)).

[1022] Human Rights Committee, General Comment No. 29, Doc. CCPR/C/21/Rev.1/Add.11 (2001), paras. 13–15.

[1023] Unlike the parallel provisions of the Covenant and the European Convention, Article 27(2) of the American Convention on Human Rights (cited *supra* note 1021) does not authorize suspension of 'the judicial guarantees essential for the protection' of non-derogable rights.

741. Some of the non-derogable human rights have no special res-onance in a NIAC, as attested by freedom from imprisonment on the ground of inability to fulfil a contractual obligation. Other non-derogable human rights, which are more apposite to a NIAC, are basically repli-cated in LONIAC. That is especially true of freedom from torture (*supra* 409, 431); freedom from slavery and the slave trade (*supra* 431); and the principle of *nullum crimen sine lege* and *nulla poena sine lege* (*supra* 448).

742. When LONIAC is silent about any germane issue, non-derogable human rights may plug the gap, complementing LONIAC. An example is the unstinting application of freedom of religion. The need to respect the religion of protected persons is enunciated in Paragraph (1) of Article 4 of AP/II (*supra* 431): this is a far cry from the full panorama of freedom of religion adumbrated by human rights law.[1024]

743. However, when LONIAC regulates a situation which is also gov-erned by a non-derogable human right, the potential for a rift between the two legal regimes is created. Here is where the *lex specialis* principle becomes particularly useful. The best illustration is that of freedom from torture. *En principe*, the fundamental prohibition of torture is shared by both bodies of law. Yet, while under the (non-derogable) human rights law torture must be committed at the instigation of a person acting in an official capacity (a State agent), LONIAC also covers acts of torture committed by non-State actors (see *supra* 533). The even-handed reach of LONIAC necessarily prevails.

D. Limitations built into human rights

744. There is a tendency to think of human rights in pithy apophtheg-matic terms. However, the contours of human rights – like those of all rights – are frequently subordinated to explicit built-in restrictions. In these cases, '[t]he proper extent of any human right can only be deter-mined by reference to the limitation clauses'.[1025] The degree of influence of the limitation clause on the application of the human right depends on the circumstantial background, but a NIAC will usually create its own gravitational field in this respect.

[1024] See Y. Dinstein, 'Freedom of Religion and the Protection of Religious Minorities', 20 *Is.YHR* 155–79 (1990).

[1025] H. Krieger, 'A Conflict of Norms: The Relationship between Humanitarian Law and Human Rights Law in the ICRC Customary Law Study', 11 *JCSL* 265, 281–2 (2006).

745. A revealing specimen of restrictive formulation – selected out of a string of similar limitations embodied in human rights law – can be found in Article 21 of the Covenant on Civil and Political Rights, where freedom of assembly (a derogable right) is presented as follows:

> The right of peaceful assembly shall be recognized. No restrictions may be placed on the exercise of this right other than those imposed in conformity with the law and which are necessary in a democratic society in the interests of national security or public safety, public order (*ordre public*), the protection of public health or morals or the protection of the rights and freedoms of others.[1026]

746. It is perceptible that, even if freedom of assembly is not derogated, its application during a NIAC may be considerably handicapped. The qualifying adjective 'peaceful', which accompanies 'assembly', already excludes riots and other violent internal disturbances (below-the-threshold).[1027] To boot, the specific mention of 'national security'[1028] presages further pervasive curtailments of freedom of assembly by law during a NIAC.

747. LONIAC norms are also subject to various limitations. Nevertheless, a limitation such as 'national security or public safety' is not among them. The presupposition is that all the special conditions of a NIAC, including national security, have already been factored into the make-up of any LONIAC rule (cf. *supra* 737).

II. Some concrete aspects of interaction between LONIAC and human rights law

748. The interplay between LONIAC and human rights law is by no means typified by a head-on collision. First, human rights law may be inbred into LONIAC. Second, even when human rights treaties are concluded separately – *dehors* LONIAC – they may impact upon it (either explicitly or implicitly) in a meaningful way.

[1026] International Covenant on Civil and Political Rights, *supra* note 233, at 184.

[1027] See *The International Covenant on Civil and Political Rights: Cases, Materials and Commentaries* 569 (2nd edn, S. Joseph, J. Schultz and M. Castan eds., 2004).

[1028] On the meaning of 'national security' in the Covenant, see A. Conte and R. Burchill, *Defining Civil and Political Rights: The Jurisprudence of the United Nations Human Rights Committee* 55–6 (2nd edn, 2009).

A. Human rights law within LONIAC

749. Common Article 3 (adopted in 1949) owed at least some of its wording to the 1948 Universal Declaration of Human Rights.[1029] Indeed, since the Universal Declaration – as a General Assembly Resolution – did not have a binding effect as such, and in 1949 it was not yet deemed declaratory of customary international law, Common Article 3 'can be dubbed the first international legislation on human rights law'.[1030]

750. The Preamble of AP/II expressly recalls that 'international instruments relating to human rights offer a basic protection to the human person'.[1031] As for the operative clauses, we have already observed (supra 450) that the recital of judicial guarantees in Article 6 of AP/II is overtly inspired by corresponding provisions of the Covenant on Civil and Political Rights. Repetition of the language of the Covenant in AP/II may seem superfluous, but it must be recalled that judicial guarantees are not tagged by the Covenant as non-derogable (see supra 740). By incorporating most of them into LONIAC, AP/II has stamped them with a non-derogable status during NIACs[1032] (see supra 737).

751. There is a paradoxical twist in the evolution of the law on judicial guarantees. The general obligation to afford such guarantees in a NIAC has been integrated into customary international law, inasmuch as it is rooted in Common Article 3 (supra 409). Specifics of due process are only provided by Article 6 of AP/II on the footing of the Covenant (see supra 448–50). Thanks to the customary standing of the relevant Covenant's stipulations, the LONIAC projection must be respected in every NIAC,[1033] and it does not matter whether the country in which the proceedings take place is a Contracting Party to AP/II. But while the original human right may be derogable (pace the Human Rights Committee; supra 740), the derivative LONIAC right is not.

[1029] See R.G. Allen, M. Cherniack and G.J. Andreopoulos, 'Refining War: Civil Wars and Humanitarian Controls', 18 *HRQ* 747, 753 (1996).

[1030] See P.H. Kooijmans, 'In the Shadowland between Civil War and Civil Strife: Some Reflections on the Standard-Setting Process', *Humanitarian Law of Armed Conflict: Challenges Ahead – Essays in Honour of Frits Kalshoven* 225, 242 (A.M. Delissen and G.J. Tanja eds., 1991).

[1031] AP/II, *supra* note 6, at 776.

[1032] See C. Droege, 'The Interplay between International Humanitarian Law and International Human Rights Law in Situations of Armed Conflict', 40 *Is.LR* 310, 316 (2007).

[1033] See San Remo Manual on the Law of Non-International Armed Conflict, *supra* note 208, at 51.

752. When LONIAC language is borrowed from a human rights instrument – as in the case of judicial guarantees – there is no sense in keeping subsequent interpretations of the text, worked out within the province of human rights law, hermetically sealed from LONIAC. There is room for synergy in the sense that parsing terminology common to the two branches of the international legal system – when done within the bounds of either one – may affect them both (*mutatis mutandis*, of course).

753. If a valid derogation of a human right relating to judicial guarantees has been made in a NIAC, this suspends only the direct application of the human right *per se*. Since the parallel LONIAC right continues to be fully applicable in a non-derogable fashion, the antecedent human right – despite its suspension – may still pulsate as an interpretive guide, indirectly shaping the LONIAC norm.[1034]

754. The fact that LONIAC can draw terminology and interpretation from human rights law does not mean that LONIAC simply photocopies all the facets of that law. Often, LONIAC has no choice but to part company with human rights law – as it does in the case of torture (see *supra* 533) – and we are back to relying on the principle of *lex specialis* (see *supra* 726 *et seq.*).

755. The special setting of a NIAC explains the formulation of any LONIAC treaty. It is no accident that some human rights enshrined in the Covenant (e.g., freedom of movement, expression or association) were never earnestly considered for inclusion in AP/II.[1035] Even when specific human rights – preeminently, judicial guarantees – were abstracted directly from the Covenant and brought into the fold of AP/II, this was not done without screening them meticulously. Thus, the right of appeal and the principle of *ne bis in idem* were deliberately scrapped (see *supra* 451).

756. Any enquiry into the inter-relationship between LONIAC and human rights law must be undertaken prudently. When the principle of *ne bis in idem* is probed, it cannot be denied that a partition must be erected between State courts and insurgents' tribunals. The fact that an individual is prosecuted for the same activity in both judicial systems (which are evidently antagonistic to each other) does not create a genuine dilemma of double jeopardy. The circumstances are such that they invite

---

[1034] See C. Antonopoulos, 'The Relationship between International Humanitarian Law and Human Rights', 63 *RHDI* 599, 632 (2010).

[1035] See M.J. Dennis, 'Non-Application of Civil and Political Rights Treaties Extraterritorially during Times of International Armed Conflict', 40 *Is.LR* 453, 498 (2007).

application of a *lex specialis*. Conversely, if the individual is prosecuted twice for the same activity before State courts – or twice before tribunals created by the insurgents – there is no real reason to forsake the principle of *ne bis in idem* even in the course of a NIAC. The omission of the principle from AP/II (owing to the desire to insulate State courts from insurgents' tribunals) does not denote that double jeopardy should be permitted within the stand-alone structure either of State courts or of insurgents' tribunals. It is submitted that this is a scenario in which human rights law can fruitfully step in and fill a gap in LONIAC.

B. *Human rights treaties* dehors *LONIAC*

(a) Explicit impact

757. A human rights treaty may be negotiated and concluded *dehors* the usual perimeter of LONIAC and still contrive (or purport) to cast its shadow on the NIAC normative regime. The consequences may be nominal. Thus, the 2006 Convention on the Rights of Persons with Disabilities provides in Article 11:

> States Parties shall take, in accordance with their obligations under international law, including international humanitarian law and international human rights law, all necessary measures to ensure the protection and safety of persons with disabilities in situations of risk, including situations of armed conflict, humanitarian emergencies and the occurrence of natural disasters.[1036]

Although the text expressly refers to 'situations of armed conflict', it is not clear what concrete measures are to be taken above and beyond the obligations of parties to the conflict pursuant to existing LONIAC.

758. By contrast, the 2000 Optional Protocol to the CRC (*supra* 497 *et seq.*) did not hesitate to raise the age bar for recruitment and participation in hostilities of child-soldiers to eighteen years of age, brushing aside the fifteen years' notch existing under AP/II and customary LONIAC (*supra* 443, 588). The outcome is straightforward: Contracting Parties to the Optional Protocol are bound by the new age bar, while others remain beholden to the preexisting norm. But the fact that the new age bar is set by an Optional Protocol to a human rights Convention rather than by an amendment to a LONIAC treaty (specifically, AP/II) is a quaint phenomenon.

[1036] Convention on the Rights of Persons with Disabilities, 2006, 46 *ILM* 443, 450 (2007).

759. The raising of the age bar in the Optional Protocol was prompted by the fact that the original CRC (signed in 1989) had dealt with child-soldiers in armed conflict in Article 38[1037] (where the age bar was left at fifteen, matching the LONIAC approach). The encroachment into the domain of the law of armed conflict was thus effected in two stages.

760. It is not detectable what value-added was envisaged by the framers of the original CRC when they stepped into the sphere of armed conflict. Once Article 38 of the CRC is studied carefully, the puzzlement only increases. The Article consists of four paragraphs, which follow two different trails in the relationship with the law of armed conflict. The first path is a direct *renvoi* to that law. Thus, Paragraph (1) of Article 38 promulgates that 'States Parties undertake to respect and to ensure respect for rules of international humanitarian law applicable to them in armed conflicts which are relevant to the child'. Paragraph (4) then adds: 'In accordance with their obligations under international humanitarian law to protect the civilian population in armed conflicts, States Parties shall take all feasible measures to ensure protection and care of children who are affected by an armed conflict'. Notably, the endorsement of the law of armed conflict is louder in Paragraph (1) and more muted in Paragraph (4). But why was an espousal of that law deemed necessary in either form? The obligations created by the law of armed conflict stand on their own feet and do not require any reinforcement in a human rights Convention.

761. The second path taken by Article 38 proceeds into the substance of the law of armed conflict. Paragraph (2) of Article 38 goes into the thick of participation of child-soldiers in hostilities, and – without distinguishing between IACs and NIACs – imposes obligations, solely on States Parties, to take 'all feasible measures' to ensure that such participation does not eventuate. Paragraph (3) enjoins States Parties to refrain from recruiting child-soldiers into their armed forces. Both Paragraphs (2) and (3) blatantly ignore armed groups.

762. The employment of the phrase 'all feasible measures' in Paragraph (2) of Article 38 has been trenchantly criticized,[1038] and rightly so. As far as NIACs are concerned, that is a distinctly retrogressive step, compared to the absolute language of Paragraph (3) of Article 4 of AP/II (*supra* 443). But the failure to mention armed groups is even worse. The omission cannot be excused, inasmuch as the gruelling record shows that armed

---

[1037] Convention on the Rights of the Child (CRC), [1989] *UNJY* 134, 144.

[1038] See G. Van Buern, *The International Law on the Rights of the Child* 342 (1995).

groups are usually the main culprits in recruiting and using child-soldiers in NIACs. This is not an inadvertence spotted by hindsight. The error in the drafting of Paragraphs (2) and (3) of Article 38, as regards NIACs, was widely noticed at the time of the adoption of the Convention. It was sharply asserted even then that the text of Article 38 might 'undermine existing standards of humanitarian law'.[1039]

763. The subsequent Optional Protocol corrects the arrant error by addressing armed groups while raising the age bar (see *supra* 497 *et seq.*). But the underlying issue remains unresolved: what advantage could be anticipated in intruding in 1989, in a human rights Convention, into the preserve of law of armed conflict texts?

764. It must be appreciated that human rights and law of armed conflict treaties – even when concluded by the same Contracting Parties – are normally negotiated by delegates with dissimilar backgrounds and expertise. What the treaty-making experience in the field of child-soldiers suggests is that a textual merger of the *jus generalis* (human rights law) with the *lex specialis* (the law of armed conflict) is not the best prescription for enhancing the quality of the ultimate product.

(b) Implicit impact

765. Some human rights treaties are negotiated and concluded *dehors* LONIAC. As such, they are not linked directly to civil strife. Yet, without referring to NIACs in any way, they may leave their imprint in an indelible way.

766. The best illustration relates to capital punishment. As noted (*supra* 449, 704), domestic courts – in a country where a NIAC is afoot – are not barred by LONIAC from imposing a death sentence on an insurgent (as long as due process of law is safeguarded and certain other conditions are met). However, this freedom of action may be impacted upon by a human rights treaty in which that country undertakes to abolish capital punishment. Preeminently, the Second Optional Protocol of 1989 to the International Covenant on Civil and Political Rights ordains that no one within the jurisdiction of a Contracting Party is to be executed.[1040] Parallel provisions exist under regional instruments, both in Europe – where it

---

[1039] S. Detrick, *The United Nations Convention on the Rights of the Child: A Guide to the 'Travaux Préparatoires'* 515 (1992).

[1040] Second Optional Protocol to the International Covenant on Civil and Political Rights, [1989] *UNJY* 130, 131 (Article 1).

was done in two phases (first, with an exception 'in time of war', and then in an unadulterated manner) – and in the American continent.[1041]

III. Non-discrimination

A. Illicit grounds of discrimination

767. Paragraph (1) of Article 2 of AP/II (cited *supra* 160) proclaims:

> This Protocol shall be applied without any adverse distinction founded on race, colour, sex, language, religion or belief, political or other opinion, national or social origin, wealth, birth or other status, or on any other similar criteria.

The underlying concept is 'the principle of non-discrimination which is nowadays universally recognized in international law'.[1042] The use of the adjective 'adverse' in relation to distinction is deliberate: in some situations 'favourable distinctions may be made quite lawfully', in order to take into account special vulnerability.[1043]

768. The menu of illicit grounds of discrimination – set out non-exhaustively in Paragraph (1) of Article 2 of AP/II – largely coincides with the classical terminology of Article 2 of the 1948 Universal Declaration of Human Rights,[1044] as well as Article 2(1) of the Civil and Political Rights Covenant.[1045]

769. The grounds of inadmissible discrimination inventoried in AP/II exceed in number those mentioned in Paragraph (1) of Common Article 3: 'race, colour, religion or faith, sex, birth or wealth, or any other similar criteria' (*supra* 409). There are a number of notable omissions from the text of Common Article 3, in particular 'political or other opinion' that may be the main driving force behind a NIAC.[1046] The lapse can be remedied by recourse to the 'any other similar criteria' saving clause, but

---

[1041] Protocol No. 6 to the European Convention for the Protection of Human Rights and Fundamental Freedoms Concerning the Abolition of the Death Penalty, 1983, *Human Rights Instruments* 105 (Articles 1–2); Protocol No. 13 to the European Convention for the Protection of Human Rights and Fundamental Freedoms Concerning the Abolition of the Death Penalty in All Circumstances, 2002, 41 *ILM* 515, *id.* (2002) (Article 1); Protocol to the American Convention on Human Rights to Abolish the Death Penalty, 1990, *Human Rights Instruments* 189, *id.* (Article 1).

[1042] *Commentary on the Additional Protocols, supra* note 95, at 1358.   [1043] *Ibid.*

[1044] Universal Declaration of Human Rights, 1948 (General Assembly Resolution 217 (III)), *Human Rights Instruments* 27, 28.

[1045] International Covenant on Civil and Political Rights, *supra* note 233, at 179.

[1046] See R.W. Gehring, 'Protection of Civilian Infrastructures', 42(2) *LCP* 86, 127 (1978).

this would probably stretch the plain meaning of the words. The AP/II text may therefore be seen as a salutary corrective to the initial oversight.

B. Nationality

770. National origin (mentioned in AP/II, albeit not in Paragraph (1) of Common Article 3) is often mixed up with nationality.[1047] However, the nub of national origin lies not in drawing a distinction between citizens and foreigners, but in a dissimilar treatment of heterogeneous ethnic groups residing in a country.[1048]

771. It is manifest that nationality (like age) is a ground of discrimination deliberately discarded from both the human rights and the NIAC instruments. The LONIAC reason for dispensing with nationality – where non-discrimination is concerned – is the ironclad legality of the unequal treatment of insurgents who are local citizens compared to foreigners.[1049] Foreign nationality could work in favour of insurgents who, after all, owe no allegiance to the State and cannot be deemed traitors. On the other hand, foreigners recruited to serve in insurgent organized armed groups may be treated as mercenaries.

772. Under the 1989 International Convention against the Recruitment, Use, Financing and Training of Mercenaries, a mercenary commits an offence.[1050] The Convention's definition of a mercenary relates to a person 'specially recruited locally or abroad for the purpose of participating in a concerted act of violence aimed at: (i) [o]verthrowing a Government or otherwise undermining the constitutional order of a State', provided that the motivation is 'the desire for significant private gain'.[1051] Granted, this is not a widely ratified treaty.

IV. Refugees and 'non-refoulement'

A. The flow of refugees

773. When a NIAC is taking place in Ruritania, armed insurgent groups may cross the border into Arcadia. In such circumstances, there may be

[1047] See N. Lerner, *The U.N. Convention on the Elimination of All Forms of Racial Discrimination* 29–30 (2nd edn, 1980).

[1048] Cf. W. McKean, *Equality and Discrimination under International Law* 152 (1983).

[1049] See D.A. Elder, 'The Historical Background of Common Article 3 of the Geneva Convention of 1949', 11 *CWRJIL* 37, 61–2 (1979).

[1050] International Convention against the Recruitment, Use, Financing and Training of Mercenaries, 1989, *Laws of Armed Conflicts* 1243, 1245 (Article 3(1)).

[1051] *Ibid.*, 1244 (Article 1(2)).

a treaty in force requiring Arcadia to disarm and intern these insurgents (or even hand them over to Ruritania). The treaty may be regional (a prominent illustration is the 1928 Pan American Convention Concerning the Duties and Rights of States in the Event of Civil Strife (Article 1))[1052] or bilateral (an example is the Iraq–Transjordan Treaty of 1947 cited *supra* 269 (Article 6(b)). Action of this nature may be easier to pledge than to carry out when the Ruritanian insurgents are not willing to submit to Arcadian exercise of territorial sovereignty. A sobering consideration for Arcadia is that, if the trespassing insurgents are not disarmed, there is a risk that Ruritanian governmental armed forces will pursue them into Arcadian territory (see *supra* 82).

774. Ruritanian insurgents need not penetrate the borders of Arcadia in formations of armed groups. Frequently, there will be infiltration by individual fighters, and their numbers may grow. An influx of Ruritanian insurgents may cause simmering unrest in Arcadia, and ultimately give rise to a second NIAC or even an IAC (see *supra* 168–9).

775. Ruritanians crossing the Arcadian border may not be fighters: many – perhaps most – are likely to be civilians who simply wish to escape the anguish of the tempestuous conditions prevailing at home due to the NIAC. The more prolonged the NIAC in Ruritania, the greater the chances of a massive exodus of civilians looking for safer surroundings. These persons may cover great distances (on foot, by boat and otherwise), in order to reach a desired destination. Still, the larger waves of Ruritanians casting about for a haven from the NIAC can be expected to descend on adjacent countries. Some of those who seek shelter in Arcadia may merely be interested in a temporary sojourn there while the NIAC is going on. Others might wish to settle permanently in what they deem greener pastures. Either way, Arcadia may be hard pressed to house, feed and look after multitudes of refugees from Ruritania, even when aided by inter-governmental agencies (led by the UN High Commissioner for Refugees (UNHCR)) and non-governmental organizations.

776. If refugee camps are established on Arcadian soil, they must not be attacked by cross-border Ruritanian armed forces, in light of their civilian character. However, if these camps function as bases for military operations directed against Ruritania, they lose their civilian immunity.[1053]

[1052] Pan American Convention Concerning the Duties and Rights of States in the Event of Civil Strife, 1928, 134 *LNTS* 45, 51.

[1053] See F. Bugnion, 'Refugees, Internally Displaced Persons, and International Humanitarian Law', 28 *Fo.ILJ* 1397, 1409 (2004–5).

Violence may follow Ruritanian refugees into Arcadia, regardless of their behaviour, for instance when a second NIAC breaks out there (see *supra* 168): if the refugees find their hopes for a sanctuary in Arcadia dashed, they may be forced to rotate between Arcadia and Ruritania.[1054]

B. Refugees and war crimes

777. The treatment by Arcadia of Ruritanian citizens seeking refuge there is anchored to the 1951 Convention Relating to the Status of Refugees (CSR), as amended by a 1967 Protocol.[1055] Under Article 1(F)(a) of the CSR, it is inapplicable to any person with respect to whom there are reasons for considering that he committed a war crime 'as defined in international instruments drawn up to make provision in respect of such crimes'.[1056] The open-ended reference to international instruments is flexible enough to cover the most recent treaties (post-dating the CSR) – preeminently, the Rome Statute – and it therefore embraces NIAC war crimes.[1057]

C. Fear of persecution

778. If the commission of war crimes is not an issue, the fundamental question is whether a Ruritanian national fleeing the NIAC into Arcadia may benefit from the status of a refugee in conformity with the CSR. This is contingent (according to Article 1(A)(2)) on whether there is 'well-founded fear of being persecuted for reasons of race, religion, nationality, membership of a particular social group or political opinion', should he return to Ruritania.[1058] Surely, flight from a NIAC *per se* does not suffice for refugee status, because the mere inability of Ruritania to secure life within its territory at a time of civil strife does not raise by itself a well-founded fear of persecution.[1059] Even violations of LONIAC (such as indiscriminate attacks) cannot be equated with persecution.[1060]

[1054] See Jacques, *supra* note 637, at 164.

[1055] Convention Relating to the Status of Refugees (CSR), 1951, *Human Rights Instruments* 343; Protocol Relating to the Status of Refugees, 1967, *ibid.*, 361.

[1056] CSR, *ibid.*, 345.

[1057] See J. Pejic, 'Article 1F(a): The Notion of International Crimes', 12 *IJRL*, Special Issue, 11, *id.*, 22–6 (2000).

[1058] CSR, *supra* note 1055, at 344.

[1059] See A. Zimmermann and C. Mahler, 'Article 1A, Para. 2', *The 1951 Convention Relating to the Status of Refugees and Its 1967 Protocol: A Commentary* 283, 370 (A. Zimmermann ed., 2011).

[1060] See *Ibid.*, 371.

Nevertheless, in Europe at least some temporary protection is given to persons evacuating areas of armed conflict.[1061]

779. Pursuant to the CSR, certain measures taken by the Government of Ruritania – especially against persons who did not participate in hostilities in a NIAC – may be regarded by Arcadia as persecution, if they are based on belonging to a specific social group or espousing a particular political opinion.[1062] There is disagreement, however, as to whether punitive measures taken by Ruritania against insurgents amount to 'persecution' or 'prosecution', and much may depend on how sympathetic Arcadia is to the insurgency in Ruritania.[1063]

780. Fear of persecution is normally ascribed to measures taken by the incumbent Government of Ruritania. But what about the state of affairs in which a part of the Ruritanian territory is under the control of the insurgents? In such circumstances, the fear of persecution is not the fault of the Government, which may simply be incapable of providing effective protection from victimization: the prime mover is the insurgent armed group in control of the area.[1064] The prevailing view seems to be that fear of persecution is to be taken into account even when the Government is merely unable to protect a person against persecution by non-State actors who are in charge (and this is also true when there is no Government at all in a 'failing State' setting; see *supra* 261).[1065]

D. 'Non-refoulement'

781. Assuming that an exile from Ruritania qualifies for the status of a refugee in Arcadia, Article 32 of the CSR does not allow his expulsion save on grounds of national security or public order (and pursuant to a decision steered by due process of law).[1066] Article 33 of the CSR[1067] prohibits the expulsion or return ('refoulement') of any refugee to any country 'where his life or freedom would be threatened on account of his race, religion, nationality, membership of a particular social group or

---

[1061] See W. Kälin, 'Flight in Time of War', 843 *IRRC* 629, 639–41 (2001).

[1062] See W. Kälin, 'Refugees and Civil Wars: Only a Matter of Interpretation?', 3 *IJRL* 435, 440–3 (1991).

[1063] See M.R. von Sternberg, 'Political Asylum and the Law of Internal Armed Conflict: Refugee Status, Human Rights and Humanitarian Law Concerns', 5 *IJRL* 153, 154 (1993).

[1064] See S. Jaquemet, 'The Cross-Fertilization of International Humanitarian Law and International Refugee Law', 843 *IRRC* 651, 665–8 (2001).

[1065] See Zimmermann and Mahler, *supra* note 1059, at 367–8.

[1066] CSR, *supra* note 1055, at 352–3.   [1067] *Ibid.*, 353.

political opinion' (Paragraph (1)). There is, of course, an 'intimate link' between Articles 33 and 1 of the CSR, inasmuch as both are governed by the criterion of well-founded fear (see *supra* 778).[1068]

782. The benefits of Article 33 may not be claimed by a refugee 'whom there are reasonable grounds for regarding as a danger to the security of the country in which he is' (Paragraph (2)). Surely, anyone bent on deposing the Arcadian Government will be deemed a danger to security.[1069] But most Ruritanian refugees do not seek to indulge in such activities: they just wish to escape endemic violence.

[1068] See G.S. Goodwin-Gill and J. McAdam, *The Refugee in International Law* 234 (3rd edn, 2007).

[1069] See A. Zimmermann and P. Wennholz, 'Article 33(2)', *The 1951 Convention Relating to the Status of Refugees, supra* note 1059, at 1397, 1415.

CONCLUSIONS

783. NIACs have to be examined not only from the vantage point of LONIAC. Issues of foreign intervention, recognition and State responsibility connected to NIACs have always commanded attention, and modern realities have only given them a keener edge. Whether or not the Security Council determines that NIACs constitute threats to international peace, civil strife presents a clear and present danger to world stability.

784. Having said that, a preoccupation with LONIAC is nowadays central to any serious discussion of NIACs. The swift upsurge of LONIAC – within the span of a single generation – from a non-subject in international law to a rich lode of both customary and treaty law (including an array of war crimes) is astounding. The process provides lambent evidence that international law is capable of unexpected velocity when the exigencies of a changing world demand it.

785. The compass point in the direction of which LONIAC seems to be accelerating is IAC *jus in bello*. As a result, legions of scholars advocate full integration of NIAC and IAC law of armed conflict. But despite the growing convergence between these two branches of the law, the notion of their amalgamation is purely academic and quite implausible. There is a fundamental divergence barring such merger, and State practice does not divulge the slightest inclination to outflank it any time soon.

786. Other scholars press for both NIAC and IAC law of armed conflict to be melded with international human rights law. This fantasy would gladly sacrifice the incalculable practical advantages of LONIAC at the altar of a theoretical and monochromatic grand design.

787. The two purely academic views about the possible synthesis of LONIAC with an extraneous legal regime should not be confused with each other. The desire to blend LONIAC with the *jus in bello* floats in a sea of wishful thinking, but – had it been empirically feasible – it might have

simplified the practice of the law of armed conflict. The urge to remove armed conflict from its special niche (be it LONIAC or IAC *jus in bello*) into the general habitat of human rights law is more complex. It seems to be linked to an ostrich-like delusion that *bellum* (including *bellum civile*) would disappear if lawyers were not fixated on an IAC *jus in bello* or its NIAC corollary.

788. Daydreaming apart, LONIAC is here to stay. The real challenge is not proving its *raison d'être* but ensuring its further development. NIAC treaty law is still lagging behind; the principal instruments are burdened by lacunae; and, in any event, many States are not Contracting Parties to them. In these circumstances, only advances in customary international law can redress the system by consolidating pragmatic solutions to grievous problems.

789. Customary international law posits general State practice (plus *opinio juris*). Again, some scholars would like to modify existing law by considering the practice of non-State actors as a new engine of customary international law. But in the second decade of the twenty-first century, there is no cue that States are willing to enable insurgent armed groups to join them in the process of international law-making. Anti-establishmentarian opinions to the contrary, it is the perspectives of States – and of States alone – that still count in this sphere.

790. The main impediment to legal progress is verifying that the incubation process of customary *lex lata* (which is unwritten) has been completed. Where LONIAC is concerned, the task has been made much easier thanks to the huge contribution of international criminal courts and tribunals since the 1990s. These unbiased rulings – rendered by impartial judges – have authoritatively endowed many LONIAC norms with a universally binding standing, with the support or acquiescence of the entire international community.

791. The incidence of NIACs steadily increases in number and in gravity. The desideratum of stemming the tide of NIACs has become a cliché. But, in reality – absent a *jus ad bellum civile* – the Security Council alone may preclude a civil strife from becoming an international powder keg. The trouble is that the Council is all too often paralyzed by discord between its Permanent Members (possessed with the veto power). This divests the Council of the ability to function effectively in the role of the 'policeman of the world', as envisaged by the framers of the UN Charter.

792. Unless and until the Security Council finds a way – through robust intervention – to curb NIACs, LONIAC remains the sole legal contrivance to lessen the injurious impact of intra-State armed conflicts. The importance of LONIAC in the scheme of international law cannot be overrated. It must not slacken its current brisk pace in constructing an even better bulwark against brutality and barbarism.

INDEX OF PERSONS

(References are to page numbers)

INDEX OF SUBJECTS

(References are to page numbers)